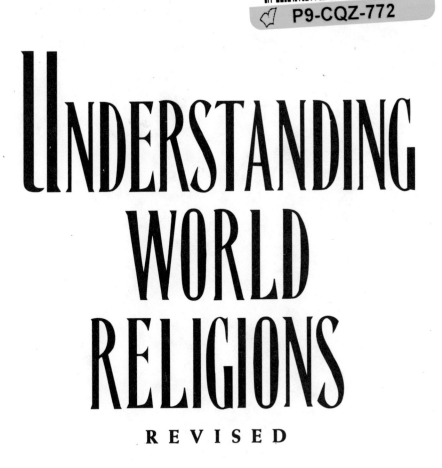

UNDERSTANDING WORLD RELIGIONS

REVISED

UNDERSTANDING WORLD RELIGIONS

REVISED

HINDUISM • BUDDHISM
TAOISM • CONFUCIANISM
JUDAISM • ISLAM

GEORGE W. BRASWELL, JR.

BROADMAN
& HOLMAN
PUBLISHERS

Nashville, Tennessee

©Copyright 1994 Broadman & Holman Publishers
All rights reserved
4210-68
IBSN: 0-8054-1068-6
Dewey Decimal Classification: 291
Subject Heading: RELIGIONS
Library of Congress Catalog Number: 93-24944
Printed in the United States of America

Library of Congress Cataloging-in-Publication Data

Braswell, George W.
  Understanding world religions / George W. Braswell.— rev. ed.
     p. cm.
   IBSN 0-8054-1068-6
   1. Religions. I. Title.
BL80.2.B724 1994
291—dc20
                                                      93-24944
                                                          CIP

To the family of Braswells

who lived among the peoples

of the Middle East

and

to the students

of Southeastern Baptist Theological Seminary

who continue to venture out among

the peoples of living religious traditions

CONTENTS

PREFACE

■   ■

W hat can one expect in reading this book? I have not intended it to be a highly technical, heavily documented, comprehensive writing on world religions. It is a book about select religions, emphasizing their historical development and growth, their major beliefs and practices, and their place in the religious community.

The basic intent of the book is to understand a variety of human beings who are religious. These human beings believe in someone or something beyond themselves. They pray, meditate, obey, and live their lives according to confessions, faith-statements, and creeds which transcend the mundane happenings of daily existence.

This book also seeks to give a Christian perspective on religions. I am writing from the experience of having lived and taught among peoples of various religions, of having friends who are actively committed to various beliefs and practices, and of my own understanding and experience of Christian faith and practice.

At the end of the book, various questions, exercises, and projects for each chapter are included. These are intended to aid one's understanding of various religions and to help one communicate one's belief and faith to others. Further readings are also suggested.

The first chapter focuses on several themes evident among the major religions, including the concept of deity, sacred writings, beliefs and practices, religious institutions, and issues from politics to peace. Chapters 2 through 7 give attention to the major religious traditions of Hinduism; Buddhism; Chinese and Japanese religions of Confucianism, Taoism, and Shintoism; Judaism; Christianity; and Islam.

Chapter 8 considers several select religious traditions including ancient Egyptian, Mesopotamian, Greek, and Roman religious traditions; Jainism and Sikhism of India; Zoroastrianism of Iran; African Traditional Religion; and the Baha'i with origins in Iran. Chapter 9 presents a brief case study of religious traditions in the Middle East, with emphasis on the Iranian context.

Chapter 10 expresses some select perspectives from Christian theologies toward religions. There is an emphasis on Christian views toward Hindus, Buddhists, and Muslims.

The last chapter offers various exercises and projects to enable one to explore the meanings of religions and to consider one's own faith and practice toward peoples of other religious traditions. A glossary and selective index are included at the end of the book.

What can one expect, then, in reading this book? I think that one will begin a journey into understanding the deep religious longings and life-styles of a variety of peoples who are rapidly becoming one large neighborhood. I also think that one will bring one's own faith and practice into relationship with other peoples; a rich conversation will develop between you and others. The Christian will confront the deepest meanings of the gospel, the good news of the Christian faith, with the challenges within the religions of revelation, authority, salvation, ethics, and peace.

UNDERSTANDING WORLD RELIGIONS

WORLD

RELIGIONS

REVISED

1

AN OVERVIEW
OF PEOPLES
AND THEIR RELIGIONS

■   ■

Introduction

Peoples of religions are no longer long distances from each other. Hindus, Buddhists, Muslims, and Christians are highly mobile populations that have crossed geographical and cultural boundaries to meet and to live among each other. A Hindu Temple, a Buddhist Congregational Church, a Muslim Mosque, and a Christian Church may be located near one another. Newspapers document the variety of worship, study, and celebration occasions of the various religious communities. Persons wearing particular religious dress are seen in the streets of both large cities and small towns. Peoples of religions have become next door neighbors and often cordial friends.

The *study of world religions* has been an academic discipline for some time. University scholars, church missionaries, and government officials have made many contributions in the written literature concerning religions. Perhaps the best way to understand world religions is to observe and to communicate with the peoples who profess and practice their religions. When conversations occur, a new world of understanding unfolds.

There are various reasons why people need to understand and desire to communicate across religious communities. The very fact of religious pluralism demands our attention of one another. Racial pluralism, ethnic pluralism, linguistic pluralism, and now religious pluralism exist. Why are

3

peoples of other religions living in our neighborhoods? Are they transient or permanent? Are they friend or foe? Are they missionary or not? Should I introduce my religion to them? The reality of religious pluralism is generating new interest in understanding who these many peoples and many faiths are.

The need to understand is also based on the common denominator that people are people regardless of their religions. People laugh and cry, are born and die, dream and plan, raise families and work, and recreate and retire. People like to talk about children and family, hardships and successes, and hopes for the future. There is a need for sympathetic understanding and appreciation of the basic human desires, frustrations, and dreams of all peoples. At the same time the religious beliefs and practices of people add depth and richness to all their experiences. Basic understanding comes, then, when the similarities and differences among various religious peoples are explored.

Religious pluralism occurs in a world of competition. Religions compete in the marketplace for both human and material resources. In order to survive and grow, religious communities seek members or patrons, personal loyalties and commitments, funds, institutional developments, and favorable public opinion.

One very practical need for understanding religions is for better methods of outreach to them or for better means of encountering their outreach. Peoples of Hindu, Buddhist, and Muslim religions may extend invitations to each other as well as to Christians to accept another religion. Persuasion and conversion techniques and methods are a vital part of many religious communities which not only teach and train their adherents to be missionaries but also send missionaries to lands of other religious communities. To understand other religions is to enable one to communicate one's faith more effectively both in missionary encounters and in defending one's faith.

Religions have increasingly become involved in the internal politics of a nation and between nations. History demonstrates that religions of world significance have vied for various kinds of power and prestige. Religion, politics, and economics have sometimes wedded themselves at a stage of history. Religious wars have occurred, for example, among Christians, among Muslims, or between Christians and Muslims. Religious communities adhere closely to sacred history, holy places, sacred persons, and holy lands. Consequently, conflict and crisis are often a fact of life for peoples of religions. Therefore, understanding and acceptance are needed to resolve conflicts and establish peace and harmony.

A sign of the times is the revival and revitalization of people's thirst for religion, for God, for gods and goddesses, for a pattern of meaning for life. People desire something and someone more than the mundane, more than the self, more than the institution, and more than what someone else says about a better life. People want a spiritual experience.

People are involved in a re-orientation of their spiritual antennas. We live in a time where rockets travel into outer space. In 1600 C.E.Giordano Bruno was burned at the stake for saying, "I hold the universe to be infinite, as being the effect of infinite divine power and goodness, of which any infinite world would have been unworthy. Hence, I have declared infinite worlds to exist beside this our Earth. I hold with Pythogoras that the Earth is a star like all the others which are infinite, and that all these numberless worlds are a whole in infinite space, which is the true universe."

Now rockets soar into outer space and there are religious rituals of celebration named after mythological deities. The Brunos are not burned, and there is excitement in the search for mystery, infinity, and divinity. We have reached a new stage in human culture. We are a planetary society containing more bits of information than the mind can stand, but holding enough space for the spirit to soar. Some of the astronauts aboard those rocket ships achieved a new or renewed cosmic orientation. One became a follower of the Transcendental Meditation of Maharishi. Another astronaut researched psychic healing and extra sensory perception. One of the astronauts, a Baptist, used his experience to enter the courts of Kings in the Middle East to proclaim the (cosmic) Christ.

Today is the day of salvation, liberation, escape, or fulfillment. The streets and the marketplaces, as well as the air waves and the temples, are the sounding boards for a plurality of religious voices, faith statements, and lifestyles. Scholars continue to research and write about religions. Governments train specialists to understand religious peoples and their systems of economics and politics in order to serve in embassies and consulates. Church agencies send missionaries to peoples of other faiths. All the while, in pluralistic societies Hindus live beside Buddhists and Christians live beside Muslims. The need is real to understand peoples of religions not only through books but also face to face.

Religions, like living organisms, are born into history, grow and mature into living traditions, and often affect the lives of hundreds of millions of followers. Some religions even face death. Zoroastrianism, the religion of ancient Iran, once flourished in the heartland of South Asia and influenced developments of both Judaism and Christianity. Zoroastrianism is now limited mostly to a few adherents in Iran and Bombay, India.

Religions seldom remain static. They tend to change their forms and characteristics over time, space, and history. Some religions give birth to reform movements from within. Buddhism may be viewed as an attempt to reform Hinduism. Other religions are formed by combining certain features of several religions; for example, Sikhism is a syncretism of Hinduism and Islam. Some religions build upon the foundations of others. Christianity's foundations upon Judaism are strong, and Islam has built upon both Judaism and Christianity.

For many religions there is no difference between religion and culture, between religion and politics, or between religion and a way of life. Hinduism in India is synonymous with being a native Indian. It is a way of life for the people of India. Similarly to Hinduism, the religion Islam offers a total way of life for the Muslims. Politics, economics, and religious life are united as parts of the whole in Islamic society. On the other hand, Christianity varies in its interpretations and impact of religion upon culture and politics.

Some religions are content to be homebound, basically affecting their own national community and remaining non-missionary. Other religions are more universalistic and migrate across cultural and national boundaries with missionary fervor. However, all religions have certain beliefs, philosophies, rituals, and institutions. In the following pages subjects will be considered such as deities and spirits, prophets, sacred writings, beliefs, religious institutions, and issues.

Gods, Goddesses, Ghosts, and Spirits: From Prophets to Gurus and Culture Heroes

Human populations have a difficult time facing life's challenges and crises without the help of deities and spirits. Supernatural beings play a significant role in the major living world religions. Some religions have a pantheon of deities who often compete for the affection and loyalty of devotees. These deities may be both male and female, representing power and control of nature's seasons, and giving health and happiness to human desires. Often a follower will seek the aid of several deities until they achieve satisfaction. A religion which offers a choice of deities to its devotees is a *polytheistic religion*. Hinduism may be considered a religion of polytheism.

Some religions claim only one deity as real and valid in human experience. There may be other gods and goddesses with names and traditions, but they are considered idols or false imitations. The one deity is universal and jealous of its own authority and power; it demands complete loyalty and allegiance from its followers. A religion which claims one deity as the only one is a *monotheistic religion*. Judaism, Christianity, and Islam may be considered religions of monotheism.

Various peoples consider ancestors important in their religious traditions. Ancestors may appear as spirits or ghosts, and they are placated in both home and community rituals. The spirit world is a common phenomenon among religious peoples, and spirits may be both good and evil. Sometimes both deities and ancestors are prominent in the same religion. Ancestors are important for tribal peoples as well as for major religions like Taoism and Shintoism.

Tribal religions and animistic traditions have their priests, medicine doctors, and shamans who serve as intermediaries between the ancestor and spirit world and the people. Where there is a supernatural deity or force present in a religion, there is a religious specialist with prescribed duties to know the supernatural and help control and mediate power to the benefit of the religious followers. Often the prophet or religious specialist is confused with the nature and being of the deity. When that occurs, the specialist may become associated with the supernatural. For example, the Buddha personally never claimed belief in deity. Yet his followers later elevated him to Buddhahood, a status of divinity.

Deities and ancestors are made known to people through certain *religious elite* in the religious community. Gods do not reveal their wills, laws, and expectations in a vacuum. In the monotheistic religions a prophet becomes the chief spokesperson for the deity. The prophet Muhammad of the Islamic religion not only heard the message of the god, Allah, but Muhammad also taught Muslims the will and law of Allah. Muhammad may be considered the founder of the religion Islam. Hinduism acknowledges no founder. Hindu beliefs and practices are ageless. Sages or gurus have taught and described the deities and truths of Hinduism, and Hindus follow the teachings.

In Buddhism there is no prophet like the Hebrew Amos, Jesus Christ, or Muhammad. Although the Buddha is acknowledged as the founder of Buddhism, Buddhists are divided in their understanding of who the Buddha was. Some see the Buddha as a culture hero, a guru supreme, who found the clue to understanding life and demonstrated the way to live out life. Other Buddhists see the Buddha as one who achieved deity, and therefore worship and emulate him as a savior. Confucians are similar to Buddhists in their understanding of Confucius.

Religious people are often surprising in their needs for deities and in their worship of deities. A particular Hindu may honor several gods and goddesses with temple worship and gift giving. However, the same Hindu may more frequently give devotion to one god, like Krishna, and may be more a monotheist in practice than a polytheist. One Buddhist may state there are no supernatural beings while another Buddhist may worship the Buddha as a supreme god. A Muslim may confess explicitly that there is but one deity, Allah, but the same Muslim may expend more time in religious energies seeking the aid of a Muslim saint.

Some Hindus and Confucians may tolerate their co-religionists' reliance upon gods and goddesses, but they, themselves, are not believers in the supernatural. The Hindu may adhere to a philosophy of monism, a belief in impersonal laws governing the universe. The Confucian may believe in the laws and traditions of society as sacred. Therefore, in some religions like Hinduism the choice of deities is unlimited. In other religions such as Christianity the choice is one of either-or, either one God or false gods.

It is important, then, in the study of religions to understand that a variety of peoples with diverse beliefs and practices compose a religion. All Hindus and all Buddhists do not believe and practice identical traditions. There may be more diversity within Hinduism than between Christianity and Islam. Hinduism may have room for atheism, secularism, polytheism, and monotheism. One perspective in the study of religions becomes clear: the human spirit, mind, and heart continue to search for someone or something beyond themselves. Often a prophet or religious hero is needed along the way.

Sacred Writings: Road Maps for Life and Beyond From the Bhagavad Gita to the Qur'an

All major living religions have sacred writings. Some religions have recorded the words of their prophets as they have uttered the message of God to the people. The Torah of Judaism, the Old and New Testaments of Christianity, and the Qur'an of Islam are examples of the recorded messages of the prophets and apostles of these religions as they have spoken the word of their god and in the name of their god. Other religions have preserved the teachings of their founders and inspired leaders. Hindu's venerable unknown sages have collected the truths inherent in the universe and have preserved them in the sacred writings known as the Vedas, the Upanishads, and the Bhagavad Gita.

Buddhism's founder, the Buddha, gave explicit teachings to his disciples, who later put them in written form. The Tripitaka contains the fundamental principles of the Buddha's teachings. The later developments of Buddhism have the Heart Sutra and the Lotus Sutra as devotional literature. In China, Confucianism was initiated by Confucius. Writings associated with Confucius and his followers are The Five Classics and The Four Books. The Analects, one of the Four Books, is the collection of sayings attributed to Confucius. Taoism, the other major Chinese religion, was begun by Lao Tzu, a contemporary of Confucius. Its major writing, The Tao Te Ching, has been attributed to Lao Tzu.

Religions may differ in the way they view their written traditions. The question of the source of the written tradition is important to a pious Muslim or Buddhist. If for the Muslim, Allah is the author of the Qur'an, and the Arabic language is Allah's language as well as the Qur'an's, then the pious Muslim questions even a translation of Allah's and the Qur'an's

Arabic into another language. The pious Buddhist, on the other hand, acknowledges that the teachings of the Buddha have been handed down in various languages and communities. The Buddhist also knows that diverse schools of monks have interpreted the teachings, and these interpretations have become a part of the Buddhist's beliefs and faith.

Sacred scriptures often become the serious business of a religious vocation. Scriptures must be preserved, interpreted, taught, and handed down to future generations. Therefore, religious communities select individuals who are religiously astute and who have the skills to work with the scriptures. Early Hinduism relied on the Brahmin priests to safeguard and teach the wisdom of the Vedas. Buddhism developed the monastery (Sangha) where the monks became the interpreters of the Tripitaka to laypersons. Islam needed religious scholars like Imams and the Ulema to know fluently the classical Arabic of the Qur'an to teach the less educated and the non-Arabic speakers. Christianity, until the time of the Reformation, relied on a priestly-scholarly religious elite to preach and teach the Christian scriptures in Latin to the less educated and non-Latin users.

Interpretation of scriptures has been a challenge and often a problem for religious communities. Priests and scholars have disagreed over translations and meanings of their sacred traditions. These conflicts have often resulted in a division in the religious community over the differing viewpoints and interpretations. Various religious schools, seminaries, monasteries, and sects have formed in variance with one another.

Buddhism is a classic example of schools of thought in disagreement over the meaning of the teachings of Buddha. The Hinayana Buddhists interpret the teachings of the Tripitaka to view the Buddha as a great teacher and example. The Mahayana Buddhists interpret the Heart Sutra and the Lotus Sutra to view the Buddha as a great being with supernatural status. Christianity is another example. Great theological debates over the nature and meaning of scripture and the nature of God have resulted in the divisions of Roman Catholicism, Eastern Orthodoxy, and Protestantism. Thus, religions develop diverse schools which in turn have renowned scholars whose viewpoints on scripture, philosophy, and theology are widely respected. Confucianism has its great scholar, Mencius; and Christianity has Augustine, Thomas Aquinas, and Martin Luther.

A variety of subjects are contained in the sacred writings of religions. If the religion focuses on a concept of deity, the scripture will describe the nature of the deity as well as the relation of the deity to the world. Themes of creation, preservation, and judgment may be prominent. Laws, rules, and guidelines for human affairs, as well as for the relationship between the deity and the person or the community may form an important part of the Scripture. The Hindu sacred writing, the Upanishad, focuses on the philosophical matter of the universal principle of the world, whereas another Hindu scripture, the Bhagavad Gita, elevates the god Krishna as the most important Hindu deity. In his writings Confucius dismisses the gods and writes of the supreme ethical relations in society. The Muslim scripture, the Qur'an, provides a complete plan for individual, community, and national life under the rule of Allah.

In all the various scriptural traditions within a single religion and between religions themselves, the *piety* of scripture readers and worship leaders stands out. The illiterate Hindu goes to the Brahmin priest to gain a thread of hope from the professional recitation of a verse from the Veda. A Mahayana Buddhist grasps for divine help beyond the words and symbols of a reading from the Lotus Sutra. A Muslim goes to the mosque to stand behind the prayer leader who recites the language of Allah from the Qur'an.

For the millions of worshipers among the major religions, scriptures provide both a rational explanation of life as well as a hope and a way to solve life's problems and to move beyond them. Scriptures become an authoritative source for the religious life. If one is illiterate, it becomes more important to place trust in a trained scriptural specialist. Often the trained specialist becomes very powerful in the religious community because of knowledge as well as trust by the community. Scriptures often become the missionary wedge a religion uses to proselytize people.

Scriptures, then, serve many purposes in religions. In the following pages attention shall be given to certain scriptural traditions in the major religions. Since all religions and their scriptures do not stress belief in deity, comparative scriptural selections on deity cannot be given. However, the attempt shall be made to highlight some of the most visible themes in the scriptures of major religions. It is important to remember that people like Hindus, Buddhists, and Muslims commit scriptures to memory, recite them at home, at work, and at worship, and teach them to their children and their children's children.

Believing and Doing: The Ideal and the Real: Head Religion and Heart Religion

Religious people have beliefs which focus their attention and motivate them to action, and they have practices which distinguish them as people of a particular religion. Beliefs are the foundations which give a view of the world. A basic belief or world view of Buddhism, for example, is that the world is filled with suffering. Since there is no personal creator and the world is not real, the Buddhist is motivated to deny the world and escape from it. On the other hand, Islam views the world as both real and good. In Islam, God not only created the world but rules over it wisely and powerfully and gives people directions to live responsibly and safely.

Beliefs may be voiced as *confessions* or statements of principles. A Buddhist states a vow of believing in the Buddha, the Law (Dharma), and in the Monks (Sangha). A Muslim confesses that there is one God and Muhammad is the prophet of God. Beliefs, then, are perceptions of the world and statements of religious fact that the religions of the world give their followers. In a sense, beliefs are a part of the *head religion* or the intellectual quality of a religion. When one says, "I believe," one may not put that belief into practice. A belief may be the ideal in the religion. A Buddhist may take a vow to support the monks but may do very little in assistance. Or a Christian may confess that Jesus Christ is Lord but may neglect the lordship of Jesus Christ in life. The vow of the Buddhist and the confession of the Christian are the ideals of their religions and are true expressions of their beliefs. However, religions attempt to have their ideals or beliefs implemented into action or practice.

Religious practice sets in motion the beliefs of a religion. Of course, beliefs may be a form of religious practice. When the Buddhist states the vow or the Muslim confesses God and the prophet daily in prayers or in devotional contexts, these vows and confessions are both believing and doing. The context for doing them may be worship, and the stated words are filled with emotion and devotion. Practice therefore is *heart religion*. Feelings and commitments are involved in action. Religious practice may occur both individually and in community. Buildings like temples, art forms like images, or the use of seating arrangements and scriptures aid in the practice of religion. Worship, prayer, pilgrimages, festivities, calendar day celebrations, and a host of other forms enable the religious individual or community to practice religion and to assist in merging the believing and doing, the ideal and the real, and the head and the heart religion into a unity.

Often, there is a great *gulf between the ideal and the real*. Some religions say that the ideal belief and practice can only be achieved by a few. Hinduism reserves its religious rewards to the Hindu holy ones who forsake family and friends and go into the forests to seek liberation (Moksha). Buddhism taught that the monks were the religious elite who had the earliest opportunity to attain Nirvana. The implications in Hinduism and Buddhism are that the road to liberation for masses of people is difficult and prolonged. Yet, it is interesting to note that in Hinduism, Krishna became the great savior for millions of Hindus who did not or could not flee into the forests. In Buddhism the Buddha and many saviors (Bodhisattva) like him became the liberators for millions of Buddhists who did not or could not become monks.

One may observe there is also, at times, a deep gap between what religious philosophers, theologians, and preachers teach and what the religious followers practice. Often, it is heard, "That is what the Bible teaches," or "The Qur'an says," or "It is written in the Vedas," or "The Swami says this is true in Hinduism." People search for authority in religious belief and practice and are ready to give their allegiance to an authoritative source, to either an individual interpreter or to a scripture. In some religions people become tired if belief is too head heavy, too intellectual. They will turn to a belief and practice which has more heart, feeling, and emotion in it.

There are two concepts which are helpful in understanding beliefs and practices. They are the *great tradition* and the *little tradition*, and they apply to differences within a single religion. The great tradition is usually associated with the oldest sacred writings and renowned teachers. It has the oldest theological schools and has orthodoxy as its position. The great tradition often has its religious building and legal and educational systems in a revered and ancient city. On the other hand the little tradition has sprung up within the great tradition. It has developed a different set of interpretations of scripture and teachers. It has its centers of activity distant from the great tradition, and it either lays claim to orthodoxy or admits to a fresher approach. Some may label the great tradition as the scholarly, intellectual, orthodox way of religion. The little tradition is considered the popular, heartfelt, flexible way of religion. The adjectives, great and little, have no numerical value as to numbers of followers of each tradition or to a greater or lesser importance.

The following examples show the nature of these traditions in belief and practice. The Hinayana Buddhists consider the Buddha a great teacher and example. This perception or belief in the Buddha is a part of the great tradition of Buddhism. On the other hand, the Mahayana Buddhists believe that the Buddha became a divine or supernatural being along with other Buddha-types like Amida. This belief is a part of the little tradition of Buddhism and grew up within the great tradition. Another example concerns Islam. The great tradition in Islam teaches the belief in one God and the pilgrimage center in Mecca. However, many Muslims give devotion to Muslim saints and make the tombs of saints into pilgrimage centers. The elevation of saints as devotional objects and saints' tombs as places of pilgrimage are part of the little tradition in Islam. Often people will participate in both traditions. However, the little tradition offers the follower a more personal and immediate religious experience. For many Muslims it is impossible to make the journey to Mecca because of distance and finances, so they opt for a saint's shrine.

There are tensions, then, within religions between belief and practice. Religions have a way of projecting the perfect or complete religious life.

Tensions come between the principles or belief, or statements of belief, and the actualization of belief into practice. Tensions come between a theology or philosophy and ethics or religious behavior. Usually, the greatest challenge within a religion is the actualization of the ideal into the real or of belief into practice.

Temples, Pagodas, Churches, Mosques, and Homes: Secure Places and Launching Pads

Religious experience is both an individual and a community experience. The home provides a place for the parents to teach the children religious ideals and values and to transmit meanings and a lifestyle. In the Muslim home, for example, the young child may emulate the father as he learns the postures of prayer or memorizes the words of the Qur'an. The Hindu home may set aside a room or a portion of the house for worship of its particular deity. The parents train the child to participate daily in the home in the various worship patterns. In the Christian home much attention may be given to teaching the child passages from the Bible and to leading the family members in devotional readings and prayer. Thus, the individual often learns the forms and patterns of religion in the home and practices them as an individual expression or within the family context.

Just as the family is often important in nurturing the religious experience of the individual, so are the larger religious communities. The major world religions emphasize *group experiences* and encourage group participation. The ideal of the Islamic community is a gathered one in which people experience worship and prayer at the mosque or at the shrine to offer prayers in unison and hear sermons. There are specialized religious leaders who call the people to prayer, lead them in prayers, give the sermon, and counsel them in matters of daily living. The Buddhist temple or pagoda may be a pilgrimage place presided over by monks where the Buddhist faithful gather for worship. The Jewish synagogue and the Christian church are similar in that they offer a place for worship, prayer, singing, and religious education. The rabbi and the minister are religious professionals, like the Muslim imam or Buddhist monk, who administer and teach the religious community. Thus, each major world religion has several key religious institutions that provide for the religious nurture of its people.

Worship centers like temples and mosques vary in size and prestige. A village may have a simple mosque made of mud, straw, and wood. A great urban area may have an enormous mosque constructed of exquisite mosaic tiles and gold plated domes. The city mosque may be the headquarters of a renowned Ayatollah or imam while the village mosque may have an itinerant Mullah. Likewise, Hindu temples, Buddhist pagodas, and Christian churches have their varieties of sizes and significances.

Important to world religions is *religious education*. Religious communities need professionals who have mastered the knowledge of the sacred writings, who have excelled in the leadership of worship and ritual, and who can give religious counsel on both legal and domestic matters. Consequently, religious schools are prominent in most major religions. Often, a religious school or monastery is located adjacent to a Buddhist temple. A theological school may be part of a mosque complex in an Islamic setting. Noted Buddhist monks (Bhikku) and Muslim religious scholars (Ulema) teach the religious curriculum to individuals of all ages. These individuals are later certified by their teachers to be practicing monks and Ulema in other temples and mosques. Often, these noted teachers are given great authority in both the religious and political spheres from their mass following of students who have been placed in temples and mosques throughout the lands. An example is that of an Ayatollah in Iran whose thousands of former students and other Muslim Mullahs delivered hundreds of thousands of faithful Muslims under his authority. The Christian Church is renowned for its emphasis upon religious education. Churches, libraries, theological seminaries, and religious education classes for all ages have been a unified approach in Christianity.

The training of religious leaders is a priority among world religions. The investments in schools, teachers, buildings, and materials are great. There are two related activities to religious education. Each religion develops its own scholars who write and publish doctrinal, liturgical, and historical books. They write curriculum materials and catechism manuals. They write apologetic works to explain their religion to strangers and to defend their faith against external attacks. Often, these writings are not only published in the native language, but also in other languages so as to positively influence outsiders. Religious communities may have their own publishing institutions with printing presses, marketing services, and book store outlets. One often sees religious publications in various temple, mosque, and church precincts.

Missionary activity is also stressed by many world religions. Both religious professionals and laypersons may be missionaries of their religious communities. They are trained in communication techniques, cross-cultural studies, and languages. They are often supported by funding from their religious communities. They are supplied with appropriate printed materials in the language of the target culture. Buddhism is an example of a missionary religion which rapidly moved from its native India to China, Korea, and Japan, and later entered the United States. Buddhist monks, armed with the printed page in the vernacular language, carried the Buddhist message to distant peoples. Temples, pagodas, and Buddhist societies were established with missionary zeal.

Likewise, Islam's missionary impetus has carried it to most territories of the globe. Mosques and Islamic centers and Muslim literature translated into the architecture and language of the population dot the landscape of some one billion people scattered across a myriad of cultures. Christianity is perhaps the best example of a missionary religion which has crossed every major population boundary with its churches, schools, hospitals, and social service projects, as well as it voluminous translations of its scriptures and teachings.

Religious institutions and places like temples, mosques, and churches serve many purposes. Certainly, they are considered by their followers as holy places where one may meet God. They are places where the individual may become a visible and feeling part of a community united in worship, and they serve as places where people expect answers to life's dilemmas and directions to life's destiny. Often, these institutions are focal points for religious leadership, education, and missionary activity. A pagoda may be known for its highly renowned monk. A temple may be visited because it is believed to be the abode of a very efficacious deity. A particular mosque may be very important because of the preaching power of its imam during the Friday sermon. A church may be chosen because of its highly rated education program for children. The temple or mosque may be one simple building, or it may be a complex of buildings including a worship center, library, school, and administrative offices. Regardless of size or overall significance, the religious institution is a place where the individual comes for an experience of security and piety. Usually, it is a place that links individual to community, home to religious institution, and piety to practice.

Issues of Survival and Growth:
From Politics to Modernization, From War to Peace

Attention is now turned to some of the basic issues that challenge religions. Religions observed thus far have demonstrated deep roots in historical consciousness, have produced and matured charismatic leadership with profound effects upon the life ideals and behavior of peoples, and have built strong institutions dedicated to worship and learning, with deep influence upon individual and community life. Yet there are challenges within religions and between religions.

A serious challenge to all religions is *secularism*. Secularism erodes the faith and practice of religions with the emphasis that religious ideals and practices need not affect the morality and institutions of a people. Confucianism and Taoism felt this impact with the communist influence in China. Muslim populations felt the influence of secularism when their national leaders refused to incorporate the state religion of Islam into the nation's constitution. Turkey under the leadership of Kemal Ataturk after World War I is a prime example of the dismantling of Islamic values and institutions through a commitment to secularism.

The relationship between *politics and religion* is another issue which religions face. Christianity has wrestled with this relationship since its inception. "Give to Caesar what is proper, and give to God what is proper," has been the statement of tension. The Holy Roman Empire, the holy commonwealth in New England in the early days of American beginnings, and the constant issue of the separation of church and state are examples which have confronted Christianity. Religion and politics have had their battles in Islam. The disagreements between the King and the Caliph and between the Shah and the Ayatollah have highlighted the tensions in Islamic history. Islam has taught that religion must inform every facet of society, including the government. Consequently, where political rulers have not been willing to establish the teachings of the Qur'an in the governing of the affairs of the nation, there has been conflict with the religious elite. An outstanding example of major conflict was the confrontation between the Shah of Iran and the Ayatollah Khomeini.

Many religious communities have formed political parties in recent times to affect the choice of candidates for government offices both on the local and national levels, as well as to influence political issues with religious values. Muslims in Indonesia, Hindus in India, and Christians in Chile are just a few examples of religious communities organizing themselves into the stream of modern political organizations to voice religious aspirations and values.

The relationship of religion and politics has several ramifications. The concept of *theocracy* means that a nation is governed by a deity through a divine king or through a sacred priesthood. In Hindu and Buddhist history there have been periods when a king would receive the blessings of the religious leaders to rule in the name of the Hindu and Buddhist value systems. Egyptian pharaohs are noted examples of theocratic rulers. Islam basically supports a theocratic rule wherein all of life is integrated through the divine rulership of Allah in the close proximity of the political and religious office.

The issue of religion and politics also raises the challenges of *religious pluralism and religious freedom*. Some nations have state religions. Usually there are religious minorities living in those nations. What is the relationship of the dominant religion to the religious minorities? What rights and privileges do the dominant and minority religions have? Many nations struggle with the question of religious pluralism and freedom.

Indonesia, with the plurality of Muslims, has a governmental ministry of religion which supervises the affairs of all religious groups. Indonesia does not have a constitution based on Islam, and it has been the scene of intense Muslim, political parties. Hindus and Muslims talked and fought until the nations of Pakistan and Bangladesh became territories mainly composed of Muslims, while India remained overwhelmingly Hindu. Thus, religions in pluralistic societies face the challenges of making accommodations to one another or face the possibilities of conflict.

History is replete with *wars* between religious communities. Western Christians fought during the crusades with Eastern Christians in Constantinople. Christianity fought Islam both in Europe and in the Middle East during the medieval era. Islamic nations have fought Islamic nations in the name of Allah during various periods of their history. A Jewish state has fought Arab Muslims and Arab Christians. In recent times Northern Ireland has witnessed the conflict between Roman Catholics and Protestants. Iran and Iraq, both Muslim nations, have waged war over disputed territory. Thus, secularism is a declared common enemy to religions while religions themselves become enemies to one another and to members of their households.

Religious nationalism is another challenge among the religions. In recent times there have been revitalizations and revivalism among some of the major religions. Some nations have been encouraged to return to their religious and cultural roots. The background of religious nationalism includes the desire of political decision makers to incur the favor of the religious majority. At the same time it is an attempt by a nation to acknowledge eras of military, cultural, and religious invasions by outsiders, and to desire something they can name and experience as their own. Hindu is the name for an Indian, a native of India, and consequently, Hindu nationalism portrays Indian culture and Hindu values. Islamic nationalism has recently been abetted by its entanglement with the state of Israel, by the oil cartel dominated by Muslim countries, and by the revival of a sense of Muslim worth and pride among the nations of the world. Muslims talk about the return to the religious, political, and cultural prominence they had during the medieval ages and the Ottoman Empire. Religious nationalism may have meaning not only for a renewed sense and status of well being for a religion, but also for religious freedoms among the minorities and for the propagation of religion of other people.

One of the enduring issues which religions face is openness or assistance to *change*. Especially in the twentieth century the impact and presence of western peoples upon religious communities outside the western hemisphere have been great. The world wars, the industrial revolution, the technological exploration, and the ease of transportation and communication have made western ideas, values, and institutions readily accessible.

On the other hand, nations have sent their youth by the hundreds of thousands to western universities for training. These youth have returned to their nations to employ learning and skills different from their homeland. Modern techniques of medicine have challenged the religious role of the shaman. Modern business principles and schedules have challenged the traditional religious calendar of Muslim peoples as to prayer times and fasting days. One of the features of modernization is to think new things and to be open to new ideas. The very process of modernization may be a threat to traditional religious communities.

Where there has been *revitalization among religions*, there has often been a renewed sense of identity and a fresh attempt to impact the world through the spread of religion. Christianity has been known as a missionary religion throughout its history, realizing a presence among the world's populations that was nearly universal by the late twentieth century. Islam, too, has been a missionary religion with a forceful resurgence since 1975. Hinduism and Buddhism have also left their native regions for missionary service in Europe and the Americas in movements such as Transcendental Meditation, Hare Krishna, Vedanta societies, Zen Buddhism, and the Buddhist Congregational Churches. As religions have become more missionary, various religious groups have been tested on their views and practices of religious pluralism and religious freedom.

One of the most challenging issues facing religious communities is the stability and integrity of the *family*. Some religions sanction large families because numbers of children demonstrate the favor of the deity upon the parents. Some religions encourage the parents or the oldest son to care for their parents and grandparents. The extended family may include several households under one roof. Monogamous marriages are favored by some religious communities, and divorce is an evil. Polygamous marriages may be the rule in other religious communities, with a husband having numbers of wives or a wife having numbers of husbands. In some religious communities divorces are easily granted to males while females are restricted.

As nations and their religions have faced constitutional crises and have been influenced by the standards of international legal principles and practices and the domestic and family traditions of other communities, they have been offered alternatives to their traditional patterns. Nations have opted for industrialization, for a work force that includes women, for expensive education for their children, and for ecological balances between numbers of people and the scarce supplies of food and survival resources. These choices affect family lifestyles in terms of having two children or ten, of having a mother at home or at work, of keeping grandparents in the home or providing for them elsewhere.

Also, in many nations the governments have taken over the education of children which formerly had been under the auspices of the religious communities. Governments have tended to play modernizing roles while religions have tended to play traditional roles. Consequently, there has often been conflict in the models of family life idealized by the government and those of the traditional religious schools.

Governments have displayed posters on city streets and village paths depicting the happy nuclear family of father, mother, sister, and brother. Sexual education has been promoted to stress family planning and the use of contraceptives. Social security and welfare programs have been government sponsored to appeal to the aged and the needy. Religious communities have traditionally cared for the indigent and the aged through the gifts, offerings, and religious taxes of the people. Thus religions have increasingly faced the government's control and influence on home and domestic matters.

Later, several issues shall be emphasized among some of the major religions to represent deep human needs, conflicts, and attempts to find religious solutions. These issues are in no way exhaustive but will serve as samples of the general issues presented.

2

HINDUISM

From Classical to Contemporary

Hinduism is a native religion to India, whose roots extend to the early Indus civilization about 3000 B.C. Hindus do not point to a prophet who founded their religion, as Muslims would name their prophet Muhammad. However, sacred writings are very important in the development of Hinduism. The Vedas, the Upanishads, and the Bhagavad Gita are among the sacred Hindu scriptures. Wise men preserved the truth of the generations in these scriptures.

Two dominant movements have characterized Hinduism throughout its development. Hindu systems of philosophy have explained the origins of the world and have interpreted the laws of life for social behavior and community relations. These philosophies have laid down the axioms of truth based upon principles and processes exclusive of divinity. On the other hand, Hinduism has been immersed in a movement based on beliefs, worship, prayer, and temples centering in gods and goddesses by the thousands. Rivers, shrines, and temples are relished as holy places and as centers of pilgrimage where the worshiper meets the deity. Hinduism, then, has become a very inclusive religion, offering contemplations and visions of truth, often arrived at through the practice of Yoga. At the same time it offers its millions of followers a devotion of the heart to some god or goddess who will aid and liberate a soul in this life and from this life.

Hinduism has a philosophy to explain life, a law to direct life, a high road to truth through contemplation and mystical experience, and a popular road of worship and devotion to a multitude of deities. It offers something to everyone and may include components of other religions.

21

To Hinduism, Jesus Christ or Muhammad may be prophets and/or deities added to the Hindu stream of truth bearers or divine helpers.

Hindus number over 500 million. Most of these live in India. The religion has never been missionary like Christianity or Islam; however, certain Hindus have advocated Hindu religious principles in other nations, especially in Europe and North America. Since the beginning of the twentieth century, Vedanta societies based on Hindu teachings and practices have been established in Western countries. Where Hindus are prevalent in numbers, a Hindu temple serves the community needs. Perhaps the most popular form of Hinduism known in the west is the Hare Krishna. Krishna Consciousness societies operate in the United States. This form of Hinduism follows the Bhagavad Gita scriptures in devotion to the god Krishna. Also, transcendental meditation societies and classes are offered in Europe and North America. These meditation practices are founded on the various Yoga disciplines of classical Hinduism.

Hinduism's greatest impact has been on the population of India, the second most populous nation on earth. Hindu traditions continue to form the solid basis of the Indian people. The gods and goddesses of Hindus, the Hindu sacred books, and the doctrines and ways of life which Hindus follow, will be examined at length in the readings ahead.

No God, Many Gods, One God

Hinduism is one of the most inclusive religions. The sophisticated intellectual may find a comfortable niche in philosophical atheism or agnosticism and remain a good Hindu. A Hindu family man may divide his devotion between the gods of his family and those of his wife. A Hindu merchant may exclusively give all his attention and devotion to one god. All may remain Hindus, accepted and respected by each other. There is also a path in Hinduism for metaphysics and speculation. Many follow a contemplative life, fixed upon a search for the principles of truth. Other Hindus follow the path of elaborate temples, colorful rituals, and sacred altars in the home; these Hindus worship countless gods and goddesses.

An important philosophical tradition within Hinduism is Advaita Vedanta. This philosophy was expounded by Shankara, who lived in India about A.D. 750. Advaita means non-dualism, and Vedanta means the summation of the Vedas, the early scriptures of the Hindus. Its teaching emphasizes the unity of all things. Only one exists: it is called Brahman. The Brahman is the true being. The Atman is the soul of individuals, but the Atman and the Brahman are one. Separate souls and gods are illusions or misrepresentations. The Brahman may be interpreted as God in an impersonal, absolute aspect. Brahman is not to be confused with Brahma, a Hindu god, or with Brahmin, a Hindu priest or caste.

This Brahman philosophy has been described as pantheism, a god or supreme principle which has presence in everyone and everything. Other Hindu philosophies have emphasized monism, the idea of a unifying purpose or principle throughout the universe with no divine or personal characteristics. Metaphysical speculation continues to be a discipline among Hindus. Various schools of Yoga mediation are based upon the philosophical principles of Hindu metaphysics. Hindu Gurus and Maharijis offer various systems of meditative speculation and practice. Transcendental meditation (TM) forums and societies trace their roots to the systems of philosophy and Yoga in early Hindu scriptures like the Vedas and in interpretations like Shankara. TM movements are part of the religious pluralism stream in American society.

Early Hindu devotion involved sacrifice to several deities. These early gods were rulers over the sky, the air, and the earth. They were nature gods but were spoken of as human. Varuna upheld the moral and physical law. Indra was the great warrior god and god of the storm. He was associated with the sacred drink, soma. Agni, the god of fire, brought both light and warmth to his worshipers. Most of the early Hindu deities have disappeared and have been replaced by a triad of gods named Brahma, Vishnu, and Shiva.

The gods of the Hindu triad have been the most popular deities of Hindu worship since medieval times. These gods represent Hindu polytheism and are worshiped in the forms of iconographic representations and symbols. Both great and small statues are found in temples and on home altars. *Brahma* is the first god of the triad and is known as the creator. Tradition says that the four castes of India sprang from the body of Brahma. In contemporary India there are only a few temples devoted exclusively to the worship of Brahma.

Vishnu and Shiva are the most popular deities. *Vishnu* has been compared to the Christian concept of God. Vishnu resides in heaven, rules over the earth as preserver, champions all good causes, and at times assumes human form. In Hinduism there is the concept of avatara, the descent of god. Avatara means that a part of divine essence is embodied in human or animal form. Vishnu has taken many human forms including Rama and Krishna.

Shiva is the third god of the Hindu triad. Shiva is more fearsome and complex than Vishnu. He has many roles and has been characterized as a creator and a destroyer, an ascetic, a fertility god, a mad dancer, and a wild-haired yogi. Shiva signifies the eternal life-death rhythm of the universe. Nandi the bull is associated with Shiva worship, and tradition says that Shiva brought the Ganges River into being. A popular image of Shiva depicts him with four arms dancing as the life-force. His common emblem is a stone pillar, the lingam, which is the sexual symbol. Shiva, unlike Vishnu, has no avatara or incarnations. However, several goddesses are associated with him as his consorts. The goddess Shakti represents female power and fertility to compliment the male Shiva. Kali, the great goddess and Shiva's consort, represents violent power. She is greatly feared and sexual orgies have been connected to her cult of worship. Another of Shiva's consorts, Lakshmi, is a goddess of prosperity and good fortune. Thus, Shiva and his goddesses represent a blend of positive and negative characteristics as demonstrated in the universe and in the human family. Temples to Shiva are located throughout India.

One of the most popular of all deities in Hinduism is *Krishna*. Stories of him are found in the Bhagavad Gita, the most popular sacred writing in India. The Gita has been called the "New Testament of India" and the "Gospel of Krishna." Krishna is the incarnation of Vishnu. He has the role of warrior and of magnanimous teacher. He is characterized as all powerful and all understanding as well as charming and compassionate. He is often depicted as surrounded by milkmaids (gopis), who represent the ideal and ultimate devotion to the Lord Krishna. Devotion to Krishna becomes the motive of action for his followers. Love becomes an end in itself. Krishna is the one who transforms earthly pursuits to heavenly ones and guarantees his devotees a Krishna paradise. With so much love and grace to offer, Krishna often becomes the only god to whom Hindus give their devotion and commitment. Krishna devotion is prevalent over India as well as outside it. The International Society for Krishna Consciousness, the Hare Krishna movement, has brought Krishna devotion to the United States. The Hare Krishna consider Krishna the supreme personality of God.

The Hindu religion has long honored its religious leaders. From earliest times the *Brahmins* were the wise men and priests who interpreted the wisdom of the gods and the ages to the people; they also performed the various sacrifices and conducted the rituals of temple worship. Since there are numerous schools of Hindu philosophy and meditative practice, spiritual masters and cult leaders known as *Gurus* developed. Gurus accept students or disciples and become their masters.

There is an understanding in Hinduism that important truths, though stored in books, must be interpreted and handed down through inspired leaders. Gurus are the reservoirs of the secrets of the universe, the gods, and life. Also, the meditative and Yoga practices are difficult to attain, and a Guru master is necessary for teaching and modeling. Gurus have taken more specific titles such as Swami and Mahariji. Often the Guru may be considered by his followers as the founder-deity of that particular school or order. Maharijis often go to other countries to found their particular schools of speculation and meditation.

Hindus may exercise choices in worshiping various gods or in giving devotion to one or several deities. Some Hindus may opt to believe in no deity. Both in India and in other countries there are Hindu Gurus, specialists in philosophy and techniques of Yoga, who stand ready to assist disciples in the multiplicity of Hindu beliefs and practices.

A Verse for All Seasons

Hindu scriptures date about 1500 B.C. when the first hymns were compiled. The oldest hymns belong to the Veda scriptures. These scriptures present diverse materials such as addresses to the pantheon of gods, rituals surrounding sacrifices to the gods, and speculation about the origin of the universe. The language of the Veda is ancient Sanskrit, and the authors are unknown. They were probably Brahmin priests.

The oldest section of the Veda scripture is the Rig Veda. A portion of the Rig Veda is a hymn to the god of fire, Agni. The following *hymn to Agni* was offered by a Brahmin priest as people gathered around the fire to offer sacrifices. Fire was looked upon as a transforming power in both creation and destruction.

To Agni

1. I laud Agni, the chosen priest, god, minister of sacrifice,
   The hotar, lavishest of wealth.

2. Worthy is Agni to be praised by living as by ancient seers:
   He shall bring hitherward the gods.

3. Through Agni man obtaineth wealth, yea, plentywaxing day by day,
   Most rich in heroes, glorious.

4. Agni, the perfect sacrifice which thou encompassest about
   Verily goeth to the gods.

5. May Agni, sapient-minded priest, truthful, most gloriously great
   The god, come hither with the gods.

6. Whatever blessing, Agni, thou wilt grant unto thy worshiper,
   That, Angiras, is indeed thy truth.

7. To thee, dispeller of the night, O Agni, day by day with prayer
   Bringing thee reverence, we come;

8. Ruler of sacrifices, guard of law eternal, radiant one,
   increasing in thine own abode.

9. Be to us easy of approach, even as a father to his son;
   Agni, be with us for our weal.[1]

The Rig Veda includes another hymn, the *Song of Creation*, which is quite different from the hymn to Agni. The Song of Creation is a speculative hymn. It raises questions about the origin of the world, and it implies that answers may not be easy to find. This hymn prepares the way for the highly *philosophical thought* in the Upanishad scriptures.

The Song of Creation

1. Then was not non-existent nor existent:
   there was no realm of air, no sky beyond it.
   What covered in, and where? and what gave shelter?
   Was water there, unfathomed depth of water?

2. Death was not then, nor was there aught immortal:
   no sign was there, the day's and night's divider.
   That one thing, breathless, breathed by its own nature:
   apart from it was nothing whatsoever.

3. Darkness there was: at first concealed in darkness,
   this All was indiscriminated chaos.
   All that existed then was void and formless:
   by the great power of warmth was born that unit.

4. Thereafter rose desire in the beginning,
   Desire, the primal seed and germ of spirit.
   Sages who searched with their heart's thought
   discovered the existent's kinship in the non- existent.

5. Transversely was their severing line extended:
   What was above it then, and what below it?
   There were begetters, there were mighty forces,
   free action here and energy up yonder.

6. Who verily knows and who can here declare it,
   whence it was born and whence comes this creation?
   The gods are later than this world's production.
   Who knows, then, whence it first came into being?

7. He, the first origin of this creation, whether
   he formed it all or did not form it,
   Whose eye controls this world in highest heaven
   he verily knows it, or perhaps he knows not.[2]

A later edition of the Veda scripture is the Upanishad which became known about 500 B.C. It contains the parables, dialogues, and maxims, and it is the most philosophical of Hindu scriptures. Its main theme is unity in the midst of diversity. It argues that unity is achieved when the individual soul (Atman) becomes unified with the world soul (Brahman). What is important is not the sacrifice as emphasized in the Rig Veda, but knowledge is the key to becoming one with the Brahman. This unity can be experienced through styles of Yoga meditation.

The following selection from the Upanishad depicts the belief in the unification of the souls, Atman and Brahman.

The Individual Soul Identical with Brahman

Verily, this whole world is *Brahman*. Tranquil, let one worship it as from which he came forth, as that into which he will be dissolved, as that in which he breathes.

Now, verily a person consists of purpose. According to the purpose which a person has in this world, thus does he become on departing hence. So, let him form for himself a purpose.

He who consists of mind, whose body is life, whose form is light, whose conception is truth, whose soul is space, containing all works, containing all tastes, encompassing this whole world, the unspeaking, the unconcerned—this Soul of mine within the heart is smaller than a grain of rice, or a barley-corn, or a mustard-seed, or a grain of millet, or the kernel of a grain of millet; this Soul of mine within the heart is greater than the earth, greater than the atmosphere, greater than the sky, greater than these worlds.

Containing all works, containing all desires, containing all odors, containing all tastes, encompassing this whole world, the unspeaking, the unconcerned—this is the Soul of mine within the heart, this is *Brahman*. Into him I shall enter on departing hence.

If one would believe this, he would have no more doubt.— Thus used Sandilya to say—yea, Sandilya![3]

Another selection from the Upanishad describes the preparation for the discipline of Yoga. In order for the individual soul to attain unity with the universal soul, the Yoga way of meditation is necessary. Yoga is a way of life of concentrated meditation and certain breathing and physical exercises. However, the Hindu must be prepared for Yoga.

How to Know God: The Yoga Aphorisms of Patanjali

1. Austerity, study, and the dedication of the fruits of one's work to God: these are the preliminary steps toward Yoga.

2. Thus we may cultivate the power of concentration and remove the obstacles to enlightenment which cause all our sufferings.

3. These obstacles—the cause of man's sufferings—are ignorance, egoism, attachment, aversion, and the desire to cling to life.

4. Ignorance creates all the other obstacles. They may exist either in a potential or a vestigial form, or they may have been temporarily overcome or fully developed.

5. To regard the noneternal as eternal, the impure as pure, the painful as pleasant and the non-Atman as the Atman—this is ignorance.

6. To identify consciousness with that which merely reflects consciousness—this is egoism.

7. Attachment is that which dwells upon pleasure.[4]

About 100 B.C. a very influential writing appeared in India known as the *Laws of Manu*. This writing described the social order of Hinduism based on the caste system. The caste system placed Hindus in groups according to vocation. It also described each group's rituals, prohibitions, and intramarriages. The castes were the Brahmin, Kshatriya, Vaisya, and Sudra. The following excerpt from the Law of Manu describes each caste.

From the Laws of Manu

But in order to protect this universe He, the most resplendent one, assigned separate (duties and) occupations to those who sprang from his mouth, arms, thighs, and feet.

To Brahmanas he assigned teaching and studying (the Veda), sacrificing for their own benefit and for others, giving and accepting (of alms).

The Kshatriya he commanded to protect the people, to bestow gifts, to offer sacrifices, to study (the Veda), and to abstain from attaching himself to sensual pleasures;

The Vaisya to tend cattle, to bestow gifts, to offer sacrifices, to study (the Veda), to trade, to lend money, and to cultivate land.

One occupation only the lord prescribed to the Sudra, to serve meekly even these (other) three castes.[5]

Other scriptural traditions are notable in Hinduism. The Ramayana is an epic consisting of 24,000 double verses. It tells the adventures of Prince Rama, who is the object of devotion of many Hindus, and his wife Sita. Another sacred writing is the Mahabharata, an epic of some 90,000 double verses. The most influential section of this epic is the Bhagavad Gita, known as the Celestial Song. In the Bhagavad Gita, Krishna tells a young warrior, Arjuna, that though death and killing are unpleasant, both life and death are minor compared with eternal values. Krishna gradually reveals himself to Arjuna as the Supreme Lord, and he teaches Arjuna to depend on him for liberation. The Bhagavad Gita is perhaps the most popular Hindu scripture both inside India and in Europe and America. It has become known as the New Testament of Hinduism and the Gospel of Krishna.

The following selection from the Gita shows the elevation of Krishna to divine status and his requirement from his followers of devotion to him.

Krishna Manifests Himself in His Glory

Of many mouths and eyes,
Of many wondrous aspects,
Of many marvelous ornaments,
Of marvelous and many uplifted weapons;
Wearing marvelous garlands and garments,
With marvelous perfumes and ointments,
Made up of all wonders, the god,
Infinite, with faces in all directions.

Of a thousand suns in the sky
If suddenly should burst forth
The light, it would be like
Unto the light of that exalted one.

Arjuna said:

I see the gods in Thy body, O God,
All of them, and the hosts of various kinds of beings too,
Lord Brahma sitting on the lotus-seat,
And the seers all, and the divine serpents.

With many arms, bellies, mouths, and eyes,
I see Thee, infinite in form on all sides;
No end nor middle nor yet beginning of Thee
Do I see, O All-God, All-formed!
With diadem, club, and disc,
A mass of radiance, glowing on all sides,
I see Thee, hard to look at, on every side
With the glory of flaming fire and sun, immeasurable.

Thou art the Imperishable, the supreme Object of Knowledge;
Thou art the ultimate resting-place of this universe;
Thou art the immortal guardian of the eternal right,
Thou art the everlasting Spirit, I hold.

Without beginning, middle, or end, of infinite power,
Of infinite arms, whose eyes are the moon and sun,
I see Thee, whose face is flaming fire,
Burning this whole universe with Thy radiance.

For this region between heaven and earth
Is pervaded by Thee alone, and all the directions;
Seeing this Thy wondrous, terrible form,
The triple world trembles, O exalted one!

Homage be to Thee from in front and from behind,
Homage be to Thee from all sides, Thou All!
O Thou of infinite might, Thy prowess is unmeasured;
Thou attainest all; therefore Thou art All!

Thou art the father of the world of things that move
and move not,
And Thou art its revered, most venerable Guru;
There is no other like Thee—how then a greater?—
Even, in the three worlds, O Thou of matchless greatness!

Therefore, bowing and prostrating my body,
I beg grace of Thee, the Lord to be revered:
As a father to his son, as a friend to his friend,
As a lover to his beloved, be pleased to show mercy, O God!

Having seen what was never seen before, I am thrilled,
And at the same time my heart is shaken with fear;
Show me, O God, that same form of Thine as before!
Be merciful, Lord of Gods, Abode of the World!

Wearing the diadem, carrying the club, with disc in hand,
Just as before I desire to see Thee;

In that same four-armed shape
Present Thyself, O Thousand-armed One, of universal form!

The Blessed One said:

This form that is right hard to see,
Which thou hast seen of Mine,
Of this form even the gods
Constantly long for the sight.
Not by the Vedas nor by austerity,
Nor by gifts or acts of worship,
Can I be seen in such a guise,
As thou hast seen Me.

But by unanswering devotion can
I in such a guise, Arjuna,
Be known and seen in very truth,
And entered into, scorcher of the foe.

Doing My work, intent on Me,
Devoted to Me, free from attachment,
Free from enmity to all beings,
Who is so, goes to Me, son of Pandu.[6]

The sacred writings of Hinduism clearly demonstrate a diversity of themes, including philosophical speculation over the nature of the world, sacrifices to a pantheon of deities, codes for moral behavior, and devotion to one supreme deity. It can be seen that Hinduism is very inclusive, being able to house a variety of beliefs and practices within the Hindu framework. Also, a Hindu may cherish and give devotion to the teachings of several scriptural traditions at the same time.

The Hindu Way: Works, Knowledge, Devotion; Transmigration, Caste, Passages

Hinduism is a religion which offers many beliefs and practices to all comers. Already Hindu beliefs in a diversity of gods, goddesses, and spirits have been presented. Also, various scriptural traditions have been shown to support this variety of beliefs. Hinduism is inclusive in that it provides for its followers a multiplicity of ways to attain its goals.

A primary belief of Hinduism is the *law of Karma* and the *transmigration of the soul*. There are two words for soul. Brahman is the world soul, and Atman is the individual soul. One goal within Hinduism is for the individual soul to unite with the world soul. Until this unity occurs, the individual soul is born time after time. This birth cycle is called the transmigration of the soul (Samsara). The law of Karma is the balancing of good and bad actions within the individual soul. As the soul attains good Karma, the chances become better to break the birth cycles and to forever unite with the world soul. However, if the soul has more bad than good Karma, then the soul faces more births, and unification with the world soul is prolonged. The ultimate goal of Hinduism is to attain freedom (Moksha), at which time Karma or good works is perfect, the birth cycle is concluded, and the individual soul and world soul become one.

How does one attain good works? Hinduism offers *three classic ways* or margas. These are the way of activity (karma marga), the way of knowledge (jnana marga), and the way of devotion (bhakti marga). One may choose one or several of these ways in hope of breaking the birth cycle and experiencing ultimate freedom.

The Way of Activity

The way of activity or works emphasizes offerings and sacrifices to gods, goddesses, and spirits in ceremonies both in temples and in homes. Hindu deities dwell on the earth and take their abodes in images and earthly forms. The temple is the place of the deity. Often temples are built by the wealthy to gain merit for themselves. In the temple there is the image of the deity. Priests called Brahmin perform the various rituals of purification and worship at the temple. The priests awaken the deity, bathe the deity, and offer food, flowers, and incense. They also commune with the deity through chanting sacred literature.

Near the temple there may be a theological school and a floral shop. Hindus bring flowers and food to the temple to offer to the temple deity, and they rely on the priests to properly care for the deity. They do not go to the temple to hear a sermon. There are no preachers, no pulpits, and no seats. They desire strength, economic success, healthy families, and the power to overcome bad omens. The temple is a place of stored power which may be set loose through the deity by Brahman. Through good works or Karma, Hindus yearn to build up enough merit to overcome all life's obstacles. Hindus may also practice good works at home. Both personal and family worship may occur at home or at a small family shrine. If worship occurs in the home, a particular space is set aside with an altar to a special deity of the family. The image of the deity is placed in a box. Each day the deity is awakened by a bell, bathed, fed, incensed, and communed with through readings and chants. At a family shrine there may from time to time be priests and singers to aid in the worship of the deity. The way of works is a popular form of Hinduism practiced by millions. It is a matter of daily duty. Performing worship (puja) to a deity helps the worshiper build up good Karma. This is the way to attain freedom.

The Way of Knowledge

Another way to freedom is the *way of knowledge*, or jnana marga. The way of knowledge offers the Hindu the secret to life and the end of life. It gives one knowledge and insight into the essence and meaning of all things. This way first was taught in the Upanishad scriptures. Later, it was detailed in the Laws of Manu. The chief belief is that a single essence, the world soul, is the basis for all things. The world soul is beyond conceptualization; however, it can be experienced through a mystical relationship. The mystical experience of the individual soul with the world soul is facilitated by the practice of Yoga meditation. At the moment of oneness there is freedom or salvation.

The attainment of this kind of knowledge is difficult. The Laws of Manu outlined the *four stages of life* (asramas) through which one must pass to accomplish the knowledge way. They are the stages of student, householder, forest dweller, and ascetic. In the *student* stage the youth studies the Veda scriptures, including the Upanishad tradition. The Guru teaches the youth the truths of Hinduism and the passages of life to reach the truth. The *householder* is the second stage of life. It is the duty of the man to wed a woman, raise a family, provide for all the sustenance of the family as well as the needy.

The third stage, that of *forest dweller*, is not a duty but a choice if the Hindu desires to continue the way of knowledge. He charges his sons to care for his wife, gives his property to his family, performs the fire sacrifice for the final time, and leaves home for the forests. He finds a Guru for his spiritual guide, becomes his disciple, and takes up the ascetic and meditative style of life, far away from family, friends, and worldly disturbances.

The fourth stage is the *ascetic* form, when the Hindu has learned the knowledge and the meditative techniques from the Guru and is ready to practice the art of Yoga on his own. Some of the ascetic practices are self-mortification. He may lay on beds of thorns. He may stare into the blazing sun until his sight disappears. He may stand on one foot for many hours. Self-torture is a way to put the body in its place so one can develop the concentration of the mind.

This concentration is what Yoga accomplishes. Yoga is the discipline in the way of knowledge that leads one to have the ultimate experience of freedom and the end of the transmigration cycle. However, certain virtues have to be a part of one's character and behavior before one can achieve this final meditative stage. Truthfulness, honesty, harmlessness, purity, and continence are among the virtues.

Yoga provides the Hindu with the method to reach freedom. The Yoga posture with head erect and spine straight and breath control enable the Hindu to attain supreme concentration. Through gazing upon certain sacred symbols and reciting certain sacred sounds, the Hindu approaches mystical union with the absolute, the world soul. This union brings him to a state of samadhi, a feeling of lightness, exemption from the laws of gravity, and peacefulness. Now he can be called a holy man, a Sannyasin. A lifetime of learning, discipline, and meditation are necessary to become a Sannyasin. The way of knowledge is an exclusive path to liberation.

The Way of Devotion

The third classic path is the *way of devotion* (bhakti). This way offers the Hindu a deity who is personal and who gives grace to overcome bad Karma. The Hindu relies on the deity through faith and devotion. It is interesting to note the differences in the three classic ways. The way of works is easily available to everyone. A home or a temple can house the deity. However, in spite of all the sacrifices and offerings to various deities, the Hindu is never certain of the outcome of breaking the transmigration and Karma cycles. The second path, the way of knowledge, is quite demanding and exclusive. Only a few can decide to leave family, home, and work to enter the forests. It is a price too costly for most Hindus.

The way of devotion is appealing to tens of millions of Hindus. In fact, it is the most popular religious belief and practice in Hinduism. The deities to whom Hindus give devotion and expect to receive grace include Vishnu and Shiva. Vishnu is a god of incarnations. Rama and Krishna are incarnations (avatara) of Vishnu. Also, Shakti, the female goddess, is prominent, especially as the divine mother. Shakti has presence in the goddess wives of Rama and Krishna. The most popular deity in the polytheism of Hinduism is Krishna. When a Hindu gives love and devotion to Krishna, as to other prominent deities, Krishna then makes liberation possible. There is no need to sacrifice countless offerings to numerous deities. It is not necessary to spend one's life deep in the forests. Devotion and grace work hand in hand to provide good Karma, break the transmigration of soul, and enable the Hindu to attain liberation.

The Caste System

The three classic ways of liberation and freedom are projected in a Hindu society built upon a caste system. The Hindu caste system has five categories of people whose duties are set according to social status. The *Brahmin* caste is the most privileged one. It is the protector and transmitter of the Veda scriptures and has general oversight of society. The *warrior* caste (Kshatriya) is the governing class. The kings, princes, politicians, army, and police populate this group. They make policy, collect taxes, and defend the people while recognizing the supremacy of the

Brahmin in faith and moral instruction. The *Vaisya* is the third caste. It includes the middle class occupations, including merchants, traders, teachers, and craftsmen. The *Sudra* caste is composed of farmers, peasants, and manual laborers. This caste undergirds the other three castes as support system. Another caste which has developed is called the *outcaste* or the untouchables. The untouchables are aliens who moved into India. They have little association with the other four castes. They perform such jobs as washing clothes, making shoes, and cremating the dead. They have no access to the religious rituals of the other castes.

According to the Laws of Manu the caste system is justified by the belief in Karma and the transmigration of souls. Hindus are not in their social position by accident, and there is no injustice in being in any caste. One gets what one merits. A Hindu may abide by the rules of the caste in a lifetime. If the rules are followed, then perhaps in another lifetime enough Karma has been built up to elevate one into a higher caste. However, while one is in a caste, one must perform the occupation of the caste, one must not intermarry with another caste, and there must be no social mingling outside one's own caste.

The caste system still remains in India. However, it was criticized and attacked by the belief and practice of Mahatma Gandhi, who died in 1947. Gandhi believed that God was in the hearts of millions in India in every caste. He said that the power of God was within the people. Where power is, there is truth. Where truth is, there is knowledge. And where true knowledge is, there is bliss. Gandhi asserted that one could realize truth or God in love and non-violence (ahimsa). Gandhi opposed not only the caste system but also British colonialism in India. He developed the practice of reverence for life (*ahimsa*) in opposition to what he considered the evils of the day. Self-suffering, courage, non-killing, and renunciation were qualities of life he espoused. India has felt the impact of Gandhi's life and teachings, yet India's population is so diverse and fragmented in ethnic, tribal, and language groups that change comes slowly and tediously.

Religious Practice

Hinduism appears to be like a mammoth ocean with enumerable vessels of all shapes and sizes bobbling in the waves. There is a proper size vessel for everyone's disposition religiously, and the ocean is large enough to carry the vessels to their destinations without collision. Beliefs are placed in animism, polytheism, philosophical systems, and in close proximity to monotheism.

What can be said about the great and little traditions in Hinduism? Certainly, the great tradition would include the beliefs and practices of the Veda scriptures, the authority of the Brahmin priests, and the Laws of Manu describing the inexorable laws of Karma and transmigration and caste. The ideal life in this tradition would be belonging to the Brahmin caste, the attainment of a holy person, the Sannyasin, and living out one's life according to the social and religious regulations of the society.

The little tradition would emphasize beliefs and practices found in the Ramayana and Bhagavad Gita sacred writings. This tradition would value the way of devotion (bhakti marga) as supreme and would challenge the caste system's rigidity and determinism. It would focus on a personal relationship between god and the individual. The little tradition would emphasize heart religion, whereas the great tradition would elevate intellectual pursuits. However, for some Hindus a taste of both traditions is a viable option.

Perhaps the spirit of Mahatma Gandhi captures the spirit of Hinduism best. Gandhi often questioned doctrinal and temporal authority. He gained value from the Bible, the Qur'an, and the Avesta. He said that his loyalty to the teachings of the Bhagavad Gita entitled him to use his faith and reason to amend it. His goal was to have self-realization, see "God face to face," and to attain freedom (Moksha). Moksha means liberation, freedom, escape, and release. So Hinduism is catholic in nature, bending to syncretism and offering a variety of beliefs and practices.

Temples and Home Life

Hindu temples in India can be found in villages, alongside roadways and rivers, and in the heartland of the cities. Temples vary in size, architectural features, and importance, according to their geography, daily worship, and community devotion. The temple may include a pyramidal gateway, a courtyard with a terrace and a source of water, a temple building with an inner shrine within which is an inner room where the sacred image is kept. A bell may grace the courtyard, and a spire may reach upward from the temple to the sky. A large temple may include a kitchen. A wall may surround all the temple features to portray a compound. The existence of the temple presupposes a clergy class which administers the worship patterns.

There is nothing haphazard about the religious life around the temple. There is a strict daily schedule, centered around the care of the temple deity. Before dawn there is an awakening ceremony, sometimes called the lamp ceremony, in which the deity is awakened with music and scriptural readings. After dawn an awakening ceremony occurs in which the image of the deity is washed. Then the image is anointed with sandal paste. With the conclusion of these initial rituals the image is worshiped through the recitation of scriptures. At noon the image is offered food, and a fire offering is performed. The image is then retired for the afternoon rest. Before evening another lamp ceremony is offered, and more food is given. After dusk the laying down ceremony occurs in which the image is dressed in beautiful clothes and flowers and laid to rest.

One may note that in large temples a retinue of priests may be involved in these numerous, technical, and highly decorative rituals. Not only are there priests who are meticulously involved but there are also the Hindu faithful who come to the temple to witness and to participate in the ceremonies. They bring garlands of flowers, perfumes, foods, various ornaments, and even sacrificial animals. The worshipers bring their lighted lamps and stand at the entrance to the inner room of the image. They also offer gifts to priests to read from the sacred scriptures and they often pay dancers and performers to enact certain dramas at the temple.

There are countless festivities and pilgrimages observed by Hindus. Festivities occur around the home and the temples and throughout the neighborhoods. The birthdays, the life stories, and the great victories of the deities like Krishna, Rama, and Shiva are commemorated. Honor is given to snails, monkeys, cows, and rivers. Phases of the moon, eclipses, stars, harvest seasons, and other seasonal cycles are observed. Hindus celebrate these festivities with worship, fasting, bathing, chanting, vows, gifts, and dancing. Pilgrimages are taken to various places, including temples, cities, and rivers. Benares, India is one of the holiest cities of Hinduism. It is located on the Ganges River and is estimated to contain some 1,500 temples and ghats (bathing places), as well as some one half million images of deities. Hindus believe that bathing in the Ganges River purifies one of all sin and cures diseases. When one's bones and ashes are placed in the Ganges, it is believed that one's place in eternity is achieved.

An important pilgrimage is the Car Festival of Jagganath (image of Krishna) at Puri, India. The images of the deities are placed on a wheeled platform and carried throughout the city. The Hindu pilgrims travel long distances for this special occasion. The following account comes from a description of the Car Festival over a century ago.

> For weeks before the Car festival, pilgrims come trooping into Puri by thousands every day. The whole district is in a ferment. By the time the great car has risen to the orthodox height of forty-five feet, the temple cooks make their calculations for feeding 90,000 mouths. The vast edifice is supported on sixteen wheels of seven feet diameter, and is thirty-five feet square. The brother and sister of Jagannath have separate cars a few feet smaller. When the sacred images are at length brought forth and placed upon their chariots, thousands fall on their knees and bow their foreheads in the dust. The vast multitude shouts with one throat, and, surging back-

ward and forward, drags the wheeled edifices down the broad street towards the country-house of lord Jagannath. Music strikes up before and behind, drums beat, cymbals clash, the priests harangue from the cars, or shout a sort of fescennine medley enlivened with broad allusions and coarse gestures which are received with roars of laughter by the crowd. And so the dense mass struggles forward by convulsive jerks, tugging and sweating, shouting and jumping, singing and praying, and swearing. The distance from the temple to the country-house is less than a mile; but the wheels sink deep into the sand, and the journey takes several days. After hours of severe toil and wild excitement in the July tropical sun, a reaction necessarily follows. The zeal of the pilgrim flags before the garden-house is reached; and the cars, deserted by the devotees, are dragged along by the professional pullers with deep-drawn grunts and groans. These men, 4200 in number, are peasants from the neighboring fiscal divisions, who generally manage to live at free quarter in Puri during the festival . . .

In a closely-packed eager throng of a hundred thousand men and women, many of them unaccustomed to exposure or hard labor, and all of them tugging and straining to the utmost under the blazing tropical sun, deaths must occasionally occur. There have doubtless been instances of pilgrims throwing themselves under the wheels in a frenzy of religious excitement. But such instances have always been rare, and are now unknown. At one time several unhappy people were killed or injured every year, but they were almost invariably cases of accidental trampling. The few suicides that did occur were for the most part cases of diseased and miserable objects, who took this means to put themselves out of pain. The official returns now place this beyond doubt. Indeed, nothing could be more opposed to the spirit of Vishnu-worship than self-immolation.[7]

Practice in the Home

Hindus practice their ceremonies in the home as well as in the temple. The following account describes a Hindu home in the United States. The descriptions are real, but pseudonyms are used to protect the family. Dr. Dharma is a brilliant and devout Hindu employed by a government department. He has a wife and five children. He is president of the Hindu Society of his region, which meets monthly for corporate worship and teaching. His father was a Brahmin priest in India, but Dr. Dharma chose to become a scientist and a teacher, and he is now an American citizen.

Dr. Dharma's family follows the Bhakti way of Hinduism, the way of devotion. He was taught the Vedas and the Bhagavad Gita by his father. He remembers arising at five in the morning to chant prayers with his father. He accompanied his father to the temple. His father chose his bride for him, and he did not see her until the wedding ceremony. They have been married some thirty years. Dr. Dharma affirms that even for his wife and himself, marriage is the responsibility of the parents. He recently arranged for his son's marriage. He and his son traveled to India to meet the girl, who was a distant relative, and the couple was married there. The Dharmas are of the Brahmin caste, so their daughter-in-law must be of the same caste.

Dr. Dharma believes that there is one universal religion and one supreme god (Krishna). He believes in one god who has no shape or figure and "no place to live." This god is everywhere and in everything. The soul is a part of god, but god is not divided. Dr. Dharma says that god is like an ocean. One may take a drop from the ocean but it is not divided. Every soul comes from god and is a part of god. Dr. Dharma says that images are representations in order to help people understand who god is. To teach that god has no form or shape or is impersonal is to hinder worship. One needs a form or figure in order to concentrate. Since god is present everywhere, god is present in the image too. Dr. Dharma and his family worship Radha and Krishna as messengers from god. Dr. Dharma also worships other figures, among which are Shiva and Shiva's son Ganesha, the elephant-headed god.

The home of the Dharma family contains a family shrine or altar. After removing one's shoes, one may go to the bedroom to view the shrine. It is a box about five feet tall, four feet wide, and three feet deep. A light is fixed to the top of the altar, and the front is open. Two statues, each a foot tall, of Radha and Krishna stand on the center shelf. They are dressed in silver dresses with leis around their necks. In front of the statues are various offerings, including stacks of quarters, dimes, and nickels. Other figures of brass and wood are on either side and on lower shelves. Several pictures of figures hang on all sides of the box. In front of the shrine box is a lamp with butter oil which is kept burning for worship.

The family worships each morning about seven o'clock for some thirty minutes. Everyone must have a bath, clean clothes, an empty stomach, calm surroundings, and the smell of incense, and the body must be in a lotus position. The figures in the shrine are bathed each morning and are offered food prepared by Mrs. Dharma. Dr. Dharma recites from the Gita in Sanskrit language and then translates for his family. He says that the vibration of the sound caused by chanting affects the environment.

The figures seem to be treated like babies in the home. While the Dharmas are on vacation, the figures are either taken along or are left with friends. They are never closed up in the house.

Worship for the Dharmas in the home is important, for it is not considered necessary for the Hindu to go to the temple for worship. In most American cities there are no Hindu temples. Dr. Dharma is proud of his religion and is also proud of being an American citizen. An American flag is placed in the corner of his living room, which is filled with large plants and modern furniture. He says that his religion is not bad or inferior to any other. Because America is a free country, as an American, he still wants to keep his tradition and his religion. He says that everyone who is a Hindu thinks his religion is best, so there is no need for change.

Cows, Castes, Krishna, and Sectarianism

Why would a people save a cow when they need the maximum production of foodstuffs and when they often have inadequate caloric and protein rations? It would appear that some people limit their survival chances in order to observe some custom and religious taboo. Hindu religion bars the slaughter of cattle, has a taboo of eating beef, and allows cows to roam the Indian countryside, clog roads, stop trains, steal food from marketplaces, and irritate tourists. What kind of sacred cow is this?

The Sacred Cow

The cow in India serves many functions. Cow dung makes an enormous contribution to the energy system in India by serving as cooking fuel and fertilizer. Among peoples of mass poverty and human survival needs, cow dung is inexpensive and available from the streets. It replaces artificial fertilizer, which is expensive, scarce, and beyond the means of the average Indian. Cow dung is cheap because the cows do not eat foods which can be eaten by people.

The taboo or ban on the killing of cows has affected the development of the meat packing industry; this might have serious consequences upon the ecological balances within India. Many families have only one cow. To slaughter it would drive the family from its lone survival technique, which is farming. Also, cows give critical quantities of milk to the people as protein value. Some beef from animals who die of natural causes is eaten by the outcastes. The taboo does solve the temptation to eat cattle in difficult times, which would mean that others would not have cattle to plant their crops when the rainy season came. Mahatma Gandhi said of the preservation of the cow, "Why the cow was selected is obvious to me. The cow was in India the best companion. She was the giver of plenty. Not only did she give milk, but she also made agriculture possible."

For those who live daily in the ultra modern reality of gadgets and bottled, frozen, canned, and packaged foods, the Indian mentality and the Hindu taboo may be difficult to understand. The cow has become an object of worship and cultic practice, but Hinduism includes a multiplicity of animals, spirits, gods, and goddesses as devotional objects. More important to the issue is the Indian and Hindu way of bringing a balance between the needs of the human family and those of nature. The preservation of the cow has served a need in an agricultural and traditional based society. The Hindu view and practice demonstrate a specific relationship to animals and the natural orders.

The sacred cow of India and Hinduism may still be worth considering, not for its divinity or veneration, but for its calling to attention the often delicate balance between the human family and nature and for using the most appropriate resources for the time and place of which we are a part. What will happen to the cow of India as that country industrializes will be an issue which both Hinduism and modernizing influences will face.

The Caste System

Indian society has been served in various ways by the caste system. The system has offered security in the economic area. With heredity vocations there was job stability. Another feeling of security is that everyone has a definite place and that everyone is necessary to the society. The Hindu world view and value teachings have the tendency to take the edge off the competitive spirit. Mundane things are not worth struggling for, and opportunities will be available in another lifetime.

The system tends to encourage and fortify the virtues of mildness, long-suffering, patience, and nonresistance. Class struggle and tension are discouraged. One outlet for escape is to go off into the forests to find peace and liberation and to become a Hindu saint or a wanderer. Millions have done this. Potential iconoclasts and dissidents of society who may have caused disruptions in society and the caste system have been lost in the forests. The caste system, then, has had its varied results.

There have been many changes in Indian society. The Islamic invasion of the seventh century A.D., British colonialism in India in the latter several centuries, and India's independence and secularistic emphases have been keynotes in the struggle of the caste system with outside influences and with change. India has one of the largest populations in the world, diversified in languages, tribes, and ethnic groups. India presents a staggering contrast in industrialization, nuclear energy potential, secularization, and deep traditional customs and religious practices. Change has come rapidly in some areas of society and slowly in others. Implications of modernizing influences on the caste system have been serious. Mahatma Gandhi opposed the caste system. He adopted a daughter who had been raised in a lower caste than his own. Many other Indian leaders have voiced the need for social change; and change has come. There has been intermingling of peoples between the castes. Intermarriages have occurred. Persons of various castes have risen above caste restraints to assume occupations and leadership positions not dictated by their caste. Yet the caste system is still a traditional aspect of the Indian people and the Hindu tradition and teachings.

Another challenge to the caste system is the alternative which Hindus may have in becoming members of other religious communities like Islam, Christianity, and Zoroastrianism. The Christian community, for example, may assume caste characteristics like its Hindu counterpart. This also raises the issues of religious pluralism and religious freedom in the context of Hinduism.

Krishna

The veneration of the cow and the complexity of the caste system are deep traditions within Hinduism which encounter the winds of change led by the leadership of India and by outside influences. There is another pattern in Hinduism which has emerged with a fresh impact. It is the devotion to Krishna, the supreme deity portrayed in the Bhagavad Gita. As previously pointed out, Hinduism has several paths to fulfillment or liberation. The paths of knowledge, works, and mysticism may lead one to break the cycle of transmigration of the soul and to balance out one's Karma. Another path is that of devotion (bhakti marga). Krishna has become the object of devotion to countless millions of Hindus, and Krishna has become the one Hindu deity to appeal successfully to peoples outside of India, namely in Europe and the United States.

There are certain tendencies with the devotional worship of Krishna by Hindus that raise challenges to other parts of the Hindu religion, as well as forbode challenges to other religions in terms of a missionary Hinduism. There are gods, goddesses, and spirits too numerous to count among Hindus. Nevertheless, Krishna emerges as a new conception of god. Krishna becomes a lord of nature rather than a god within nature. Hindus push beyond the metaphysical speculations about the origins of the world and the principles which govern it to find a personal god in Krishna who rules over the world. The Hindu comes near to monotheism in supreme devotion to Krishna, although there are other deities in the framework of Hinduism.

Krishna can accomplish several tasks for the Hindu which other deities cannot easily accomplish. Krishna can overcome the laws of Karma and break the cycle of transmigration through love and grace toward the individual and through a loving and obedient response of the individual to Krishna.

In the worship of Krishna, caste restrictions are often ignored and forgotten. There is a different understanding of the nature of humankind. Persons are not identical with deity, a divine principle, or a world soul. Persons are separate from the deity and dependent upon the deity. Krishna becomes the beloved, a friend, personal, affectionate, able to do for one what one cannot do for oneself. In this pattern of devotion escape to the forests is not necessary, and asceticism and extreme practices of meditation are not essential. One needs to keep company with Krishna in the company of their devotees. There is a congregational aspect to worship, and there is the idea of fellowship with Krishna and with one another, not union with a deity.

Thus, later developments of Krishna worship, devotion, and consciousness have had an impact on orthodox doctrines, traditional rituals, and the caste system within Hinduism in India. Devotion to Krishna has also served as a vanguard movement for the migration of Hinduism to other lands. Particularly in the United States, the gurus, the swamis, and the maharishi have come from India to teach the truths of Hinduism. In 1965 Swami Bhaktivedanta Prabhupada came to New York City, and shortly thereafter, the International Society for Krishna Consciousness, better know as the Hare Krishna, became established in cities across the United States. Swami Prabhupada had obtained his devotional knowledge (Bhaktivedanta) from gurus of the Krishna way in India. He came to America in time to reap some spin offs from the drug culture, and his movement especially appealed to the youth counter culture. Many of his followers who entered the Krishna communes and temples viewed the Swami as the incarnation (avatar) of Krishna for their time. Hare Krishna became a missionary movement within the religious pluralism stream of America. Alan Ginsberg, the poet, and George Harrison, one of the Beatles, praised the Swami's work in both poetry and song. The Swami's magazine, *Back to Godhead*, became a tract in the hands of eager members as they handed them out on the streets and in the airports of the nation.

Another movement of Hinduism to the United States is the transcendental meditation school. Maharishi Mahesh Yogi brought this school to America in the late 1950s. Other gurus came from India to promote its teachings. Guru Krishna, named after the deity Krishna, set up his classes in meditation. These classes offered a path to self-realization and fulfillment. The path would enable one to build a bridge between spirit and matter through a discipline of unifying body, mind, and spirit into a posture perfectly manifesting the presence of god. When the Guru stops his heart for seventeen seconds at the Menninger Clinic under conditions of precise, scientific observation, he is insisting that matter will be spiritualized and that consciousness is being raised to new levels. The Guru offers his followers a new dimension of life and faith, springing out of the background of the Yoga paths of Hinduism.

There are other issues which Hinduism has faced and is facing as it is challenged by national and world events. India has millions of religious minorities, including Muslims, Christians, Jains, and Sikhs. Hinduism as the dominant religious community faces the continuing experiment of living with diverse religious groups. Hindus and Muslims have had their difficulties, resulting in wars and new nations, namely, Pakistan and Bangladesh. Through all the issues of sacred cows, caste system, modernization, and war, Hinduism has shown a remarkable capacity for absorption, accommodation, and tenacity. Hinduism continues to offer to the Indian people a series of alternatives for life and faith and to the world at large a piece of its religious heritage.

3

BUDDHISM

■ ■

India is the homeland of Buddhism. The Buddha, born of the Gautama clan in the sixth century B.C., founded the religion named after him. He grew up in the Hindu tradition. However, as a young man he faced the crucial issues of life—suffering, old age, and death; he was dissatisfied with the answers which Hinduism offered. He left his home, wandered in the forest, and had an experience which came to be known as "the enlightenment."

The Buddha taught that the problem in life is suffering, and the cause of suffering is misplaced desire. The solution to life's predicament is the path of right thoughts, right actions, and right deeds. After this experience of enlightenment the Buddha gathered a core of disciples and preached his doctrines. A Buddhist way of life centered around the teachings of the Buddha, the Buddhist pathway, and a community of monks. His teachings were handed down in written form in the Tripitaka and the Sutras.

From A to Zen

Although Buddhism is present in India, it has spread widely since its beginnings. There are several main branches of Buddhism. The *Hinayana* (Theraveda) Buddhists are particularly prevalent in South and Southeast Asia in Burma and Thailand. The Hinayana view the Buddha as a great teacher, and they emphasize the life of the monastery. Another branch, the *Mahayana* Buddhists, has wide influence in its expansion through China and Korea to Japan. The Mahayana have developed elaborate Buddhist pantheons which have elevated the Buddha and other great Buddhist teachers into deliverers who enable their followers to attain the bliss of life and the world to come.

45

The Buddhism of Tibet is known as Tantric Buddhism or *Vajrayana*. It is a mixture of Mahayana with mystical and magical thoughts and practices. Perhaps the most popular form of Buddhism in western countries is *Zen* Buddhism. A Zen master teaches and leads a follower through certain techniques of meditation and exercises to experience supreme enlightenment (Satori). Besides Zen Buddhist groups in the United States, for example, there are also Buddhist Vihara societies and Buddhist Congregational churches.

Expansionism and missionary zeal have been more characteristic of Buddhism than Hinduism. Also, flexibility and adaptation have enabled Buddhism to appeal to diverse populations like China, Korea, and Japan. The Buddha grew up within the heart of Hinduism, and even attempted to reform it through his teachings and his disciples. However, Buddhism had to leave its homeland in order to gain favor with others. It has spread to over thirty countries, and has affected the philosophy, literature, music, drama, and art of many cultures, including western Europe and North America. Buddhism claims over 300 million adherents, including 100 million Hinayana, 185 million Mahayana, and 15 million Vajrayana.

Altogether, India has given birth to Hinduism and Buddhism, which claim nearly a billion followers. India also includes a large population of other religions, including Jainism, Sikhism, and Islam.

The Buddha:
From Reformer to the Blessed One to Buddhahood

Siddharta Gautama, popularly known as the Buddha, was the founder of Buddhism. Born about 560 B.C. in India, he was a contemporary of Confucius and Zoroaster. The Buddha was raised in a wealthy family. Tradition states that wonderful signs were attached to his birth and that his mother miraculously conceived him. A Hindu sage told his father that his son would be a world famous king or a Buddha, which means the enlightened one. The father attempted to shield his growing son from the unpleasantries and evils of life. His son was married and had a child. However, one day Buddha saw four sights which caused him deep concern. He saw an old man, a dying man, a dead man, and a holy man. The sight of age and death alarmed him, and the Hindu sage intrigued him, and he left his family to begin a life of spiritual pilgrimage in the forests. He became a student of Hindu Gurus. He meditated on Hindu philosophy. He followed the strict discipline of an ascetic life, often in self flagellation, but there was no satisfaction in his quest for the Hindu holy life.

Then the experience of *enlightenment* came to him. He was in meditation under a fig tree when truth apprehended him. He then formulated his teachings, which he called the Four Noble Truths and the Eightfold Path. Through sermons and invitations, the Buddha gathered a corps of disciples who followed him and formed the first monastery. Buddhism was on the way to becoming an alternate choice for the people of India.

As Buddhism migrated from India to other eastern lands, it encountered the religious traditions of native populations and it evolved its own interpretations and expressions from the teachings of Buddha and the traditions of the early Buddhist monks. The Buddha was represented to his followers as an example to emulate and often as an ultimate religious symbol. Temples were built to house statues of him. Offerings and prayers before his image became standard ceremony. The Buddha was granted a more than human status—he was the Blessed One.

As Buddhism stretched to China, Korea, and Japan, it formed various sects. A belief arose that many individuals had attained the same enlightenment as Gautama Buddha, and therefore other Buddhas were qualified for Buddhahood. They had decided after reaching enlightenment not to leave this life but to remain and help others toward the same goal.

A prominent Buddhist sect is Pure Land. This sect has elevated Amitabha as a Buddha. Amitabha is the merciful father of a pure land or western paradise. His followers gain salvation by having faith in him. Buddhists throughout China, Korea, and Japan voice a daily prayer, "I flee to thee Amitabha, glory be to Amitabha." The paradise which this Buddha presides over and offers to his devotees is described in vivid material terms.

Unlike Hinduism, then, Buddhism has a definite founder in Gautama Buddha. The Buddha has been viewed and venerated by his followers in both humanistic and metaphysical terms. Being the enlightened one he is seen as a Teacher, a Master, a Great Man, a Lord, and the Exalted or Blessed One. Later Buddhist communities considered him a Bodhisattva (a savior and universal ruler). Still later, other great men who attained the enlightenment of Gautama were elevated to Buddhas, and an elaborate pantheon of Buddhas emerged.

Thus, there are diverse interpretations within Buddhism concerning the nature of Buddha. Some Buddhists insist that Buddhism is atheistic or at least agnostic. Others not only state but also express in devotional practices that god is real in such figures as Amitab. Buddhists, like Hindus, have a variety of human needs to be met. Their religious experience raises questions and faces problems that are not solved in the human context. They extend their minds, hearts, and hands to a source, persons, or deity beyond themselves. So there is a Krishna in Hinduism and an Amitab in Buddhism who offer grace and reward to the devoted and faithful.

Buddhist Literature:
Buddha's Teachings and Disciples' Interpretations

Buddhism has a variety of sacred written traditions based on the teachings of the Buddha and the numerous interpretations of his disciples. The two main schools of Buddhism, the Hinayana (Theraveda) and the Mahayana, have their distinctive canons and scholarly interpretations. The Hinayana sacred writings are in the Pali language, and it is estimated to be about twice the size of the Bible. The Mahayana sacred writings have translations from the Sanskrit language as well as original writings in Chinese, Japanese, and Tibetan languages. Although some of the Mahayana writings are similar to the older Hinayana Canon, many Mahayana texts have no similarity to Hinayana writings. The two schools are quite distinct in their interpretations of both the meaning of the Buddha as well as his teachings.

The Hinayana Canon is prevalent in Southeast Asia in Burma and Thailand. The texts of the canon are called the Tripitaka, literally meaning division into three baskets. The Tripitaka contains the sermons and lectures of Buddha, rules for the monks in the monasteries, and metaphysical treatises. The canon circulated in an oral tradition from the time of the Buddha in the fifth century B.C. until the third century B.C., when it came into written form.

In the following text, the Buddha, who is called the Blessed One, discusses the problem of life—desire or false clinging to attachment groups.

> Thus have I heard. On a certain Occasion The Blessed One was dwelling at Savatthi in Jetavana monastery in Anathapindika's Park. And there The Blessed One addressed the priests.
> "Priests," said he.
> "Lord," said the priests to the Blessed One in reply.
> And The Blessed One spoke as follows:
> "I will teach you, O priests, the burden, the bearer of the burden, the taking up of the burden, and the laying down of the burden.
> "And what, O priests, is the taking up of the burden?
> "Reply should be made that it is the five attachment-groups. And what are the five? They are: the form-attachment-group, the sensation-attachment-group, the perception-attachment-group, the predisposition-attachment-group, the consciousness-attachment-group. These, O priests, are called the burden.
> "And who, O priests, is the bearer of the burden?
> "Reply should be made that it is the individual; the venera-

ble So-and-so of such-and-such a family. He, O priests, is called the bearer of the burden.

"And what, O priests, is the taking up of the burden?

"It is desire leading to rebirth, joining itself to pleasure and passion, and finding delight in every existence—desire, namely, for sensual pleasure, desire for permanent existence, desire for transitory existence.

"This, O priests, is called the taking up of the burden.

"And what, O priests, is the laying down of the burden?

"It is the complete absence of passion, the cessation, giving up, relinquishment, forsaking, and non-adoption of desire. This, O priests, is called the laying down of the burden."[8]

The teachings of the Buddha stress dependence on the individual to work out one's own problems and destiny. A Buddhist's goal is to arrive at Nirvana, and one must be freed from this world to accomplish Nirvana.

In him who depends (on others), there is wavering. In him who is independent, there is no wavering. Where there is no wavering, there is tranquility. Where there is tranquility, there is no passionate delight. Where there is no passionate delight, there is no coming and going (in rebirth). Where there is no coming and going (in rebirth), there is no falling from one state to another. Where there is no falling from one state to another there is no "here," no "beyond," no "here-and-yonder."

That is the end of woe.[9]

The practice of meditation is highly important for the Buddhist. The Buddha taught that meditation leads to tranquility and to insight.

Two things, O brethren, are conducive to knowledge. What are the two? Tranquility and insight. When tranquility is developed, what happens? Mind is developed. When mind is developed, what happens? Whatever passion there is is abandoned. When insight is developed, what happens? Right understanding is developed. When right understanding is developed, what happens? Whatever ignorance there is is abandoned. The mind soiled with passion is not greed. When there is soiling through ignorance, right understanding is not developed. Thus through unstaining of passion there is freedom of mind, and through unstaining of ignorance there is freedom of right understanding. (Anguttara Nikaya.)[10]

The Mahayana Scriptures are a later edition of Buddhism. As Buddhism spread to China, Korea, and Japan, it encountered Confucianism, Taoism, and Shintoism, and was influenced by these religions. Mahayana scriptures became codified about A.D. 100. It is said that a Buddhist monk cannot read all the Mahayana sacred writings since they are so numerous. These scriptures expand the interpretations of the Hinayana Canon and teach the doctrine of the heavenly Buddhas and the Bodhisattvas (the Enlightened Ones).

Perhaps the most important Mahayana texts are the Lotus of the True Law and the Discourses on the Perfection of Wisdom, which includes the famous Heart Sutra and the Diamond Cutter Sutra. All of these texts emphasize the nature of Buddha, which has become infinite and universal. The Buddha has attained perfect wisdom and knows the way to Nirvana, the other shore. Also, these texts stress that others like Gautama Buddha may become Bodhisattvas, those who have attained enlightenment or perfect wisdom and aid others to cross to the other shore.

The following extract from the Lotus Sutra writing emphasizes the Buddha who is called Tathagata as a Savior ready to help others attain deliverance from this world.

> I am the Tathagata, O ye gods and men! the Arhat, the perfectly enlightened one; having reached the shore myself, I carry others to the shore; being free, I make free; being comforted, I comfort; being perfectly at rest, I lead others to rest. By my perfect wisdom I know both this world and the next, such as they really are. I am all-knowing, all-seeing. Come to me, ye gods and men! hear the law. I am he who indicates the path; who shows the path, as knowing the path, being acquainted with the path.
>
> I shall refresh all beings whose bodies are withered, who are clogged to the triple world. I shall bring to felicity those that are pining away with toils, give them pleasures and final rest.
>
> Hearken to me, ye hosts of gods and men; approach to behold me: I am the Tathagata, the Lord, who has no superior, who appears in this world to save. To thousands of kotis of living beings I preach a pure and most bright law that has but one scope to wit, deliverance and rest.
>
> I preach with ever the same voice, constantly taking enlightenment as my text. For this is equal for all; no partiality is in it, neither hatred nor affection. I am inexorable, bear no love nor hatred towards anyone, and proclaim the law to all creatures without distinction, to the one as well as the other. I re-create the whole world like a cloud shredding its

water without distinction; I have the same feelings for respectable people as for the low; for moral persons as for the immoral; for the depraved as for those who observe the rules of good conduct; for those who hold sectarian views and unsound tenets as for those whose views are sound and correct. I preach the law to the inferior in mental culture as well as to persons of superior understanding and extraordinary faculties; inaccessible to weariness, I spread in season the rain of the law.[11]

Buddhist scriptures, then, are multifaceted and voluminous. Unlike Hindu scriptures, written by countless nameless sages, Buddhist writings are either in the name of the Buddha or refer to his teachings. It is to be noted that in the scriptural traditions the Buddha is described in a variety of ways from a teacher, an ideal, and an exemplar to a deliverer, a lord, and a supernatural being.

Another form of Buddhism, Zazen or Zen Buddhism, also has its varied and complex writings. Zen Buddhism is perhaps the best-known expression of Buddhism in North America, having migrated from Japan. Zen teaches enlightenment (Satori) through highly disciplined meditation and mental exercises called Mondo and Koan, which have been handed down from Chinese and Japanese forms. Mondo is a rapid question and answer exercise between master and pupil. Koan is a riddle-like statement or question. The four following exercises indicate the complexity and the difficulty of Zen practice, whose purpose is to push beyond the intellect and the emotions to intuition and enlightenment.

A Zen Master met an Emperor. The Emperor began to boast before him. "I have built many temples and monasteries. I have copied the sacred books of the Buddha. Now what is my merit?"

The Zen Master said to him, "None whatever your Majesty."

The Emperor tried again, "What is the first principle of Buddhism?"

The Zen Master replied, "Vast emptiness."

The Emperor then asked, "Then who now confronts me?"

The master replied, "I have no idea."

Two monks were returning home and came to a stream across the path. A beautiful girl was waiting at the stream, fearful of getting wet if she crossed. One monk picked her up in his arms, crossed the stream, and having put her down, walked on. The other monk was horrified at what his friend had done, to touch a beautiful girl, and berated his fellow monk as they walked on. The first monk, suddenly aware of the harsh words of his friend, said to him, "That girl! I put her down at the stream. Are you still carrying her?"

Two hands when clapped together make a sound. What is the sound of one hand clapping?

A man hangs over a precipice by his teeth which are clinched in the branch of a tree. His hands are full and his feet are dangling. A friend leans over the precipice and asks him, "What is Zen?" What answer would you make?[12]

The Buddhist Path: From Suffering to Nirvana: Ethics and Enlightenment

Buddhism offers its followers choices in beliefs and practices. It has been pointed out that Buddhism is divided into several large movements including the Hinayana and the Mahayana. The Hinayana fit the great tradition while the Mahayana demonstrate characteristics of the little tradition. Consequently there are great differences between the movements. However, there is a core of belief and practice to which all Buddhists adhere. The Buddhist world view centers in the Four Noble Truths, and Buddhists look to the Eightfold Path as a way to live ethically and to achieve enlightenment.

The Four Noble Truths

Gautama Buddha formed his teaching from his experience growing up as a Hindu in India. He pondered upon the meaning of disease, the aging process, death, and the holy life lived by Hindu ascetics. The Buddha rejected the Hindu beliefs in the Veda scriptures, in the Brahmin authority and the caste system, and in the idea of an individual and world soul. He accepted the beliefs in karma and transmigration. However, the Buddha taught that there is no soul. The individual is composed of predispositions or psychological forces called Skandas. These Skandas are made of atoms, but they are not eternal. They are the means by which karma or good action is transferred from one life to another. The five skandas are body, sensation, perception, the aggregates, and consciousness. There is no permanent self. There is only a changing collection of the Skandas.

The Buddha rejected many Hindu beliefs and practices. He formulated his own teachings in the Four Noble Truths. These truths emerged from the Buddha's rejection of Hindu beliefs and practices and the formulation of his own teachings. The truths are the following:

- All life is suffering (dukkha).

- All suffering is from desire or craving (tanha).

- If there is no craving, there is no suffering.

- If you follow the Eightfold Path, there is no craving and, hence, not suffering.

Birth is suffering. Decay is suffering. Illness is suffering. Death is suffering. The presence of objects we hate is suffering. The separation from objects we love is suffering. Not to obtain what we desire is suffering. Everything from A to Z is suffering. The Buddha issued a judgment upon all of life and rejected the current ways of answering the dilemmas of life.

On the walls of early Buddhist monasteries a wheel was painted depicting the wheel of becoming. The spokes of the wheel symbolized Buddhist beliefs about life. One spoke focused on growing old and dying. To the Buddhist this was unsatisfactory. What preceded it? Birth preceded growing old and dying; but if there was no birth, one would not grow old and die. Another spoke symbolized the process of becoming, of being born from one existence to another. What happens on the deathbed of the previous life? One clings to life. One desires to live and not die, and throughout life there is a craving thirst, a clinging desire to have more things, more life. One dies in ignorance (avidya) not knowing how to end desire. One needs wisdom and enlightenment in order to break the cycle of the wheel, birth to death to birth, and to attain Nirvana.

Knowledge for the Buddhist is essential. One must know the Four Noble Truths and what lies behind them. Of course, there is suffering. Pleasure, itself, is not only a prelude to pain but is a form of pain. There is also impermanence (anicca), a continual succession of becoming in the form of the Skandas. There is no soul, no ego (anatta). Behind these truths there is no belief in a deity or deities. There are no prayers to the gods. There is no reliance upon external help. The Buddha taught that one should work out one's own salvation. He was aware that people believed in gods, goddesses, and spirits. He knew they made their sacrifices and offerings, but he offered another way of understanding the world and of living life.

Some have argued that the Buddha and early Buddhism were atheistic in their beliefs. Others have said that they were agnostic at best. It is safe to say that early Buddhism emphasized the importance of knowledge and ethics and basically ignored the animistic and polytheistic trends of Hinduism. Later developments in Buddhism, especially the Mahayana, introduced whole sets of beliefs and practices that differed with those of earlier periods.

The Noble Eightfold Path

After one believes in the Four Noble Truths and the themes underlying them, then what does one do? How does one act to overcome suffering and cease desiring? How does one reach the goal of enlightenment? What kind of experience does Nirvana hold for the Buddhist? The *Noble Eightfold Path* is the Buddhist answer. It is the fourth noble truth. The Eightfold Path can be divided into three larger divisions which are the right beliefs and resolves, the moral life, and the mystical or meditative life.

In the category of *right beliefs and resolves*, there are right views and right resolves. A good Buddhist has right views when the Four Noble Truths are understood and accepted. Basic to this path is having the correct knowledge about the origin and cessation of suffering. A right resolve is when one takes a solemn oath to break the wheel of becoming and eliminate sensuality, craving, and malice. The two paths affect the understanding and the will of the individual.

The next stage in the Eightfold Path includes the *moral life* with the three components of right speech, right conduct, and right occupation. One refrains from gossip, rumors, and harsh talk. A good Buddhist practices nonviolence (ahimsa) toward all creatures. Stealing is forbidden. Celibacy is ideal. One takes up a proper occupation. A good Buddhist does not trade or sell armaments or butcher animals.

The third division describes the *disciplined life of reflection and thought*. This includes the right endeavor, right mindfulness, and right meditation. These three paths necessitate seclusion from others and withdrawal to a favorable place for quiet and serenity. Right endeavor means to get one's mind under the control of one's will. It implies eliminating evil thoughts and focusing on good qualities. Right mindfulness means to direct one's thoughts to prescribed topics which root out distraction, inattention, and physical objects. It is achieving pure attention in the meditation exercises.

The eighth stage in the path is *right meditation*. The proper form and content of meditation is important. There are a variety of postures and exercises used in this state. Breath control exercises are essential. One may focus vision on an object or symbol. One may repeat certain sacred words from the sutras, Buddhist sacred writings. The Buddhist who arrives at this last state will then experience certain trances. The trances (dhyanas) are characterized as the serenity of body and mind, the freedom of the intellect, rising above joy and suffering, and the conquest of mind over all ignorance. One can see beyond birth to see the cause of rebirth. One has rooted out all craving and has overcome suffering. The wheel of becoming has been overcome. The Eightfold Path has been completed, and one has arrived at enlightenment. The Buddhist in this stage and in this experience is ready for Nirvana. One has become an Arahat.

Buddhists are reared to know the Four Noble Truths and the Eightfold Path that compose the Dharma or conduct of Buddhism. They know that the Buddha taught those truths in the context of a middle path. He did not advocate the extreme pleasure of a hedonistic life nor the stringent life of asceticism. The Buddhist middle way of ethics and enlightenment includes a respect for all of life. The Buddhist is to abstain from unchastity and intoxicants. One is counseled to eat moderately and to refrain from frivolous activities.

Buddhist Devotion

Each Buddhist takes a vow to the Buddha, the Dharma, and the Sangha (monastery). The Buddha served as the supreme example for his followers. He gave them the principles and practices to guide them through life. But what about the monastery? The monastery provides a superior life and the best opportunity for one to achieve enlightenment. Buddha taught the ideal was to live as a monk. The traditional monk's orange robe, shaven head, and temple lodging separate him from laypersons. He must observe some 227 rules. He must not grow his own food for fear of taking the life of some animal form and breaking one of the rules. The monk demonstrates to laypersons his ethical superiority by his cloistered and restrained life. A layperson may observe some of the qualities of the Eightfold Path, but only a monk can have the time and disposition to complete the Eightfold Path. A discrepancy, therefore, exists between the monk and the layperson. Persons with families and work responsibilities simply cannot take up the monk's life.

The laity must support the monks. In Thailand, a Hinayana Buddhist country, one may see monks pass along the roads each morning accepting in their bowls the alms given by the laity. Laity go to the temples at festival times to take the monks special gifts. In the Buddhist understanding there are reciprocal blessings or karma gained by each party. The monk gains good karma by renouncing the world. The layperson gains good karma by aiding the monk. Therefore, the system works well for both parties. The monk is supported in the latter stages of the Eightfold Path, and the monk furnishes the laity with an opportunity to gain merit. The vow which a monk takes is not binding for life; one may enter the monastery for a short time. The monastic life symbolizes a basic Buddhist belief that one gains merit by renouncing the world. It is interesting to note that just as the Buddha rejected the elitism of the Brahmin priests, he formulated the monastery as an elite group in Buddhism.

Nirvana in Hinayana and Mahayana

After understanding the truths and following the paths to enlightenment, what is Nirvana like? How can one experience it and describe it?
Nirvana is perhaps one of the most difficult and enigmatic religious terms
to define or clarify. Etymologically, it means extinction. A fire is extin-
guished or dies out. Other words are used to describe Nirvana. It is the
end of suffering. It is the medicine for all evil. It is detachment or the cessation of becoming.

Buddha saw personality as a collection of material, volitional, and
mental elements. The elements were held together by craving. Once
craving is overcome, the elements disperse. There is no history in transmigration once craving ceases. Buddha's very theory of the "non-soul"
or "non-self" implies extinction. There is no god to restore the elements.
Where does the fire go when it goes out? It does not go north or south.
It just goes out. Nirvana, then, is not existence. Nirvana is not to be
born. Buddha refuses to speculate about life after death. Does the saint
(Arahat) exist after death? The Buddha would say not to worry over it. It
is an attainment of freedom, and it is an escape from ignorance and
greed. However, millions of Buddhists are dissatisfied with the emptiness
of Nirvana and seek another answer.

Buddhism, like Hinduism, has a belief and practice system which
emphasizes a personal relationship to deity and a response of faith to
grace. In Hinduism the way of devotion to a god like Krishna appealed to
millions who became tired and frustrated with philosophical systems,
impersonal principles, and mystical knowledge. In Buddhism, the Hinayana path, which highlights the life of the monk and serious meditation
practices that demand extended time and isolation, became a problem for
the millions. Also, as Buddhism migrated from India to lands where it had
to compete with other religions, it was willing to adapt to the religious consciousness of peoples. Consequently, it emphasized different beliefs and
practices from its native India and from earlier Buddhism. This later form
is known as *Mahayana*. The Mahayana are the little traditions as the
Hinayana, who sometimes are called the Theraveda, the great traditions.
The Mahayana compose the largest number of Buddhists.

What are the Mahayana like? Perhaps three words may characterize
the Mahayana: accommodation, universalism, and transcendence. In
their historical development these Buddhists were willing to change or to
accommodate their beliefs and practices to the religious expectations
and ideas of people. They were willing to move beyond considering the
monk as the only religious elite and beyond the monastery. They
appealed to more people and became missionaries to other lands. They
looked upon themselves as a universal religion. The Mahayana interpreted and transformed the Buddha and his teachings into a divine being

of personal nature and transcendence. The Buddha became like a god. Others could become like him. These transcendent divine beings offered more than a way of enlightenment. They offered grace to those who would have faith in them and give them devotion.

What happens to the concept of Nirvana among the Mahayana? Again, Nirvana is an ambivalent term. The Mahayana first speak of a heaven, a Buddha land, to which faithful Buddhists are transported at death. The Amida Buddha, so prominent among Japanese Buddhists, is a cosmic deity who has attained the Buddha nature. He has a heaven of bliss called the Pure Land, he offers compassion to people who honor him, and he promises them a heavenly reward in his paradise.

The Lotus Sutra, a sacred Buddhist writing, says that there have been an infinite number of Buddhas saving people. Many people can attain Buddhahood. When one has made this achievement based on ethics, enlightenment, and the compassion and mercy of a Buddha, one may become a Bodhisattva, a savior, who helps others. In Mahayana there are hierarchies of Buddhas and Bodhisattvas. There are heavenly realms. The teaching of Nirvana by the Buddha gets pushed into the background; it becomes transformed or fleshed out in a more personalistic and understood form. Thus, images of the Buddha and other Buddha-types like Amida fill Buddhist temples, and they serve as focal points for worship and devotion by the Mahayana.

Both Hinayana and Mahayana forms of Buddhism are good examples of the great and little traditions within a single religion. They both stand upon the teachings of the Buddha, but they make various interpretations upon the noble truths and the Eightfold Path. Perhaps the following sketch may be helpful in distinguishing key differences:

	Hinayana	Mahayana
Person	individualistic self–emancipation	community oriented dependent–salvation by grace
Key Virtue	wisdom	compassion
Religion	full–time job monk elitism	normal in life laypersons and saints
Ideal	Arahat (saint)	Bodhisattva (savior)
Buddha	saint	savior
Prayer	meditation	petition
Orientation	traditional	innovative (flexible)

Buddhism offers its followers a deep variety of beliefs and practices similar to the kinds of choices in Hinduism.

Shrines and Monasteries

Buddhism has had a colorful history as it has moved from India through Southeast Asia into China, Korea, and Japan. It has both influenced the cultures of other peoples as well as accommodated itself to those cultures. Consequently, unlike India with its unity and uniformity of temple worship and organization, Buddhism has a variety of shrine forms and monastic communities. In the following paragraphs there will be select descriptions of Southeast Asian shrines, a Thailand monastery, and a Japanese Zen Buddhist monastery.

Southeast Asian Shrines

The earliest shrine, out of which the pagoda emerged, was the stupa, a burial mound with a relic of the Buddha. These stupa became places of popular worship. During the third century B.C. the missionary-minded King Asoka constructed over 84 thousand shrines within a three-year period. An umbrella-type roof covered the burial mound, and the stupa itself became an object of worship and a pilgrimage site. Two of the most famous shrines are the Tooth Temple in Kanday, Sri Lanka, housing a tooth of Buddha, and the Shyway Dagon Pagoda in Burma, containing eight of his hairs. These shrines continue to exist as places of veneration, but shrines are also included in a larger system of Buddhist organization.

The vow of a Buddhist includes belief in the Buddha, the Dharma (Law), and the Sangha (monastery). The monastery, sometimes called the Vihara or the Wat according to the culture, has been an important community for Buddhists since the time of the Buddha. Equivalent to the Christian church or the Islamic mosque in importance to the community at large, the Buddhist monastery grew. A modern understanding of the Vihara or the Wat is a building or temple which houses the image of the Buddha and usually includes a greater complex of buildings. Larger temples have an area for important rituals and higher ordination and recitation. A separate building might include a hall for sermons preached to laypersons during holy season.

Other sacred places are often found within the Vihara holding relics of the Buddha, wall shrines for meditation, and often a bo tree, like the one under which the Buddha sat to attain enlightenment. The Vihara complex may also include quarters for monks (bhikkus), open courtyards, kitchen and dining hall, store house, bell tower, library, and a bathing pond. A school may be attached to the temple for the education of novice monks.

A Hinayana Monastery in Thailand

During the season of heavy monsoon rains monks remain in their own Wat for religious observances. After this season monks may leave their Wat and travel to visit other Wats or to make pilgrimages to sacred stupas. Some four to six hundred monks may reside at the same time in the Wat. Their daily life is a highly disciplined one. A bell is rung at 4 a.m. to awaken them. After bathing, each puts on three yellow robes. Each residence has an altar on which a Buddha-image is placed. The monk bows before the image and recites the vow. Then, in a cross-legged position the monk sits and meditates. Having meditated, the monk goes into the courtyard, finds another monk, and confesses his shortcomings. Having accomplished these exercises before sunrise, the monks retire to their residence for rest.

Shortly after sunrise the monks with their alms-bowls go into the road-ways to receive the food-offerings from the people who await their emergence from the Wat. They eat their breakfast in their individual residences. In smaller Wats monks may sit together for breakfast. After eating, they pronounce a blessing upon their alms-givers. A bell rings about 8 a.m. to call the monks to the sanctuary for the morning chanting ceremony. They take their seats in rows according to seniority with the elder monks in front, followed by the younger monks and the novices. They bow and recite in the Pali language before the Buddha altar, after lighting the candles. New monks are then given basic instructions while the older monks retire to their residences.

By 11:30 a.m. the main meal is taken either from food left over from the morning alms from the laity, or it may be prepared in the Wat kitchen. There is rest and study after lunch. At 6 p.m. the bell sounds to call them once again to the sanctuary. In groups of two they confess their failures, and then they bow and chant to the Buddha-image as was done in the morning. Evening classes are held for new monks. Afterward, there may be visitation among the monks before retirement for the evening.

There are various ceremonies and celebrations held in the Wat according to the Buddhist calendar. On occasion the laity will visit the Wat to take vows and to hear a sermon. The laity will bow and chant to the Buddha-image along with the monks, although they will be segregated in the seating arrangement. A prominent layperson will request the director of the Wat for a sermon. On other special occasions all the monks will assemble in the sanctuary to hear a specially trained monk recite the 227 rules of Buddhism clearly and fluently. Another monk checks the recitation from the printed Pali text. There is a special time during a holy season when the laity present new yellow robes to the monks. Then there is the ceremony when men who have become monks for only a short time of several months leave the Wat to return to their families and their jobs. In Thai society there is an expectation that an adult male will spend several months in a Wat.

A Zen Monastery in Japan

Zen Buddhism has its origins in the Mahayana tradition in China and Japan. The goal of the Zen life is to experience Satori, which is enlightenment. Also, Zen strives for moral and social virtues which enable the individual to promote peace and welfare in the community. The Zen life may be observed in terms of a life of humility, of labor, of service, of prayer and gratitude, and of meditation.

Humility is a virtue which the Zen monk attains through a life of begging. Begging is not only a way for the monk to survive physically, but also it is a system of merit giving and merit receiving between the monk and the laity. Begging teaches the monk humility and the giver self-denial. The monk goes out into the streets with several other monks. A broad hat enables the monk to see only several feet ahead, keeping the monk from seeing who places money or rice in his begging bowl. Charity is to be free from personal relationships and from favoritism either on the part of the monk or the layperson. There are also families who consistently contribute rice and other produce to the monastery. Monks go out monthly with sacks or hand carts to these families to collect quantities of food.

Labor is an essential feature of the Zen life. "A day of no work is a day of no eating." Of course, the Zen life is filled with hours of meditation and abstract thinking, but Zen masters have taught their monks to work on the farm, and in the forests, to use axes, to pull carts, and to carry water. The master works as well as the pupils. There is a democratic spirit about Zen life in which both the high and the low in the hierarchy do the same work.

All work in the monastery is looked upon as a life of service. The management of the monastery is handled by the master and senior members. Divisions of service include the supervision of the procurement and preparation of food, administration of the Buddhist shrine and related facilities, and general supervision of life in the Meditation Hall under the leadership of the master. Eating is a highly ceremonial event. Breakfast consists of gruel and pickles. The main meal is taken about 10 a.m. and consists of rice mixed with barley, soup, and pickles. Supper is the leftovers from lunch. Since Zen monks are to have only two meals each day, emulating the Buddha, the evening meal is called "medicinal food."

As the monks are seated before eating, they recite the names of the great Bodhisattvas. Then they recite the five subjects of meditation: their own worthiness of eating, their virtues, their detachment from defects, their commitment to a strong and healthy body, and their devotion to the truth. They conclude with the vows to destroy evil, to do deeds of goodness, and to help all beings and themselves to attain Buddhahood. There is silence during the meal itself. Monks take turns serving the tables. Upon finishing the meal each monk wipes his bowl and stores it in a cloth. Then the monks return to their residences. The spirit of brotherhood, mutual help, and service to one another characterize the monastery.

A life of prayer and gratitude governs the Zen community. Prayers are offered to the Buddhas and the Bodhisattvas. Sutras are also recited. Sutra readings and recitations aid one to understand the thoughts of the founders of the sutra scriptures as well as to gain spiritual merit. The monks demonstrate their gratitude to all the Buddhas, Budhisattvas, teachers, and other beings through their reading and recitation of the sutras, incense offering, bowing, and individual reflections. At New Year there are special sutra recitation ceremonies in which the monks pray for the welfare of the nation and for the peace of the world. This recitation carries special merit for both the reciters and for those to whom the recitation is dedicated. The monks recite at the top of their voices, and the occasion is a colorful and lively one.

The life of meditation among the Zen is a rigorously disciplined one. The Meditation Hall or Zendo is the central abode of the monk. The interior of the Hall has raised platforms call Tan, which run along the sides of the Hall. The Tan is eight feet wide and three feet high. The shrine for the Bodhisattva stands at one end of the empty floor between the Tan. The empty floor provides space for monks to walk during the meditation times to keep their minds fresh and bodies agile. Each monk has a space of three to six feet on the Tan which is his abode. In this space the monk sits, meditates, sleeps, and lives out his existence in the Hall. A shelf is provided for bedding and individual necessities. The monks retire about 9 p.m. after recitations and bowings before the Bodhisattva. They arise at 3:30 a.m. to practice Zazen.

The basics of the Zendo life are to study the sayings, writings, and actions of the past masters and to practice meditation. The practice of meditation is called Zazen, and the study of the masters includes attendance of the lectures of the teacher of the Zendo known as Roshi. The teacher or master (Roshi) attempts to help the monk help himself in understanding the ancient teachings.

It is incumbent on the monk to master the Koan exercise—this is one of the most important disciplines in the life of meditation. The Koan is a question or riddle which the monk is asked to solve. As one Koan is mastered, others are given to the monk. In the Meditation Hall (Zendo) the monks sit along the Tan facing each other. At certain times of the year the monks are exempt from work and practice Zazen from 3:30 a.m. until 9 p.m. except for meals. In order for Zazen to bear fruit, the monk must do Sanzen. During Sanzen, the monk presents his views on the Koan to the Master. This usually occurs twice daily. A Zen monk may leave the monastery to take up life in another if the master gives permission. Usually several times each year each monk is evaluated according to his behavior and his dedication to the disciplined life. He may remain in the monastery, or he may petition to leave for another one. If his behavior has not been agreeable, he may not be able to continue in any Zen monastery.

Buddhism, then, provides a clear and precise system of temple, shrine, and monastery which unites the monk and the layperson in religious activities and satisfactions. Buddhist laity rely heavily on the religious professionals in the shrines and monasteries for religious merit and security. On the other hand, the religious professionals depend on the laity for their economic and physical survival through a well defined and accepted method of merit giving and merit receiving. Throughout Buddhism there is a mutual reliance between the monks and the laity for religious organization, religious practice, and religious survival.

Militancy, Missions, and Messiahs

Basic to Buddhist teaching is a world view that sees the world as illusory or evil and that promotes a path to escape or liberation from the world. An obvious challenge within Buddhism is the tension to live in the world and affirm it, to flee the world through isolation within it, or to negotiate a path of discipline through it. Buddhism has offered a more universal approach to life than Hinduism. Buddhism has opposed the caste system and has emphasized the individual. The individual has been given the responsibility to achieve one's destiny. Buddhism has kept the Hindu teachings of reincarnation and karma, but an internal challenge within Buddhism has been the diversity of thought it has incorporated as it accommodated itself to other religious traditions in China and Japan.

There are several ways that Buddhism has made adaptations to the world. It has found patrons to protect it and give it sustenance. It has interpreted the Buddha's teachings to include Bodhisattvas or savior types to offer assistance to individuals to achieve their destinies. It has spread its teachings to other populations so that Buddhism might continue in vitality and stability. Thailand is an example of a country in which Buddhism found a patron in a king. The relationship between the monks (Sangha) and the state in Thailand has been close. Until recently, the king was regarded as the Buddhist World Emperor. He was given divine characteristics. He was the protector of the Buddhist tradition and a patron to the monks. Court ceremonies were symbolized by Buddhist institutions and values. In modern Thailand there continues to be a working relationship between Buddhist institutions and government, but with social and political change tensions have emerged between church and state. In a process of modernization religion tends to be compartmentalized along with other important social and cultural matters.

Buddhism, then, is challenged in its development to consider political theory and practice. In the case of Thailand the king was to protect the Buddhists from all threats and invasions. In the case of South Vietnam in the 1960s a crisis developed between the Buddhists and the Roman Catholic government which had repercussions for politics, militancy, and religious freedom. Fourteen Mahayana sects led by their monks merged into the United Buddhist Church. The monks addressed thousands of Buddhists in the pagodas with speeches denouncing the Roman Catholic regime. Soon there were eight ritual suicides by monks as they burned themselves in protest of governmental actions. They were led by the Venerable Thich Quang Duc, a seventy-three year old monk who burned himself to death on a Saigon street in 1963. Although the regime attempted to stamp out the Buddhist opposition with massive retaliation, it failed. The United States withdrew its support from the regime, and a military coup occurred. Buddhism has struggled with the ways of the world in relating to the political order.

A militant and missionary form of Buddhism arose in Japan after World War II known as Soka Gakkai, meaning the Value Creating Society. The Soka Gakkai trace their roots to Nichiren Daishonen, a Buddhist leader of the thirteenth century A.D. This leader placed emphasis upon the Lotus Sutra as the primary Buddhist scripture. He taught that a particular chanting of the Lotus Sutra would bring one happiness, bliss, and material success. There was no need for other forms of Buddhism. Nichiren said that Japan only needed the Sutra and his own understanding of it. As Nichiren taught and gained followers, they believed as he did that he was the new Buddha for the ages to come.

In post-war Japan the Soka Gakkai grew by the millions. They used coercion and other methods of fear and intimidation to recruit members. They formed a political party, the Komeito, which became the third most powerful political influence in Japan. The Soka Gakkai came to the United States in the 1960s and became known as the Nichiren Shoshu. It was organized in many of the major cities. It claims over three hundred thousand followers, most of whom are non-Asians. This Buddhist group demonstrates militancy and missionary outreach, and they give devotion and obedience to a man who claimed to be Buddha.

Another movement of Buddhism which migrated to the west from China and Japan is Zen Buddhism. Zen Buddhism is missionary to the extent that it came to the United States to attract Americans. However, Zen is not militant, and it proposes no Bodhisattva or savior for its adherents. In fact, Zen is opposite from the Soka Gakkai. It teaches self-discipline and self-realization. Reliance upon the self and upon the meditative exercises of the Zen master are the essentials. Peace, serenity, and order are ingredients of Zen. When one travels to Japan, one sees the evidence of Zen influences in the gardens, tea ceremonies, and the flower arrangements, as well as the arts. Zen Buddhism has quietly established over a dozen centers in the United States, with trained Zen masters as leaders. It beckons to those who through self-help will find a fulfilling path without militancy or a savior.

Buddhism, then, which began quite exclusively and passively with the Buddha's teachings and example, changed its teaching and forms over time and space. Like Hinduism, it became inclusive. It made room for deities, speculation, and Yoga disciplines. It broke out of the rigidity of the monk system, which restricted the fruits of liberation or Nirvana only to the monks, and it established a system of Buddhas and saviors who offered the masses a better and swifter way to fulfillment. It also was willing to fight for its place in the political and economic and social systems of the nations and made not only an accommodation but an impact upon politicians, statesmen, and governments. Like the Krishna movement within Hinduism, it became aggressive and missionary and expanded to other peoples and continents.

As the process of modernization penetrates traditional societies of which Buddhism is a part, it will face the continuing challenge of change. What influence will the monks and the monasteries (Sangha) have as laypersons become more educated, skilled, and exposed to the processes of secularism? What impact can Buddhism have upon nations and governments in the currents of nationalistic and revolutionary movements as it teaches individualism or passivity or escape from cravings and desires? What further adaptations will Buddhism need to make to continue to influence its own native populations and non-Buddhist peoples? Buddhism, like other major religions, has faced challenges for several millennia. It faced the opposition of Hinduism at its inception, and migrated to more fertile fields. It has learned to make adjustments.

4

CHINESE AND JAPANESE RELIGIOUS TRADITIONS

■   ■

Confucian, Taoist, Shinto, Buddhist

Two native religions of China are Confucianism and Taoism. China, like India, had various religious traditions among its people before either Confucianism or Taoism developed. Chinese ancient religions emphasized spirit worlds and ancestor worship. However, by the sixth century B.C. two religious geniuses came along to offer other religions.

Confucius was born about 550 B.C. in the Shantung province. He worked as a civil servant, traveled widely in China, and made friendships with government leaders and princes. His learning and counsel were sought, and he gathered disciples and founded a school. His teachings were collected later in the Analects. There was little mysticism and supernatural inclination about Confucius. He was more rationalistic and humanistic.

Confucianism was built on the importance of right order in the family and in the society. According to Confucius, people are basically good and will respond to goodness if they have the proper models. There are appropriate relationships of family, society, and work which are to be followed. Confucius taught an ethic for society that governed duty, demeanor, and all relationships. Confucianism fits well the Chinese propensity for ancestor worship, close family relations, and obedience to various levels of authority.

The second major religion that developed in China was Taoism. Its founder Lao Tzu also was prominent in the sixth century B.C. Taoism began as a philosophy of laissez-faire, emphasizing principles of noninterference in the lives of others and of quietism. In later development Lao Tzu was divinized in a pantheon of other deities with an elaboration of Taoism temples, monks, and scriptures. Both Confucius and Lao Tzu were given divine status by Chinese emperors. Confucianism and Taoism developed at a time when Mahayana Buddhism was impacting China. The emperors may have been reacting against the acceptance of Buddha by offering their people indigenous Chinese gods and rituals.

Shintoism is the major native religion of Japan. It is practiced both on the national level and in the family. The Japanese government supports Shinto shrines and rituals which closely align the sun deities with the emperor. The Bushido Code of ethics promotes the Samurai spirit of loyalty and obedience to the gods and to the emperor. Shintoism in the home includes god-houses, offerings, and rituals which the family performs daily.

Besides Shintoism, Mahayana Buddhism has influenced Japanese society. One Japanese Buddhist group is called Pure Land. This group worships Amida, who offers them deliverance to a heaven called Pure Land. Over 14 million Japanese adhere to this group. Another Buddhist expression in Japan is the Soka Gokkai, a twentieth century expression of Japanese Buddhism claiming over 16 million adherents. It is dogmatic, militant, and missionary. A third group is the Zen Buddhists. Professor D. T. Susuki has made Zen of Japanese flavor very popular in western countries.

Ancestors, Rice-Gods, and Buddhas

China and Japan offer their people various religious experiences and many divine beings and spirits to believe and to worship. Basic to both peoples is the *ancestor cult* in which deceased family and national figures like emperors are honored and venerated. In China the sage, Confucius, emerged as a great teacher. Confucianism became a way of life based on the right relations within the family and society; later Confucius himself was honored with temples and worship in his name. Likewise the founder of Chinese Taoism, Lao Tzu, established his religious teachings, and he, too, was later deified and included in the pantheon of Chinese gods.

In Japan there is a pervasive practice of honoring ancestors with daily offerings. Japanese Shintoism is the native religion based upon the way of the gods or spirits. The word for God, Kami, means superior and is used to describe those persons or objects like heaven, earth, mountains, animals, and emperors whom the Japanese honor and venerate.

Confucius, like Gautama Buddha, was a founder of a religious tradition. Confucius desired to strengthen the family and social fabric of

China by emphasizing the authority and obedience relationships between father and son, ruler and citizen, and the elders and youth. Some scholars have said that Confucius was a moralist and a skeptic. However, he accepted the religious practices of his day with reverence for ancestors and spirits. In his writings, the Analects, he counseled the people to remain aloof from the spirits. It is evident that he approved of some religious practices, especially those associated with ancestors, while he disapproved of others.

Shintoism offers the Kami, a pluralism of spirits and powers. Various stories tell of the activity of the gods throughout the Japanese island nation. Izanagi the god and Izanami the goddess gave birth to the islands as well as to the nature spirits and other deities. Amaterasu, the sun goddess and offspring of Izanami, is the most important Shinto deity. One of the greatest Shinto shrines is dedicated to her at Ise. Her brother, Susanowa the Storm-god, and his son, the Earth-god, have a large shrine at Izumo. Tradition states that Amaterasu gave her son Ninigi all of Japan for his kingdom. Ninigi married the goddess of Mount Fuji. One of their great-grandchildren became the first emperor of Japan. This story validated the later belief in the divinity of the emperor and the National Shinto cult.

The *Rice-god*, Inari, has a shrine in most villages. Inari is continually worshiped during the agricultural seasons of planting, transplanting, and harvesting rice. There are countless family and village deities called upon over Japan. Shintoism is expressed in over a hundred thousand shrines. The deities within the shrines protect the families and the land surrounding them. An organized priesthood supervises the rituals in the larger shrines. Also, within the homes there are small shrines to family ancestors, and daily offerings are made to the ancestors.

Buddhism entered Japan in the sixth century A.D. and found Japanese people receptive. Buddhism interpreted the Shinto deities as Bodhisattvas, manifestations of various *Buddha figures*. Buddhist monks presided over the Shinto shrines, and there was an intermeshing of Shinto and Buddhist deities and rituals. Later there were reactions of these religions against one another, and each attempted to purify and express its own religious patterns. However, in Japan today many Japanese families simultaneously have ancestor shrines, attend Shinto festivities, and adhere to a Buddhist monk's teachings. The Jodo sect in Japan is the same as the Pure Land sect in China. It reveres Amida Buddha (Amitabha in China) and claims him as the Lord of the Western Paradise. Amida, through his own enlightenment, has stored enough merit to save anyone who recites his name in faith. Amida gives salvation even to one at the point of death who can pray, "Hail Amida Buddha."

Japan, then, can claim no religious founder like the Buddha or Confucius. Yet it has a multitude of shamans, priests, monks, and great teachers who have influenced the people's beliefs in deities. Especially in Buddhism, charismatic leaders like Kobo, Kaishi, Honen, Shinran, and Nichiren have arisen in Japan to foster various interpretations. Even some of these leaders were characterized by their followers as more than mortal beings. Modern times have brought drastic changes with the communist takeover in China emphasizing atheism and the defeat of Japan in World War II, when the emperor repudiated any association with divinity. However, religious loyalties and beliefs in ancestor gods and spirits are difficult to subdue, much less to erase, and the Chinese and Japanese continue to search for realities beyond.

Confucian Classics and Taoist and Shinto Writings

The primary literature of *Confucianism* may be grouped into two main categories: The Five Classics and the Four Books. This literature is not considered as divine revelation like the Bible or the Qur'an, for it was written either by Confucius or his disciples. There is some question of the authorship of the materials. Some scholars think that some of the writings in the Classics came before Confucius' time and that he may have edited them. Some think that The Four Books were written during and after the time of Confucius.

The Five Classics are composed of the Book of Changes (I Ching), the Book of History (Shu Ching), the Book of Poetry (Shih Ching), the Books of Rites (Li Ching), and the Spring and Autumn Annals (Ch'un Ch'iu). These writings include a manual for fortune telling, civic duties, ballads and satires, rituals, and love songs.

The Four Books are the Analects (Lun Yen), the Book of Mencius (Meng Tzu), the Doctrine of the Mean (Chung Yung), and the Great Learning (Ta Hsueh). The Analects include the sayings of Confucius. Mencius was a noted disciple of Confucius, and he writes about the good qualities of human nature and civic duties. The Doctrine of the Mean is attributed to Confucius' grandson, Tsu-Ssu. It describes a moderate way of life in harmony with the Tao, the way of Heaven. The Great Learning describes the cultivated and cultural life of the individual, the family, the nation, and the world.

The following selection from the Doctrine of the Mean written by the grandson of Confucius provides a brief summary of the teachings in Confucianism. Confucius was not primarily concerned with deity. He was more interested in the development of individual and social nature and harmony so that right and good relationships could exist in families and societies. Tao is the word used for nature.

Personal Source of Social Harmony

What Nature provides is called "one's own nature." Developing in accordance with one's own nature is called "the way of self-realization." Proper pursuit of the way of self-realization is called "maturation."

One's own nature cannot be disowned. If it could be disowned, it would not be one's own nature. Hence, a wise man pays attention to it and is concerned about it, even when it is not apparent and when it does not call attention to itself.

One's external appearance is nothing more than an expression of his invisible interior, and one's outward manifestation reveals only what is inside. Therefore, the wise man is concerned about his own self.

Being unconcerned about (attitudes toward others and by others involving) feeling pleased, angered, grieved, or joyful is called "one's genuine personal nature." Being concerned (about such attitudes), each in its appropriate way, is called "one's genuine social nature."

This "genuine personal nature" is the primary source from which all that is social develops. This "genuine social nature" is the means whereby everyone obtains happiness.

When our "genuine personal nature" and "genuine social nature" mutually supplement each other perpetually, then conditions everywhere remain wholesome, and everything thrives and prospers . . .

Nature's Way Is Self-Correcting

Nature's way is not something apart from men. When a man pursues a way which separates him from men, it is not Nature's way.

In the *Book of Verses* it is written: "When one molds an axe handle, his pattern is not far away." The model for the handle is in the hand which grasps it, (even though) when we compare them, they appear different. So likewise, the wise man influences men by appealing to their natures. When they revert (to nature's way), he stops.

When one develops his nature most fully, he finds that the principles of fidelity and mutuality are not something apart from his nature. Whatever you do not want done to you, do not do to other.

Social Relationships

The nature of social (i.e., mutual) relationships may be illustrated by five (social relationships), and the traits needed to fulfill them (may be summarized as) three.

The relationships are those (1) between sovereign and subject, (2) between father and son, (3) between husband and wife, (4) between elder brother and younger brother, and (5) between friend and friend associating as equals. These five exemplify the nature of all social relationships.

The three traits—concern (*chih*), good will (*jen*), and conscientiousness (yung)—are required in all social relationships. In effect, the way in which these (three) traits function is unitary.

Some persons seem born with social aptitudes. Some acquire them by learning from teachers. And some develop them through trial-and-error experiences. But no matter how obtained, they operate in the same way.

Some persons express their concern for others spontaneously, some by calculating the rewards in prospect, and some by reluctantly forcing themselves. But when concern (and good will and conscientiousness) for others is expressed, then regardless of whether they are expressed spontaneously, calculatingly, or reluctantly the results are the same.

To be fond of learning is close to having wisdom (*chih*). To try hard is close to having good will (*jen*). To have feelings of guilt contributes to conscientiousness (yung).

When a person understands these traits, then he knows how to develop his character. When he knows how to develop his character, then he knows how to guide others. When he knows how to guide others, then he knows how to govern the whole country, including its states and communities.[13]

The major literature of Taoism includes the Tao-Te Ching, the Chuang Tzu, and the Tao-Tsang. The Tao-Te Ching is attributed to Lao Tzu, although scholars differ in their assessment of him as the author. The other writings are by later Taoist thinkers. Early Taoism stressed philosophical thought about the nature of life and the universe. The word *Tao* means the way and is quite complex in its full meaning. *Te* means power or virtue, and it is an ethical approach to Tao. Later development of Taoism brought magical practices, a pantheon of deities, and temple worship. Also literature which described this later Taoism developed the Eight Immortals, the Jade Emperor, and others which portrayed the popular side of Taoism.

The following excerpts are from the Tao-Te Ching. It is philosophical and mystical. Answers are not easy as one searches for the Way (Tao).

> There was something undifferentiated and yet complete
> Which existed before heaven and earth.
> Soundless and formless, it depends on nothing
> and does not change.

> It operates everywhere and is free from danger.
> It may be considered the mother of the universe.
> I do not know its name; I called it Tao.

> The all-embracing quality of the great virtue
> follows alone from the Tao.
> The thing that is called Tao is eluding and vague.
> Vague and eluding, there is in it the form.
> Eluding and vague, in it are things.
> Deep and obscure, in it is the essence.
> The essence is very real; in it are evidences.

> From the time of old until now, its name
> (manifestations) ever remains.
> By which we may see the beginnings of all things.
> How do I know that the beginnings of all things are so?
> Through this way (Tao).[14]

The Chinese and Japanese Way: Family, Friends, and Nation

Attention has already been given to the importance of family relationships, national pride, and patriotism among the Chinese and Japanese peoples. This section, then, shall deal with the effects of Confucianism, Taoism, and Shintoism on these people's lifestyles.

The Chinese Way of Life

At the time of Confucius, China was in the midst of internal strife. The ancient feudal society was in disintegration. Confucius sounded the alarm through his itinerant travels and teachings and called the people to return to the ethics and values of former generations. This view of humankind was optimistic. Although the Chinese had failed to honor their ancestors and to seek the good of others, Confucius saw the good in people and encouraged them to express that goodness in family and social relationships. How was one to be good? One can be good by observing a moral and social code of propriety. The linchpin of propriety is *Li*, the way things should be done. Li is good conduct and etiquette, observing what is traditional and expected by time-honored customs. It also means ritual or ceremony.

Confucius did not necessarily believe in the ancestors and spirits to whom sacrifices were offered in his day, but he believed in the value of ceremony and ritual, for it was good for the well-being and stability of society. He desired to establish a highly ritualized code of conduct so that an individual at whatever age and state of life would know exactly what was expected and what to do.

The primary expression of the virtue of Li is found in the *five overarching relationships*. There are relationships of ruler to subject, father to son, husband to wife, older brother to younger brother, and the patron or older friend to client or younger friend. In each relationship one member is dominant while the other is subordinate. There is also respect between the two. The ruler, the father, the husband, the older brother, and the older friend should show benevolence, kindness, gentility, and humaneness to the subordinate members. On the other hand, the subject, the son, the wife, the younger brother, and the younger friend should demonstrate loyalty, obedience, deference, and piety to the dominant members.

Other virtues taught by Confucius which support the five relationships are the will for good (jen), righteousness through justice (yi), wisdom (chih), and faithfulness (hsin). For example, the virtue of jen gives an attitude of benevolence which produces loyalty, good will, and right conduct. It is jen which helps one give service to one's ruler or parents. Not only does jen direct good will toward others, but it also enables one to have proper respect for one's own dignity as a human being.

Confucianism teaches an ideal person for an ideal society. The ideal person is one who possesses the virtues, who follows the conduct and ritual of propriety, and who is courteous, loyal, benevolent, and sincere. In the ideal society there is a perfect relationship between motives and manners. Duty, demeanor, and decorum are always appropriate. Love is never vexed; wisdom has no doubts; courage is without fear. How does one attain these idealisms? Confucius placed great attention on proper education to form good character and good relationships in society. He encouraged the study of Chinese literature, music, arts, and ancient rites.

Harmony and conformity are two themes inherent in Confucianism. Being in harmony with the will of heaven, the eternal way (Tao) which is expressed in moral code, is essential for correct living. Being in conformity to the manners of the ancients is worthy to emulate. Confucius had little to say about the nature of heaven or the origin of things. There was little mysticism or supernatural inclination within him. He was more rationalistic and humanistic, but he liked the values behind the rites of ancestor worship, which brought solidarity and harmony to individuals, families, and the nation. Confucius taught his moral and ethical qualities and codes of conduct as if they were grounded in the very nature of things. What was good for the individual and family was good for the nation. Confucius remained an optimist with regard to the goodness and possibilities of human nature and society.

After the death of Confucius certain Chinese emperors incorporated the teachings of Confucius into the nation's education. Other emperors established a national cult in honor of Confucius. Miracles and legends were associated with him. Temple worship was begun with pictures of Confucius placed on altars. Offerings were given in his honor. The national cult may well have been fostered by emperors to shore up their own prestige and power by association with Confucius. Also, Buddhism became a threat to Confucianism in China with the elevation of the Buddha into supernatural status. The national cult to Confucius may have been a reaction to Buddhist intrusions. The communist invasion of China in 1949 severely curtailed the expressions of Confucianism. However, with such a pervasive moral code and emphasis upon individual, family, and national virtues, communism could manipulate Confucian forms to fit its own goals.

Taoist influences

Taoism (pronounced dow ism) in China began about the time of Confucianism. Taoism reminds one of Hinduism with its diverse beliefs and practices. Its founder, Lao Tzu, emphasized philosophy and mysticism. Later Taoism stressed religious devotion to deities and spirits, priest and temple organizations, and magical practices. For Lao Tzu a life of harmony with nature was the ideal. The word *Tao* signified a way of life in conformity with the nature of the universe and also the principle or power which governs or regulates nature. The goal in life is to follow the Tao, which gives harmony and unity to everything. The primary qualities or virtues found in the Tao Te Ching are passivity, nonaction, nonstriving, and the simplicity and usefulness of yielding to nature, to spontaneity, and to appreciation of the beauty of life. Be like a newborn child or an uncarved block. Flow with the nature of things. Love, contentment, and kindness will emerge.

The related concepts of *yin* and *yang* are very important for Taoism. In order to attain harmony or Tao, both yin and yang must be blended into a balance. Yang is the force in the universe associated with the masculine, the positive, and the assertive. It is symbolized by the color red, and it gives warmth, brightness, firmness, and strength. The sun, the day, and fire are a part of the yang. Yin, on the other hand, represents the feminine, the passive, and the mysterious force in the universe. The night, shade, and water are a part of yin. Both yin and yang are necessary in proper balance to achieve the Tao. Neither of them is evil. Perhaps Taoism stresses yin more than yang because of the imbalance in Lao Tzu's time of the masculine and assertive. While Confucius called for a right order based on dominance and deference, Lao Tzu taught a withdrawal from society to commune with nature. The moral life was not some allegiance to a system of principles, but it was unity and kinship with the underlying natural forces. Lao Tzu and his early followers withdrew from the corrupt and "overcivilized" world of his day and returned to the simplicity of nature. It was a laissez-faire way of life.

Another side of Taoism is the *religious devotion and magical beliefs and practices*. This expression blended with the ancient Chinese reverence for nature and the spirit world. Both good and evil spirits were worshiped to gain benefits and to keep away evil. The spirits of ancestors were placated to honor family tradition, to give security, and to bring good fortune. The spirits of mountains, rivers, and animals were honored. For example, if one could build one's house over the nest of a dragon, good fortune would be forthcoming. Later Taoism incorporated magical rites, incantations, and divinations with a full-blown priestly and temple organization. The priests perform exorcisms of demons and communicate with the spirit world. In some temples the most important object is the incense burner, which symbolizes unity with the Tao. Also, the Tao was represented in later Taoism by supernatural beings like the Jade Emperor and the Eight Immortals, and even Lao Tzu became a deity, Lord Tzu. Popular Taoism today in Taiwan has numerous gods like the kitchen god who is honored in the home.

Taoism has developed in a more mystical direction than Confucianism. Both physical and spiritual self-discipline fashioned on the Yoga methods of Hinduism and Buddhism have influenced disciples who have reportedly achieved astonishing physical and occult powers. Taoist philosophy and mysticism influenced the developments of both Chinese and Japanese Zen Buddhist sects.

In conclusion, Taoism fits well the great and little tradition typology. Early Taoism was based on the philosophy and teachings of Lao Tzu, encouraging a withdrawal from the civilized world and a reunion with nature. It emphasized the great tradition of the teacher, his teachings, and the narrow way and goal to live life. Later Taoism became assimilated with indigenous Chinese beliefs and practices of ancestors, spirits, and magic. Deities became prominent with temples and priests as sustainers of the little tradition. More variety and flexibility of religious ways became prominent. Thus, Taoism and Confucianism sprang out of the soul of the Chinese past, offered correctives for living, and blossomed into visible and tenacious ways of life which have influenced not only the Chinese but other cultures as well.

The Japanese Way of Life

The Japanese have been influenced by several religious expressions, including Confucianism, Buddhism, and Shinto.

Shintoist influences

Shinto is the native religion. It means the way of the gods. Kami is the name given to deities and spirits which are honored both in shrines as well as in homes. Shinto has its stories of the god Izanagi and the goddess Izanami, who through procreation gave birth to gods and the Japanese islands. Amaterasu is the goddess who is associated with the sun and who is honored at the Grand Shrine of Ise. The emperors of Japan have long been identified with kinship with the high gods. The Grand Shrine of Ise has served as the focal point for imperial worship. Shinto shrines serve as the places of offerings to the kami, of festivities commemorating ancestors, new births, and national occasions, and of feelings that the shrine is an atmosphere of safety, purity, and sacredness. In the homes there are god houses containing the kami of the family. The names of ancestors are also included on the altar, and daily offerings are made to them. The Japanese, then, view their world as divinely created and housed by various gods who give life, happiness, and family and national stability.

Shinto gave support to a society based on a hierarchy of gods, ancestor veneration, strong family and national identity, and social divisions. The Tokugawa period (A.D. 1600-1868) provides a good observation of Japanese society undergirded by Shinto beliefs, values, and ethics. Tokugawa society was composed of feudal fiefdoms presided over by the shogun (military ruler), who acted in behalf of the emperor. The emperor, who claimed divine kinship, was at the apex of society. In descending order were the shogun, the feudal lords who ruled over the individual fiefdoms, the samurai or bushi warriors, and the peasant farmers, artisans, and merchants. Each level was to perform its explicit duties and to give loyalty to one another. In this system the military (samurai) became very prestigious, and the Bushido code (way of the warrior) became the idealized way of life. This code promoted loyalty and obedience from one group to the other, emphasizing the virtues of politeness, honor, courage, and reserve. The samurai spirit became one of ultimate loyalty to one's emperor and one's nation. One would give one's life for the nation. Or one would take one's life before dishonoring family or nation through a failure or a defeat. "Saving face" is important among the Japanese.

Other influences

Of course, Confucianism and its loyalty-obedience patterns in the five great relationships added support to Japanese values of group identity and leader-follower roles. *Mayahana Buddhism*, through its encouragement of devotion to the Buddha, lent its influence to group dependence on leadership. One may note the strong sense of group formation in Japanese society. Groups like the family, the clan, or the nation are thought of as natural arrangements blessed with the sacred quality. The head of each group relates its members to divine ancestors and to protective deities. The father of the family or the elder of the clan relates them to ancestor worship. The village elder or priest relates its members to local kami. The emperor of the nation relates all the people to the imperial ancestors and deities. Individuals exist because of the continuous flow of blessings from the ancestors and deities through the various heads of the groups. In return for those blessings individuals work within the group to repay those blessings and to sacrifice themselves for the group if necessary. Ethics, then, consist in acting as one should in one's group.

Confucianism, Taoism, Buddhism, and Shintoism are the major religious traditions among the Chinese and Japanese. Each tradition has a uniqueness of its own, and each meets a need among the people. The explicit ethics of Confucianism and Shintoism regulate individual and community conduct. People often rely upon several of the traditions. The Japanese will celebrate the births of their children and marriages in Shinto temples, but they will observe funeral ceremonies in the Buddhist temples. In all the traditions there are diversities of beliefs and practices which include deities, ancestors, spirits, temples, priests, specific religious lifestyles, and a sacred quality to the family, the clan, and the nation.

Confucian and Taoist Temples and Shinto Shrines

Confucianism and Taoism in China began as philosophical and ethical movements. In time priests and temples developed in both religions. Taoism as a living religion may be viewed in Taiwan, while Confucianism and Taoism as living religions in China still remain to be explored within the context of Chinese communist ideology and practice. Japanese Shintoism portrays a lively shrine complex with priests and rituals. A continuing pattern to be observed among religions is the elaboration of teachings into a cult of religious professionals and temples which attracts individuals and families from their homes to larger institutions of ritual and worship.

Confucian Temples

Confucianism has lent support to the ancient practices of ancestor worship among the Chinese. Ancestor worship occurred in the home or at the family temple as members gathered around the altar. On the altar there was a wooden tablet with the name of the ancestor. The altar also contained a Buddha image and a tablet or image of Confucius. So Confucianism in home and temple practice has long been associated with ancestor worship. After all, Confucius strongly supported the integrity and significance of the family.

After the death of Confucius a cult developed honoring him with temples, altars, and images. Although it had the support of the government, it was basically begun by Confucian scholars and loyal followers who excelled in their study of the Confucian classics and who believed his teachings should be the basis for Chinese life. The Confucian temple was called the Hall of Fame for scholars in A.D. 647. Each district had its temple in which images and tablets of Confucius were conspicuously displayed. Confucius was labeled the Supreme Saint in A.D. 1013. Ceremonies by scholars were conducted periodically in the temples since there was no priesthood. The cult surrounding Confucius, with its temples and ceremonies, was basically engineered and administered by the intellectually elite to foster the teachings and moral values of their teacher and sage. However, with the advent of the People's Republic of China, the cult of Confucius was severely curtailed. The temple of his birthplace was destroyed. His tomb with its altar and tablet was vandalized. However, there are contemporary signs that Chinese recollection and honor to Confucius are still alive.

Taoist Temples

Taoism has developed many ceremonies, rituals, and religious professionals to meet the needs of popular religion. In China in the second century A.D. a revivalistic healing movement was begun by Chang Ling, who claimed inspiration from a spirit appearance by Lao Tzu. Ling's followers have honored his descendants as "Taoist Popes," holding wide control over priests and their rituals. Other deities in Taoism include the Jade Emperor, the Three Pure Ones (Lao Tzu, the Yellow Emperor who is the first mystical ruler of China, and Penku, the primal man), the Eight Immortals, and various other deities. The priests of popular Taoism varied in their functions. Some were married, while others were celibate and monastic. Some administered the rituals of temples with images of the various deities. Other priests were involved in divination, in exorcism, and in serving as mediums to the spirit world. Some temples had a large abacus or calculating machine to remind the worshipers of the tallying of good and bad deeds. Like Confucianism, Taoism in the People's Republic of China has been greatly influenced by the communist view of religions.

Taiwan offers the best view of liturgical practices in Taoism. There are three groups of religious leaders in a Taoist temple. Laypersons are in charge of the administration of the temple. A category of priests named "Red Heads," from the color of their headdresses, performs rituals to the ordinary gods. They exorcise demons and supervise the mediums who communicate to the spirit world. A third group called "Black Heads" are the orthodox priests who trace their descent to Chang Ling. Consequently, their priesthood is hereditary. They perform rituals to the higher deities of Taoism, conduct dedication ceremonies at temples, and preside over other significant services for the larger religious community. The two groups of priests in the Taoism of Taiwan illustrate the classic division in the great and little traditions. The Black Heads are urban centered, use literary language in the rituals, honor the high deities, frequent the large temples in cities, and enjoy government sanction.

This is a classic description for the great tradition in understanding religions. On the other hand, the Red Heads represent the little tradition, as they are rural oriented, use the vernacular language, perform rituals and shamanistic practices to varieties of deities and spirits, and have an unorganized priesthood. These priests appeal to folk religion with their magic, charms, and alchemy, while the Black Heads relate more to the intelligentsia and to the traditional concept of Taoism as a way (Tao) to reality.

Shinto Shrines

Shinto Shrines in Japan reveal a fascination with tradition in the midst of a rapidly changing and technological society. The shrines vary in size, shape, and status, but there are common motifs that bind them together. The shrine is a pure place in the midst of an impure world. When one enters the shrine, one washes and uses a green branch to sweep away the impurities in one's path. A dead body would never be brought into a shrine, for it would pollute it. Shinto affirms the goodness of life as it has been handed down through the generations of spirits, families, and clans. The Japanese emphasize tradition and natural relationships of life, and the ceremonies and rituals at the shrine mirror this view. Shinto festivals at the shrine demonstrate through ritual and dance a mood of joy, affirmation, and relationship to a spiritual reality.

The shrine itself has basic features. One enters under the crossbeams of the torii and passes a font for purifying rituals. The porch contains a drum, paper streamers, and other decorations. A hall or larger room is for prayer and dancing. At the front of the hall is an eight-legged table for offerings. A set of steps behind the table lead to a decorous door, behind which is a room (honden) much higher than the shrine itself. The kami or god lives in this enclosure. In a Shinto worship experience the priest, dressed in white, purifies the worshipers gathered in the courtyard by waving a branch or sprinkling salt water over their heads. The priest enters the hall and presents offerings of various foodstuffs on the eight-legged table. On high occasions the priest may open the door to the room of the kami and lay the gifts on the floor. After recitations of prayer, there may be a sacred dance in honor of the kami and participation by the worshipers by eating a portion of the offerings upon the table.

At the annual festival (matsuri) the shrine becomes a lively place full of color and activity which includes the entire community. The priest officiates the taking of the kami from the shrine to be placed in a palanquin and carried through the street by joyous, shouting, and zigzagging young people. The shrine grounds become like a carnival with cotton candy booths, wrestling exhibitions, folk dances, archery displays, and fireworks. The festival is a time when the community and the shrine are symbolically and physically united. It is also a time when the kami leave the shrine to be carried through the community.

Shinto shrines are places of joy, security, purity, and festivity. The Japanese celebrate their happy moments of marriage and dedication of children in the shrine, and they dance in the shrine. On the other hand, the Japanese hold their funeral and memorial rituals in Buddhist temples, for they associate Buddhism with suffering and death. Shrines may be so small that offerings are made only several times a year with a visiting priest. Larger shrines may have a resident priest who performs daily rituals as well as the important special rites and festival occasions. The Grand Shrine of Ise, located on the east coast of Nagoya, is the shrine of the chief imperial ancestress. The emperor presents offerings to the Grand Shrine on significant festival days.

5

JUDAISM

■   ■

When one moves from South Asia and the Far East to the eastern Mediterranean Basin and Arabian Peninsula, a different kind of religious tradition is encountered. Judaism, Christianity, and Islam focus on monotheism, the belief in and devotion to one God. That God, named Yahweh or Allah, is revealed to the human family through a prophetic tradition. The prophet speaks in the name of the God of all universes and times with a specific message to the peoples. Judaism is the foundation for Christianity, and Islam developed from both its predecessors.

God-Covenant-People

The history of the Jewish people extends some thirty-five centuries. Its patriarchs are descended from Abraham, Isaac, and Jacob, who came out of Mesopotamia to Palestine. Moses led these descendants out of Egyptian bondage, and after receiving the Ten Commandments from Yahweh, Moses and then Joshua led the people to Palestine. Prophets arose among the Jewish people bringing messages of direction, judgment, and hope in the midst of crisis, conflict, and invasion by surrounding nations. With the Roman occupation of Palestine and Jerusalem, the last in a series of Jewish rebellions was ended, and Jews, for the most part, dispersed from Palestine.

Judaism centers on the worship of God, the practice of good deeds, and the love of learning. The Jewish calendar is followed in observance of festivities, holidays, and community and family celebrations. There is a deep unity within Judaism of history, literature, liturgy, prayer, and religious way of life. Jews are represented in most parts of the globe; however, they are not a missionary religion.

81

Yahweh and the Prophets

Judaism's view of Yahweh is a personal one. Its prophets had a direct and personal encounter with Yahweh. For example, Moses received a "call" from Yahweh with specific content and direction. Yahweh initiated the relationship with Moses, and while Moses did not see Yahweh, he was certain of Yahweh's holy presence and word. Yahweh, then, is personal, has particular purposes to which He calls people, establishes covenants with the people who listen to the messages of His prophets, and acts in historical events to achieve His purposes.

Yahweh is the creator, preserver, sustainer, judge, and end of life. Yahweh gives the law and the commandments through His prophets. Yahweh is characterized by such concepts as righteousness, justice, love, mercy, and power. Yahweh has spoken to the world primarily through the Hebrew people, who have preserved His words and laws in the holy Scriptures, the Torah.

The relationship between Yahweh and the people is primarily an ethical one. The people had Yahweh as their protector as long as the law was observed. Any disobedience incurred the wrath of Yahweh and threatened the partnership in the covenant relationship. At various times Yahweh would raise up prophets from within the Hebrew people to warn them of impending disasters, invasions by nations, the evils of the people, and specific teachings for their guidance. Prophets like Amos, Hosea, Micah, and Ezekiel have varying messages from Yahweh for the people of their particular era.

Judaism has no stories of Yahweh which characterize Him as desiring a consort or marrying a goddess. Yahweh is not a warrior god who is superior to other gods. There are no images of their God. He is austere, transcendent, and is not subject to the weaknesses which humans experience. Judaism arose in a religious environment of many gods and goddesses, of human sacrifices to the deities, of images made of deities, and of myths of romance and marriage in a pantheon of deities. Early Hebrew concepts of deity interacted with this religious environment. However, the Hebrew prophets were the charismatic leaders who spoke in the name of the one God against idols and false images, which the Hebrew people of various times adopted and associated with the worship of Yahweh. Judaism today continues to be a strong monotheistic religion based on a prophetic and ethical tradition.

Torah and Writings

Jewish and Christian peoples claim revelation, inspiration, and teachings from the part of the Bible known as the Old Testament. Christians also consider the New Testament of the Bible as the completion of the

Old Testament for their faith and practice. Thus, both Judaism and Christianity hold to sacred writings which parallel in age those of Hinduism, Buddhism, Confucianism, and Taoism.

The two primary foci of Jewish sacred writings are the Bible (Torah) and the Talmud. Torah means law or learning and specifically means the Pentateuch, the first five books of the Bible. These five books are Genesis, Exodus, Leviticus, Numbers, and Deuteronomy. Moses has been traditionally considered the author of these books. The Pentateuch contains the basic law for Jewish self understanding as well as history, religious statutes, and ethical rules for individuals and community, ceremonial rituals, stories of the creation of the world by Yahweh God, and the beginnings and development of humankind.

More generally, the Torah includes the entire Old Testament. Books named for the prophets like Isaiah, Jeremiah, Ezekiel, Amos, Jonah, and Micah tell of the prophets' messages in the name of Yahweh to common people, priests, and kings about the salvation, the law, and the judgment of Yahweh. The Torah also includes the wisdom literature, with books like Psalms, Proverbs, Job, and Ecclesiastes. These books are devotional classics, wise axioms, and personal stories of individuals who seek to know and practice the righteousness of Yahweh. The Torah or Old Testament of the Bible includes thirty-nine different books.

The other sacred literature of Judaism is the Talmud. Talmud means study. Talmud is a collection of the studies and interpretations of the Torah made by Jewish rabbis. It includes various materials of law, moral codes, and various commentaries on the Torah. The Talmud is composed of three parts, namely, the Mishnah, the Gemara, and the Midrashim. The Mishnah, written about A.D. 200, means repetition or a restatement of the law by an authoritative opinion. The Gemara is another strand of interpretation and completes the Mishnah—it includes folklore, sayings, and legends. The Midrashim includes commentaries and folklore collected through the nineteenth century.

The following passages from the Old Testament present a sampling of Jewish Scriptures. The passage from Deuteronomy shows the covenant God established with Israel. Through Moses God led the people out of bondage in Egypt on the way to a land across the Jordan. God acted mightily in history on behalf of Israel and expects Israel to keep the ordinances. The passage from Micah 6 shows the prophet's message to the people of the Northern Kingdom, before the Kingdom's collapse. Micah called the people to do justice and mercy. The passage from Exodus 20 is the Ten Commandments, which God gave to Moses to govern the life of the people of Israel. The last selection is Psalm 100, a devotional hymn, recognizing the goodness and love of God.

Deuteronomy 7:6-16

6 For you are a people holy to the LORD your God; the LORD your God has chosen you to be a people for his own possession, out of all the peoples that are on the face of the earth. 7 It was not because you were more in number than any other people that the LORD set his love upon you and chose you, for you were the fewest of all peoples; 8 but it is because the LORD loves you, and is keeping the oath which he swore to your fathers, that the LORD has brought you out with a mighty hand, and redeemed you from the house of bondage, from the hand of Pharaoh king of Egypt. 9 Know therefore that the LORD your God is God, the faithful God who keeps covenant and steadfast love with those who love him and keep his commandments, to a thousand generations, 10 and requites to their face those who hate him, by destroying them; he will not be slack with him who hates him, he will requite him to his face. 11 You shall therefore be careful to do the commandment, and the statutes, and the ordinances, which I command you this day. 12 And because you hearken to these ordinances, and keep and do them, the LORD your God will keep with you the covenant and the steadfast love which he swore to your fathers to keep; 13 he will love you, bless you, and multiply you; he will also bless the fruit of your body and the fruit of your ground, your grain and your wine and your oil, the increase of your cattle and the young of your flock, in the land which he swore to your fathers to give you. 14 You shall be blessed above all peoples; there shall not be male or female barren among you, or among your cattle. 15 And the LORD will take away from you all sickness; and none of the evil diseases of Egypt, which you knew, will he inflict upon you, but he will lay them upon all who hate you. 16 And you shall destroy all the peoples that the LORD your God will give over to you, your eye shall not pity them; neither shall you serve their gods, for that would be a snare to you.

Micah 6:1-8

1 Hear what the Lord says: Arise, plead your case before the mountains, and let the hills hear your voice. 2 Hear, you mountains, the controversy of the Lord, and you enduring foundations of the earth; for the Lord has a controversy with his people, and he will contend with Israel.

3 "O my people, what have I done to you? In what have I wearied you? Answer me! 4 For I brought you up from the land of Egypt, and redeemed you from the house of bondage; and I sent before you Moses, Aaron, and Miriam. 5 O my people, remember what Balak king of Moab devised, and what Balaam the son of Beor answered him, and what happened from Shittim to Gilgal, that you may know the saving acts of the LORD."

6 "With what shall I come before the LORD, and bow myself before God on high? Shall I come before him with burnt offerings, with calves a year old? 7 Will the LORD be pleased with thousands of rams, with ten thousands of rivers of oil? Shall I give my first-born for my transgression, the fruit of my body for the sin of my soul?" 8 He has showed you, O man, what is good; and what does the LORD require of you but to do justice, and love kindness, and to walk humbly with your God?"

Exodus 20:1-17

1 And God spoke all these words, saying 2 "I am the Lord your God, who brought you out of the land of Egypt, out of the house of bondage. 3 You shall have no other gods before me. 4 You shall not make for yourself a graven image, or any likeness of anything that is in heaven above, or that is in the earth beneath, or that is in the water under the earth; 5 you shall not bow down to them or serve them; for I the Lord your God am a jealous God, visiting the iniquity of the fathers upon the children to the third and fourth generation of those who hate me, 6 but showing steadfast love to thousands of those who love me and keep my commandments. 7 You shall not take the name of the LORD your God in vain; for the LORD will not hold him guiltless who takes his name in vain. 8 Remember the sabbath day, to keep it holy. 9 Six days you shall labor, and do all your work; 10 but the seventh day is a sabbath to the LORD your God; in it you shall not do any work, you, or your son, or your daughter, your manservant, or your maidservant, or your cattle, or the sojourner who is within your gates; 11 for in six days the LORD made heaven and earth, the sea, and all that is in them, and rested the seventh day; therefore the LORD blessed the sabbath day and hallowed it. 12 Honor your father and your mother, that your days may be long in the land which the LORD your God gives you. 13 You shall not kill. 14 You shall not commit adultery.

15 You shall not steal. 16 You shall not bear false witness against your neighbor. 17 You shall not covet your neighbor's house; you shall not covet your neighbor's wife, or his man-servant, or his maidservant, or his ox, or his ass, or anything that is your neighbor's."

Psalm 100

1 Make a joyful noise to the LORD, all the lands!
2 Serve the LORD with gladness!
Come into his presence with singing!

3 Know that the LORD is God!
It is he that made us, and we are his,
we are his people, and the sheep of his pasture.

4 Enter his gates with thanksgiving,
and his courts with praise!
Give thanks to him, bless his name!

5 For the LORD is good;
his steadfast love endures forever,
and his faithfulness to all generations.

The Jewish Way: Faith, Worship, Life

Judaism is quite distinctive from the eastern religions in its beliefs and practices. At the same time, Judaism serves as a major source for many of the beliefs and practices of the religions that follow it, especially Christianity and Islam. Its focus is monotheism, prophets, history, ethics, and a strong sense of community. God is the creator of everything, including nature, the animal world, and the human family. The human family is called upon to worship God and to give obedience and service to God through both worship and work. God both sustains life and redeems life. He is creator, judge, and redeemer. He is the only God, although the human family makes its idols and false deities.

God has revealed Himself in history through the messages of prophets. This revelation is found in the law of Judaism, the Torah. History is important, in fact is crucial, for Judaism. History has a beginning and an end. The human family lives out its life in history for better or for worse. Unlike Hinduism and Buddhism, there is no transmigration of the soul. There are no second or infinite chances for an individual to return to the world. Judaism views the relation between God and the people as covenant. In this view the people called the Jews have been favored by God to be a special people through whom He makes His revelation and will known to others. God is their God, and they are God's people. The covenant is reciprocal. Since God is holy, righteous, and just, the people are to mirror these qualities in their obedience to God and in the relations among themselves. This covenant relationship gives the Jews a strong sense of community identity, expressed in the Jewish home, in ceremonies and festivities around the Jewish calendar, and in worship and education in the synagogue.

A special belief in Judaism is the idea of the Messiah. The Messiah is the anointed one of God who inaugurates a new era of justice, righteousness, and peace in the world. There have been various interpretations within Judaism concerning the Messiah. One interpretation focuses on the Messiah as a descendant of King David of Israel. Others have viewed the coming Messiah as an ideal King, a superhuman deliverer, or an ordinary human being. The messianic hope has been an important part of Jewish life in its exile, dispersion, persecution, and suffering. Associated with this expectation is the messianic age and an understanding of last things and last days.

Jews speak of the Kingdom of God, the world to come, Paradise, and the resurrection of the dead as views within the context of the messianic age. Some Jews believe in the immortality of the soul while others reject the resurrection of the body. Jews traditionally believe that the new age will find the covenant people in Zion and that peace, righteousness, and justice will triumph over all opposition. Jews continue to expect the Messiah to come, to bring this new era into existence. Recent Jewish expectations have focused on Palestine and Jerusalem as signs of the beginning of a new era. Zionism was the movement that brought to fruition the state of Israel in 1948.

Perhaps it was Maimonides, the Jewish theologian, who best summarized the faith of Judaism in thirteen statements.

1. God is the author and guide of everything that has been and will be created.

2. God is Unity, there is none like unto His Unity and He alone is our God.

3. God is not body and He has no form whatsoever.

4. God is the first and the last.

5. We must pray to God alone and to no one else.

6. All the words of the prophets are true.

7. Moses is the chief of all prophets whose prophecy is true.

8. The Torah which we possess is the same that was given to Moses.

9. The Torah will never be changed and there will never be any other law of God.

10. God discerns the hearts of all men, knows all their thoughts and deeds.

11. God rewards those who keep His commandments and punishes those who transgress them.

12. Messiah, though he tarry, will come.

13. There will be resurrection of the dead.

Faith, worship, and life form a unity within Judaism. The family at home and the community at the synagogue express their worship and obedience to God through various ceremonies and festivities. The family is the central unit in the religion. The family takes primary responsibility for worship, religious education, and moral behavior. The Sabbath is a holy day of prayer, meditation, and rest. It begins at sunset on Friday and ends with sunset on Saturday. In the home candles are lighted, blessings are said, and devotions are observed. It is a time of family closeness. In the synagogue there is common worship on the Sabbath, led by the rabbi.

Ceremonies abound both in the home and in the synagogue. Circumcision for males is performed as a sign of the covenant relationship with God, when the child is thirteen years old. The child recites benedictions from the Torah, and this ceremony is called Bar Mitzvah. Girls have a similar service called Bat Mitzvah. Other significant life events such as marriage and death are surrounded by religious meanings and are observed by both family and synagogue with special ceremonies.

There are many feasts and festivals observed by Jews. The Jewish liturgical calendar follows a lunar cycle. It is composed of twenty-nine and one half days. An extra month is added every seven years out of nineteen to make it coincide with the sidereal year. The religious calendar begins in the spring with the Passover, to commemorate the exodus from Egypt. Shavuot, known as Pentecost or the Festival of Weeks, celebrates the grain harvest and commemorates the giving of the Torah. Rosh Hashanah observes the New Year. Yom Kippur is the Day of Atonement. Sukoth, or the Feast of Tabernacles, celebrates the autumn harvest. Hanukkah is a feast of dedication celebrating victory in 165 B.C. over the Syrians. Purim, or the Feast of Esther, remembers the deliverance from the Persian Empire. Israel's independence day is observed by many Jews since the State of Israel was formed. Belief and practice are very much shaped by the observances around the calendar. Below is a brief outline of the dates of the major celebrations in the Jewish calendar with their approximation in the regular calendar.

Jewish month (approximate secular month)

Nisan (March or April)
   14 – Passover Eve
   15–21 – Passover

Iyyar (April or May)
   5 – Israel Independence Day

Sivan (May or June)
   6, 7 – Shavuth (Festival of Weeks; Pentecost)

Tishri (September or October)
   1 – Rosh Hashanah (New Year Day "Days of Awe"
      (Orthodox: Tishri 1 and 2)
   10 – Yom Kippur (Day of Atonement)
   15 – Sukkoh (Feast of Tabernacles) begins
   21 – Hashanah Rabbah (seventh day)
   22 – Shemini Atzeret (eighth day)
   23 – Simchat Torah (Rejoicing in Torah) (ninth day)

Kislev (November or December)
   25 – Hanukkah begins (eight days), to the second
      of Tebet (December or January)

Adar (February or March)
   14 – Purim (Feast of Esther)

Life is to be lived in Judaism according to the ethics of the Torah, the revealed law of God which has universal meaning and implications. The Ten Commandments found in the Book of Exodus of the Torah are fundamental for Jewish behavior. They apply both to individual and to community relationships. Justice and righteousness are two primary virtues incumbent upon Jews. God is just and righteous and expects the people to be and to do likewise. Jews are taught to hate evil, to love good, and to do justly.

There are over seventeen million Jews worldwide. Some six million live in the United States and populate over four thousand synagogues. There are three major groups of Jews: Orthodox, Conservative, and Reform. These groups differ according to how much tradition they adhere to and how open to change in pluralistic societies they are. Orthodox Judaism observes the Torah and the Sabbath very strictly and practices the dietary laws. In the synagogue the Hebrew language is used in liturgy, and there are separate pews for women. Orthodox Jews form the union of orthodox Jewish congregations. Reform Judaism is much more adaptable to the views and habits of the culture in which it lives. It emphasizes that the moral laws of the Torah are important and that faith must be rational. There is equality of the sexes in worship, and prayers in the synagogue are said in the vernacular language. Reform Jews are organized into the Union of American Hebrew Congregations, and they founded Hebrew Union College in Cincinnati in 1875. Conservative Judaism strikes a balance between tradition and change. It follows the pattern of traditional Judaism for the most part but uses the vernacular in its religious services. Its synagogues form the United Synagogue of America, and it has the Jewish Theological Seminary in New York City.

Many Jews practice the kosher laws, which are dietary rules. The more traditional Jews look upon these laws as God's special rules for His covenant people. They basically are derived from the Book of Leviticus in the Torah. Certain foods are forbidden such as pork, rabbit, and some shell fish. Meats must be slaughtered according to ritual and must meet certain health standards. Meat products and dairy products must not be eaten together. Jews view these kosher laws as a lesson in self-discipline, as a part of their God-given heritage, and as a way to relate to other living things.

Judaism, then, is a way of faith that brings a close sense of identity and unity to the family and to the community. Religious devotion, religious education, and moral values are central to Jewish life. The beliefs and practices of Judaism have highly affected western culture and values. Its ethical monotheism has been the foundation for the development of Christianity and Islam. Throughout its long history it has weathered the storms of adversity and has maintained its faith, worship, and life in the home and synagogue.

Sabbath and Synagogue

The bedrock of Jewish practice is the observance of the Sabbath. The Old Testament passage of Exodus 20:8 provides the scriptural authority for the Sabbath: "Remember the sabbath day to keep it holy." A period of twenty-four hours from sunset Friday to sunset Saturday marks the observance. The time is intended for rest, when the body and soul may be refreshed, and no work is to occur. The Jew keeps the Sabbath as a memorial to creation and also a reminder of the Exodus from Egypt and redemption. There is celebration and inspiration during this time in Jewish homes and in the synagogues.

Sabbath observance begins on Friday afternoon, when one concludes work, bathes, and dresses for the evening activities. The family gathers in the home. As the wife lights the candles, she may say, "Blessed art

Thou, O Lord our God, King of the Universe, who has sanctified us with Thy commandments, and commanded us to kindle the Sabbath lights." Special blessings are said, and the Sabbath meal is taken with the full cup of wine. After the meal the family may attend the Sabbath Eve services at the synagogue.

Synagogues or temples are places of worship, instruction, and fellowship. During the Sabbath period services may be held on Friday evening and Saturday morning and afternoon. The architecture of the synagogue is similar to that of a Christian church. Seats face an elevated platform on which are one or two lecterns and chairs. The Ark, which contains the scrolls of the Torah, is the central feature at the platform. A curtain veils the Ark, and a lamp burns before it. During the service the rabbi will remove the curtain and open the door of the Ark to retrieve the Torah to read from it.

Although a Jewish layman may lead the worship services if there are ten adults present, usually a trained rabbi is the religious leader. The Sabbath services may include hymns, chants, prayers, readings from the prayer book, and congregational responses. Often a choir and an organ will accompany the singing. The rabbi will deliver a sermon and often interpret the Torah readings. Families return to their homes after Sabbath worship for meals and final ceremonies to end the Sabbath observance. Sabbath ends at sunset with a blessing of farewell. It should be noted that Sabbath practices may vary in both the home and the synagogue according to whether one is an Orthodox, Conservative, or a Reformed Jewish practitioner. For example, in Orthodox synagogues men and women will sit on separate sides, the liturgy will be spoken in Hebrew, and rituals may be more in line with traditional European Jewish practices. In Reformed synagogues, the service may be very dignified, with emphasis upon the rabbi's sermon and with English used throughout the service. The synagogue provides the Jewish community a place for worship not only on the Sabbath but also for daily prayers, festivals, and the Day of Atonement. Religious education and benevolence projects also occur in the synagogue. The rabbi serves the role of pastor, administrator, and counselor, using the synagogue as a place of worship, religious nurture, and benevolent activity.

Identity and Family, Rights and Territories, Tradition and Change

Perhaps there is no greater symbol in all religions of the issues of religious identity, rights, territories, and "family of God" than the city of Jerusalem. Three of the major religions of the world were birthed in and around Jerusalem and still lay claim to that holy place. Religions throughout their histories have made sacred places out of territories, buildings, and various objects of veneration and pilgrimage. The Hindu lives a lifetime to be buried in the sacred Ganges River. The Buddhist waits for the time to visit the spot of the Bodhi tree where the Buddha had his enlightenment. The Jews, Christians, and Muslims look to the city of Jerusalem as a place to claim as their own.

Judaism traces its history of association and ownership of Jerusalem through its prophets, kings, and patriarchs like Abraham, Moses, David, Solomon, and Isaiah. The kingdoms of Judah and Israel in Jewish history were some of the best and worst days of Jewish association with Palestine and Jerusalem. With the destruction of Jerusalem and the dispersion of the Jews in the first century A.D., the city and its peoples served under many rulers and were composed of diverse ethnic and religious groups. In 1948 the state of Israel was formed after decades of conflict among the landed Jews, the immigrant Jews, and the Arab Muslims and Christians of Palestine. Since 1948 there have been major conflicts between the state of Israel and her neighbors, mainly Arab Muslim states, over the rights of territory and the control of the city of Jerusalem. Jews have demonstrated that they would fight their way to the old wailing wall in the old city of Jerusalem and kneel down and pray to Yahweh, the God of Abraham, Isaac, and Jacob, to allow the temple of Solomon to be rebuilt from the ruins of the wall stones. They pray for the messiah to come and to restore Israel. The Jews will give their lives for what they believe to be their territorial rights.

Within several hundred yards of the wailing wall is the Dome of the Rock, a sacred place of Muslims. The present building was designed during the Umayyad period of Muslim history to demonstrate the movement of Islam from the Arabian peninsula to Palestine. The Dome of the Rock is a mosque where Muslims come to pray. However, it is symbolic of various religious identities for both Jews and Muslims. The mosque houses the rock on which the Jews believe Abraham attempted to sacrifice Isaac. In the Muslim tradition it is the son, Ishmael, whom Abraham attempts to sacrifice.

For the Jews the rock is also a part of the wall of King Solomon's temple. For both Christians and Muslims the mosque is over the place where both Jesus Christ and Muhammad often visited. For Muslims it is the place where Muhammad ascended to heaven to be with Allah. The late King Faisal of Saudi Arabia once said that Muslims by the hundreds of millions have the right to their holy territory. He asserted that they would claim it through the use of the holy sword or "holy oil." The king's threats included not only Jerusalem but also Palestine.

Not far from the wailing wall and the Dome of the Rock are two Christian landmarks. They are Golgotha, the place of the skull and the place of the crucifixion of Jesus Christ, and the garden of Gethsemane housing the tomb of Jesus Christ with the stone removed from the door opening to signify the resurrection of Jesus Christ. Both Christian places remind one of the history of the Christian church in its conflicts with both secular and religious powers, especially during the Middle Ages, for the territory of Jerusalem and its environs. The crusades marked the hostile relationships between Christians and Muslims as they fought for land and peoples.

Thus, Jerusalem is the city and Palestine is the land where Jews, Christians, and Muslims have lifted their religious territorial flags, planted their deep loyalties, and sacrificed the lives of their family members and friends, as well as their enemies. Jerusalem is the city of eschatological significance for many Jews, Christians, and Muslims, where history will culminate and new kingdoms will begin. However, wars and rumors of wars continue to exist to retake or to defend these holy territories. The religious symbolism of the city of Jerusalem calls attention to each religious community's sense of identity, its religious duties, and its relationship to the impending forces of change.

The challenge to Jewish identity has been a constant one over several millennia. In dispersion the Jews lived among diverse cultures, rulers, governments, and religions. Usually, they lived as a minority people, and often, they experienced deprivations in social, economic, political, and religious life. Periods of persecution and attempts of annihilation of Jews have been explicitly documented, most notably in the attempt of Nazi Germany. Jews have been affected by their cultural environments as well as by their religious in-house differences of orthodoxy, conservatism, and reformism. The nineteenth-century flowering of Zionism fostered by twentieth-century policies of large nation-states encouraged Jews worldwide to consider returning to Palestine to form a homeland for the Jews. In the State of Israel's declaration of independence, the only reference to divine help was in the last paragraph, where a national term for God was used, "with trust in the Rock of Israel we set our hand to this declaration." Jewish identity, then, has been challenged by forces without and within.

Judaism as a religion has been the representative of a covenant community based on the teachings of the Torah, of a special relationship between Yahweh and the people of Israel. The Jews have viewed themselves as a representative of a blood community nurtured by a religious calling to be a chosen people to represent Yahweh to the nations. The identity challenge has arisen between universalism and particularity. Religiously viewed, is Judaism to be a religion which depicts Yahweh as the God of the nations whose acts are to be universalized in history, or is Judaism to be a religion which depicts itself as the particular people with rights and privileges of Yahweh to be acted out in history which are not available to other peoples? What kind of chosen people are they? Are they to be involved in an elitism like the Hindu Brahmins, the superior priest-caste, who are exempt from the struggles of one reincarnation after another until they reach perfection? Are they to be a servant people serving Yahweh as a vessel of the reflection of the righteousness of Yahweh? Or are they to be a people who lay claim to territory and raise a flag to demonstrate their identity? The Jews have known what suffering is. The Jews have known what claiming a land and defending it is. However, there is a dilemma in the people's sense of identity and their expression of identity.

Jews themselves are raising the flag of the identity crisis. Who is a Jew? Is a Jew a Jew by birth, by decision, or by conviction? There are various answers. Religiously, a Jew is one who accepts the faith of Judaism and who participates in Jewish ritual and ceremony. Culturally, a Jew may regard the folkways and literature of Judaism as one's own without affiliation with the rituals, synagogue, or religion proper. Practically, a Jew may consider being a part of a predominant Jewish neighborhood as reason for Jewishness, or may be considered such by others. In the state of Israel, a Jew, by law, is one born of a Jewish mother who has not converted to another faith. Also, in the state of Israel there is ambivalence among the people about how secular the principles of government and the principles of society ought to be and how religious or even theocratic they should be. Political parties in the state of Israel have both secular and religious orientations. Theocratic leanings are prevalent in religious parties to make the state a theocratic one based on the teachings and law of the Torah, with the Rabbinate as the authoritative interpreter.

These identity challenges face individual Jews and Jewish communities in a variety of ways, including inter-marriages with non-Jews, relations with other religions, the nature and implication of Zionism, and the shape and direction of the state of Israel. The issues which face the Jews are complex and urgent. They have been exposed to environmental changes for much of their history. The forces of change which externally confront them are not new, but each succeeding generation often faces a new set of conditions. Some Jews have begun to take a fresh look at the meaning of messiah both in their tradition and in the Christian tradition. There have been inter-marriages between Jews and non-Jews with accommodations made in both communities. President Sadat, an Arab Muslim, upon the invitation of Prime Minister Begin, an Israeli Jew, visited Jerusalem to discuss both Muslim and Jewish territorial questions. The question of Jerusalem once again raises the challenge of religious communities' identities as families of Allah and/or Yahweh and to their rights and privileges to the land of their sacred histories.

6

CHRISTIANITY

■　　　　　　　　　　　　　　　　　　　■

Christianity arose out of the Judaism of the first century of the modern era. It is founded upon the life and teachings of Jesus of Nazareth, known to Christians as Jesus Christ. Christianity has a sacred Scripture, the Bible, which contains the Old Testament and the New Testament. The New Testament especially focuses on the life of Jesus Christ. The Wise Men of the East gathered around the birth of Jesus, symbolizing the universal appeal of Christianity. The crucifixion of Jesus between criminals showed the tragic side to human life. A primary teaching of Christianity is that the death of Jesus brings the possibility of new life for the believer. The resurrection of Jesus signaled that He overcame death not only for Himself but for the believer. It offers a new future for the Christian community, the church.

Christians believe that Jesus Christ is the Son of God, the Savior of humankind, and the Lord of the world. Christians follow the teachings of Jesus Christ in the gospels of the New Testament and in the writings of the apostles in other books of the New Testament. Christian worship is of great variety and richness, including preaching, praying, singing, meditation, baptism, and communion. The Christian life is to live in the world by the good news of Jesus Christ with the help of God.

Three major groups of churches compose Christianity. The Roman Catholic Church, under the leadership of the papacy in Rome, comprises over 600 million members. The Eastern Orthodox Church, with its several patriarchs in leadership, has its greatest strength in the Middle East. It numbers some 125 million followers. Protestant churches represent a variety of denominations, including Lutheran, Episcopal, Methodist, Presbyterian, and Baptist. Membership in Protestant churches is over

300 million. The Southern Baptist Convention is the largest Protestant body, comprising over 15 million.

Christianity has had a universal appeal through its twenty centuries of development. It acknowledges its heritage in Judaism. It also has been one of the most mobile and missionary religions and now includes over 1,400,000,000 followers.

God, Jesus Christ, Spirit

Christianity emerged out of Judaism. Jesus Christ, its founder, and His early disciples were Palestinian Jews who frequented the temples and learned from the Jewish teachers, the rabbis. When Jesus Christ prayed, He spoke his words to Yahweh. When Jesus read the sacred writings, they were from the Torah. When Jesus Christ taught the people, His teachings were filled with Jewish law and the words of the Hebrew prophets before Him. Christianity and the church which developed after Jesus Christ continued to stake its teachings and life on the Scriptures known as the Old Testament as well as the Christian Scriptures known as the New Testament. For Christians, then, Yahweh as the God of Jesus Christ is the God whom they worship and to whom they give obedience.

The fundamental message of Jesus Christ was that the *Kingdom of God*, the reign and power of God, was about to enter history. Jesus Christ called for the repentance of the people, including the Jewish religious leaders of the day. He was an itinerant teacher and preacher in the heartland of Palestine for several years while in His early thirties. He was arrested, tried, and crucified on a wooden cross by Roman authorities at the instigation of Jewish religious leaders. After three days His followers reported that Jesus had been resurrected and had appeared to them in several places, including Jerusalem. His disciples and apostles, including Peter and Paul, proclaimed the death of Jesus as a sacrifice in order to instigate the Kingdom of God. His resurrection was a victory over sin and death, and those who accepted His death on the cross and resurrection from the tomb could share in the triumph over sin and death. The Christian church, then, was founded upon the teachings, ministry, death, and resurrection of Jesus Christ.

Christianity, like Hinduism and Buddhism before it, has had a diversity of philosophers and theologians. There have been a variety of interpretations of *Jesus Christ*. Controversies have occurred in the church about His person and work. Church creeds have evolved affirming both the humanity and the divinity of Jesus Christ. Various Christian communities like the Roman Catholics, the Eastern Orthodox, and the Protestants have expressed their understanding and experience of Jesus Christ through theological statements and art. Among some Christian commu-

nities images of Jesus Christ are prominently displayed in church sanctuaries and are used in worship. Other communities disdain this use of
images. Two thousand years of church history continue to present lively
theological discussion of the nature and work of God and of Jesus Christ.

The New Testament contains both the teachings of Jesus and the
writings of His disciples and apostles. Jesus is characterized as Truth,
Light, Way of Life, Good Shepherd, one with God, born of the virgin
Mary, Word, and Messiah. He is accepted not only as a great teacher
and as a human model for ethics, behavior, and life style, but also He is
proclaimed and followed as Savior and Lord. He offers and mediates
God's love and will for humankind.

Christian theologians have developed a concept to interpret and
explain the relationship of God and Jesus. It is called the doctrine of the
Trinity. God is one; however, God is expressed in three personal ways,
roles, or functions: God the Father, the Son, and the Holy Spirit. The
unity of God is preserved in oneness while the richness of the nature and
work of God is demonstrated in diverse ways. Jesus Christ is the expression of God's love and will in the context of humanity and history. Jesus
is referred to as the incarnation of God—God's Word became flesh. The
church teaches that faith is a necessary condition for a Christian to
accept Jesus Christ as the Savior and Lord of Life.

Christianity presents a diverse and often complex religious development over two thousand years. Yet its concept of God is expressed out of
a deep heritage within Judaism. Its Christology, the doctrine of Jesus
Christ, finds an orthodoxy in the mainstream of Christian thought and
practice. Christianity is a prophetic religion, as is Judaism and Islam. It
also presents a rich tradition of reverence for saints, especially evidenced
in the Roman Catholic Church. The virgin Mary, mother of Jesus, is
deeply revered by Roman Catholics as are other saints, and the Pope,
Bishop of Rome, has power to canonize others into sainthood. However,
the protestant churches have not emphasized Mariology and sainthood.
Christianity also has its priests, monks, and ministers who interpret the
sacred traditions and Scriptures for the church. Christianity, then, has
remained a strong monotheistic religion with a focus on its founder as
Jesus Christ, who is both the Savior and Lord for His followers.

The Bible: The Revelation and Word of God

The Christian sacred writings are found in the Bible. Christianity
began from a background in Judaism with the life and teachings of Jesus
Christ. Jesus was not only familiar with the Torah but taught from it and
expanded its meanings by His interpretations. Consequently, Christianity
considers the thirty-nine books of the Old Testament and the twenty-
seven books of the New Testament as its sacred Scriptures.

The New Testament tells about the life, teachings, ministry, death, and resurrection of Jesus Christ. It also describes the origin and early development of the Christian church and guidelines for the church's existence in the world. The New Testament falls into several divisions. The first four books are called the Gospels—Matthew, Mark, Luke, and John. Their main content is the description of the life of Jesus Christ. They trace Jesus' genealogy through Abraham to Adam, record His birth of the virgin Mary, describe His years of teaching and ministry, and document His death by crucifixion and His resurrection from the tomb outside of Jerusalem.

The Book of Acts in the New Testament records the sayings and actions of the young Christian church. The church was led by Simon Peter, Paul, and other companions who were disciples and apostles of Jesus Christ, and then was extended from Palestine through Asia Minor into Europe in Acts. Most of the remaining books of the New Testament are called epistles, many of which are written by the apostle Paul, who is considered the leading theologian of the Christian church. The epistles include the Books of Romans, Corinthians, Ephesians, and Galatians. Paul interpreted the lordship of Jesus Christ in the life of the church.

The following passages from the New Testament are samples of its thought and practice which have influenced the Christian church. The selection from the Gospel of Mark portrays Jesus in a healing ministry among townsfolk. Jesus' healing of the paralytic and His declaring forgiveness of sins give evidence of who He was, the Servant of the Lord, who had been spoken of in the Book of Isaiah in the Old Testament. The passage from the Gospel of Matthew includes a portion of Jesus' Sermon on the Mount known also as the Beatitudes. Two passages are included from the Book of Acts describing the early preaching in the young Christian church. Simon Peter in these sermons asserted that Jesus was a man approved, indicating the humanity of Jesus, and Simon Peter also preaches the core of belief of the early Christians that Jesus was made both Lord and Christ by God through His death and resurrection. The last selection comes from the Apostle Paul's epistle to the Philippians. Paul states the themes of obedience and Lordship as modeled by Jesus Christ.

Mark 2:1-12

1 And when he returned to Capernaum after some days, it was reported that he was at home. 2 And many were gathered together, so that there was no longer room for them, not even about the door; and he was preaching the word to them. 3 And they came, bringing to him a paralytic carried by four men. 4 And when they could not get near him

because of the crowd, they removed the roof above him; and when they had made an opening, they let down the pallet on which the paralytic lay. 5 And when Jesus saw their faith, he said to the paralytic, "My son, your sins are forgiven." 6 Now some of the scribes were sitting there, questioning in their hearts, 7 "Why does this man speak thus: It is blasphemy! Who can forgive sins but God alone?" 8 And immediately Jesus, perceiving in his spirit that they questioned within themselves, said to them, "Why do you question thus in your hearts?

9 "Which is easier, to say to the paralytic, 'Your sins are forgiven,' or to say, 'Rise, take up your pallet and walk'? 10 "But that you may know that the Son of man has authority on earth to forgive sins"—he said to the paralytic— 11 "I say to you, rise, take up your pallet and go home." 12 And he rose, and immediately took up the pallet and went out before them all; so that they were all amazed and glorified God, saying, "We never saw anything like this!"

Matthew 5:1-12

1 Seeing the crowds, he went up on the mountain, and when he sat down his disciples came to him. 2 And he opened his mouth and taught them saying: 3 "Blessed are the poor in spirit, for theirs is the kingdom of heaven. 4 Blessed are those who mourn, for they shall be comforted. 5 Blessed are the meek, for they shall inherit the earth. 6 Blessed are those who hunger and thirst for righteousness, for they shall be satisfied. 7 Blessed are the merciful, for they shall obtain mercy. 8 Blessed are the pure in heart, for they shall see God. 9 Blessed are the peacemakers, for they shall be called sons of God. 10 Blessed are those who are persecuted for righteousness' sake, for theirs is the kingdom of heaven. 11 Blessed are you when men revile you and persecute you and utter all kinds of evil against you falsely on my account. 12 Rejoice and be glad, for your reward is great in heaven, for so men persecuted the prophets who were before you."

Acts 2:22-24

22 Men of Israel, hear these words: Jesus of Nazareth, a man attested to you by God with mighty words and wonders and signs which God did through him in your midst, as you yourselves know— 23 this Jesus, delivered up according to the

definite plan and foreknowledge of God, you crucified and killed by the hands of lawless men. 24 But God raised him up, having loosed the pangs of death, because it was not possible for him to be held by it.

Acts 2:32-36

32 This Jesus God raised up, and of that we all are witnesses. 33 Being therefore exalted at the right hand of God, and having received from the Father the promise of the Holy Spirit, he has poured out this which you see and hear. 34 For David did not ascend into the heavens; but he himself says, "The Lord said to my Lord, Sit at my right hand, 35 till I make thy enemies a stool for thy feet." 36 Let all the house of Israel therefore know assuredly that God has made him both Lord and Christ, this Jesus whom you crucified.

Philippians 2:5-11

5 Have this mind among yourselves, which you have in Christ Jesus, 6 who, though he was in the form of God, did not count equality with God a thing to be grasped, 7 but emptied himself, taking the form of a servant, being born in the likeness of men. 8 And being found in human form he humbled himself and became obedient unto death, even death on a cross. 9 Therefore God has highly exalted him and bestowed on him the name which is above every name, 10 that at the name of Jesus every knee should bow, in heaven and on earth and under the earth, 11 and every tongue confess that Jesus Christ is Lord, to the glory of God the Father.

The Christian Way: A Way of Light, Life, Love

The Life and Teachings of Jesus Christ

Christianity began in the first century founded upon the teachings and ministry of Jesus of Nazareth, a Palestinian Jew. It arose within Judaism but soon separated from it as Jesus reinterpreted the Jewish law on the basis of His own authority. He healed the sick and taught the coming of the long-awaited Kingdom of God. The Kingdom of God would come when God's will was accomplished in the lives of people. Jesus taught many things, among which to obey the will of God was to love God and one's neighbor completely. Jesus emphasized that love was central to the coming of the Kingdom.

Jesus was a controversial figure, so much so that He was charged with blasphemy by the Jewish leaders of the day and was crucified for treason. The accusations against him were that He had usurped God's authority and that He claimed to be king of the Jews. His disciples proclaimed that He was resurrected on the third day after death and appeared to them on several occasions. The later Christian community, the church, made the belief in Jesus' life, teachings, death, and resurrection the central core of faith and practice.

Christianity accepted a number of Jewish beliefs without major changes. Christians profess a monotheistic faith in one God who acts in history. Christians affirm humanity's tendency to disobey God and believe that God offers salvation to humanity. The major distinction from Judaism is the Christian understanding and proclamation that Jesus was the long expected Messiah of whom the Jews spoke. Christians believe that God revealed His love for humanity in the life and teachings of Jesus, and they believe that through His death and resurrection there is a triumph over humanity's death and a promise of resurrection for those who follow Jesus the Christ.

For Christians Jesus came to mean the incarnation of God in human form, a unique and unrepeatable event. Among the early Christians a belief arose that God, who revealed himself in Jesus, continued to be present in a unique spiritual presence. This presence was the Holy Spirit. Later the church would speak of a doctrine of the Trinity: belief in God the Father (Creator), God the Son (God in Jesus Christ), and God the Holy Spirit (God present in history). The doctrine of the Trinity was the church's way to acknowledge the unity of God in the diverse ways that God manifested Himself to humanity.

Perhaps the Sermon on the Mount provides the most basic teachings of Jesus on the Christian way. It is found in the fifth, sixth, and seventh chapters of the Gospel of Matthew. The teachings are the ethics of a new order, the Kingdom of Heaven (or Kingdom of God). The words of Jesus are contrasted with the Torah of the Judaism of His day. Jesus' emphasis on the purity of motives and the love of neighbor contrasts with the Pharisee's stress upon ceremony and strict legalism. In one broad stroke Jesus painted a portrait of the possibilities of life to be lived presently as well as a hope and a promise of what humankind might become. It is a total moral code proclaiming the absolute demands of God. At the same time it elicits complete obedience while stating that God's mercy and grace are abundant.

The distinctives of Christian ethics, then, focus on the life and teachings of Jesus. He becomes the way, the paradigm, for disciples to emulate and follow. The concepts of righteousness, mercy, justice, and the Ten Commandments of the Torah are dealt with and refined by Jesus. Love and forgiveness become central to the Christian life. He taught that one shall love God with one's total strength, mind, will, and heart. In the same breath He said that one shall love one's neighbor as one loves one's self. The neighbor concept and relationship become vital in the Christian way. The neighbor is the person in need of understanding, of love, of sustenance of life, of healing. The neighbor may be the stranger, the enemy, the near or distant one.

Especially, Jesus teaches concern and action for the afflicted and the less fortunate. The Christian way demands willingness to suffer with others and for others in matters of justice and moral right. Jesus denounced acts of violence and encouraged relationships based on understanding, reconciliation, and peace. He did demonstrate an intense impatience with legalism and hypocrisy. One needed to have matters of the heart corrected before one's obvious activity could be correct. In other words, worship and prayer were to be integrated with ethics. Grace and hope were to be translated into life's relationships.

The Christian way affirms life in this world. It is positive toward history in that God reveals Himself and His will through creation, nature, His acts in history, and particularly in Jesus the Christ. All of creation, including humankind, nature, and the animal orders, have been given by God to live together in order and in affirming relationships. There is placed upon the human family the responsibility to live in peace and harmony with one another as well as with all the environment.

The Historical Church

The New Testament, which includes the Gospels and the Epistles of the Apostle Paul, also provides the basis for the Christian community, the church. The early church was a loosely organized community with its local leaders assuming the authority and responsibility for matters of belief and practice. As the church became more universal, councils were formed to make policy and decisions. Because the church grew in diverse cultural environments, various theological and ritual practices emerged.

Two branches of Christianity formed: Roman Catholicism in the West and Orthodoxy in the East. Roman Catholicism emphasized a more rationalistic theology, accepted the authority of the Bishop of Rome (Pope), and interpreted the Eucharist as a reenactment of the death on the cross. On the other hand, Orthodoxy stressed the more spiritual forms of worship in terms of the poetic and mystical, accepted the authority of various archbishops, and viewed the Eucharist as a celebration of the resurrection of Jesus from the dead. Protestantism later became a branch of Christianity. It reacted against the authority of the Pope and the emphasis that grace came explicitly through the church sacraments. Protestantism championed the authority of the Scriptures and the grace of God through the faith of people. It later proliferated into numerous branches called denominations like the Lutheran, Methodist, and Baptist. These various branches have had a variety of theological interpretations, church practices, and ethical concerns.

Christians of all branches have accepted at least two sacraments or ordinances. Baptism is an initiation ceremony portraying the experience one has of God's love and forgiveness and one's fellowship within the Christian community. The resurrection of Jesus demonstrates that evil and death are overcome by God and that the followers of Jesus and the church have a new beginning. The ceremony of baptism, in which a new Christian is placed underneath the water and is raised up from the water, symbolizes death to the old self and resurrection or new birth to the life given by the death and resurrection of Jesus. The resurrection implies for the Christian community a positive approach to life, history, and beyond history to an eternal life with God. Baptism also affirms the individual's decision to be a Christian and to be active in the church. The Eucharist, or the Lord's Supper, is the ordinance in which bread and wine are taken to commemorate the life, death, and resurrection of Jesus and to ensure the believer's participation in its meaning. The Roman Catholic Church and the Orthodox Church recognize seven sacraments.

The early church faced persecution as a minority movement in a hostile environment. One of the ideals of the ancient church was the monastic life and the monasteries. Evil was acknowledged, and one way to combat it was to withdraw, to pray, and to live an ascetic life. The ethics of scarcity and celibacy were prominent. As the medieval age approached, the church found itself growing internally and expanding geographically. For a thousand years (A.D. 500-1500), the church became powerful with the papacy, cathedrals, monasteries, land holdings, huge followings, and alliances with rulers and governments. Europe and Christendom were synonymous. Heresy was fought with the Inquisition. The ethics of affluence and power and holy war were prominent during those times.

In 1517 Martin Luther, a priest-scholar, nailed the ninety-five theses to the church door at Wittenburg, Germany, unleashing a series of church reforms that initiated the Protestant Reformation. Issues at stake in the church were corruption, clerical power and authority, and the ethics of faith and life among the masses, with justice and righteousness as prime concepts. One of the rallying cries came from the Book of Romans found in the New Testament, "The just shall live by faith" (1:17).

The modern church era of the nineteenth and twentieth centuries has seen the extension of the church in a missionary enterprise which has taken Christianity around the globe. Africa, Asia, the Middle East, and Latin America have become strong Christian areas. Many indigenous

Christians from these continents have become able to send their missionaries to other continents. The modern era has also witnessed strong ecumenical currents and church union organizations. The World Council of Churches and the National Council of Churches have been formed by various participating denominations. The theology and ethics of the era have emphasized unity, mission, and the Lordship of Jesus the Christ. A rallying cry for the modern church has been, "one Lord, one faith, one baptism" (Eph. 4:5).

Fundamentals of the Christian Faith

In summary, the fundamentals of the Christian faith may be expressed as the following, remembering that the richness of the Christian tradition has been its unity in diversity.

1. Jesus of Nazareth became the crucified and resurrected Christ.

2. Jesus' teachings centered on the Kingdom of God.

3. The Christian Church was founded upon Jesus' teachings and inspiration.

4. The Christian Bible includes the thirty-nine books of the Jewish Scriptures (Old Testament) and twenty-seven books such as the Gospels, and the letters of Paul which are called the New Testament.

5. An important doctrine of Christianity is in the Trinity: God as Father, God as Son, God as Holy Spirit.

6. Christian worship is of great variety and richness including emphasis on preaching, praying, singing, meditation, baptism, and the Lord's Supper.

7. Christian life is to live by teachings of the New Testament in the world, sustained by the help of God in Jesus the Christ.

The Christian Church: From Worship to Mission

Since its inception Christianity has emphasized and encouraged a gathered community, the church. Its scriptural tradition, the New Testament, has described the church as a holy people, the body of Christ, a living organism to do the work and ministry of Jesus Christ, the Lord of the church. The church, throughout its nearly two thousand years, has demonstrated a variety of shapes and a diverse pattern in its architecture and organization. The early church met in the homes of Christians. It was led by informed and often itinerant leaders. The medieval church developed magnificent cathedrals with lofty spires and exquisite art work. Monasteries were organized promoting ascetic disciplines, church scholarship, education, and missions. With the reformation came a proliferation of church structures, liturgies, and activities. The contemporary Christian church presents a plethora of organizations and leadership.

The four words that best describe the Christian church are worship, education, benevolences, and missions. The *worship* function is clearly in mind when churches are constructed and when one observes the building. The sanctuary or auditorium is usually the largest building. Seating arrangements include rows of benches, pews, or chairs which face an elevated platform. On the platform there may be one or two lecterns and several chairs for presiding priests or ministers. A table closely associated with the platform, either on the level in front of it or on the same level, is used for the Lord's Supper. A special seating arrangement for a choir is obvious, as well as a place for an organ and/or a piano. A baptismal pool may be closely associated with the platform area. Various artifacts depicting Christian symbolism may decorate the sanctuary, including a cross, a Christian flag, stained glass windows, and table and pulpit ware. Often a Bible may be opened on a table near the platform.

Worship services in Christian churches may be just as diverse as their architectural features. However, there are common patterns that fit most churches. Singing is shared by both the congregation and the choir. Prayers are offered by both the congregation and the ministers. Scriptures are read by the ministers, and the congregation often participates in a responsive reading. A focal point in the worship service is the sermon delivered by the minister. The sacraments or ordinances are observed in worship services. When an individual becomes a member of the church, he or she is baptized by water in the context of community worship. The Eucharist or the Lord's Supper is also observed by the entire congregation as the bread and the cup are shared from the communion table.

Many churches have a dedication service for young babies and their families. Weddings are held and marriage vows are said in sanctuaries in the context of congregational worship. Funeral services are sometimes observed in the sanctuary in the spirit of worship. Perhaps one of the most universal facts of the church is that Christians meet once each week, usually on Sunday from 11 a.m. until noon for congregational worship in the sanctuary. The Christian calendar also provides special worship services throughout the year. The Christmas and Easter seasons commemorating the birth, death, and resurrection of Jesus Christ are celebrated in church sanctuaries with special music, decorations, pageants, and dramas.

Education is another prominent feature represented by the church architecture. Christian education is a large enterprise in the church, which demands personnel and material resources. Church schools or Sunday Schools are highly organized around age levels from preschool children and babies to adults. Each church has teachers and classrooms for these various age levels. Consequently, a large unit of the church building houses the educational program. Christian education includes the study of the Bible, doctrines and ethics, missions, and training skills in communication, like music education. Church schools meet weekly, usually before the Sunday worship service. Some churches have week-day schools. Churches through their denominations and federations produce and publish literature for their church curricula, as well as for their religious bookstore outlets. Churches also support private church schools as well as colleges, universities, and theological schools. Theological schools and seminaries prepare men and women as professional priests, ministers, educators, and musicians.

Benevolence is stressed in the church. The church building has become a focus for community voluntarism and projects to meet the needs of the less fortunate. Churches usually have kitchens and fellow-ship halls. The church members often gather for meals at the church or they may have special days when the indigent come to the church to be served hot meals. There are clothes closets in churches that receive clothes from its members and distribute them to the people who frequent the church for aid. Churches may conduct literacy, English language, and skill classes for internationals and a variety of peoples. The handi-capped and senior citizens are provided programs. Organizations like the Girl and Boy Scouts and Alcoholics Anonymous are given meeting rooms in the churches. The building is a physical expression of the church's good will and availability to the community.

Missions are an integral part of the church. Sermons stress the mis-sionary nature of the church. Missionary education abounds in the church school classes, and churches participate in personnel and funding to sustain missionaries both home and overseas. Mission agencies aid the churches in recruiting, training, and placing missionaries. In local set-tings there are mission opportunities for church members to go into the neighborhoods to invite others into membership in the church, to build other churches, and to aid in relief projects of food, medicines, and other survival supplies.

Worship, religious education, benevolences, and missions are integral parts of Christianity. However, it is to be noted that the church traditions of Roman Catholicism, Eastern Orthodoxy. and Protestantism have vari-ous theologies and practices which color these four expressions.

The Roman Catholic Church until recently used the Latin language in their liturgy of the Eucharist, similar to the Orthodox Jews' use of Hebrew in their formal worship. Within Protestantism baptismal rites vary between the Baptist churches which practice immersion and the Methodist church, which practices sprinkling. Monasteries within the Roman Catholic Church have traditionally been the training centers for missionaries like the Jesuits and the Dominicans, whereas in Protestant churches pastors and laypersons in local churches have become missionaries. The liturgy in worship services varies throughout Christianity from high church with formality of dress, music, and ritual to low church with its informality. Church architecture comprises both Gothic features as well as contemporary designs using stone and brick, as well as wood and glass.

Perhaps the Christian church offers the greatest variety among religions with regard to architecture, liturgy styles, and organizational patterns. It may also portray groupings of people based on class and social and economic lines in distinct church membership and attendance. Group experience tends to be the premium in the Christian church, where services, programs, and activities are structured for larger gatherings. Hindu temples and Buddhist shrines offer more individualistic and smaller family-oriented services. Because of its missionary advance upon all continents and its presence in most cultural groups, the Christian church has faced the challenges of cultural diversity and flexibility. Consequently, it is appropriate to remember that the Christian church is a rich mosaic of racial, cultural, ethnic, theological, and organizational diversity.

Religious Identity and Family, Rights and Territories, Tradition and Change

Since the sixteenth century A.D. Christianity has proliferated in a variety of churches, denominations, and sects. These divisions have caused religious identity crises among various Christian groups, especially among religious minorities. In predominantly Roman Catholic areas, there have been concerns among Protestant minorities for their religious freedoms and rights. In Protestant areas Roman Catholics often have been concerned about their religious status. In the presidential election in the United States in the early 1960s, Protestants were greatly concerned over the candidacy of John F. Kennedy, a Roman Catholic. The issues of religious pluralism and religious freedom were substantially aired and debated during that period of American history.

In Northern Ireland the religious and political differences between Roman Catholics and Protestants have exploded in conflict and terror, aided by the interests of international groups. In Lebanon, a small but populous country, dissensions based on religious, political, and ethnic factors have cast Christians and Muslims as protagonists against one another, as well as Christians against Christians. In Lebanon it is often a matter of religious, ethnic, and land identity of one group versus that of another. Rights and power are tied to clan and land which may be Christian or Muslim. When rights, power, and land are threatened, Christian may fight Muslim, or Christian may fight Christian.

Unity has been a heralded cry within Christianity during the twentieth century. Leadership in the Roman Catholic Church, in the Eastern Orthodox Church, and in the Protestant churches has worked through such structures as the World Council of Churches and other organizations to discuss common concerns and to implement specific programs together. Some churches and denominations have organically united into one church or denomination.

At the same time of movements toward unity, there have also been greater sectarian movements and the growth of mainline denominations which refrained from deep involvement in unity discussions or programs. The Southern Baptist Convention, the largest Protestant denomination in the United States, has refrained from membership in the World Council of Churches, and for the most part functions within the structures of Baptist organizations.

An issue for Christianity, then, is unity. It is that religion which holds to the ideal of "one Lord, one faith, one baptism." Unity may mean many things. It may involve the merging of churches into organic union. It may mean formal participation among churches of various denominations in making decisions about issues which face the church and all humankind and in the pooling of church resources, both personnel and finances, to meet those challenges. It may mean the informal partnership among churches and denominations on local levels to apply their resources together to face common threats and meet human needs. Christianity is a diverse religion with its theologies, confessions, polities, ethnic groupings, and historical backgrounds, but a constant issue before it is its unity.

Perhaps one of the greatest challenges to Christianity is its encounter with *secularism*. Christianity, especially in Europe and the United States, has flourished with the rise of industrialization, technology, and modern forms of communication and transportation. However, by the 1960s and 1970s Christianity was faced internally by the death-of-God theology and by the decline in church memberships. Secularism, with its detachment from Christian values and ethics, challenged societies where Christianity had been dominant. The demise of the influence of Christian values and teachings upon the nature of the family and its responsibilities is influenced by the impact of secularism upon society.

Christianity faces the issues of ever-increasing divorce rates, single-parent homes, parentless children, and the integrity of the family unit. Abortion, homosexuality, and the relations of church and state are among some of the issues that face Christianity and divide her in terms of solutions. Secularism confronts Christianity in terms of another alternative to the values and institutions of society. Christianity has to wrestle with the questions of the separation of church and state, with religious liberty, with the guarantees that the constitutions of nations offer for various freedoms, and with the authority and power that it feels it has to impact society with its teachings and values and institutions.

The universality of Christianity has brought it to impinge upon every major human population. A challenge it has had to face is its flexibility and adaptability to other cultures. On one hand it has had to deal, for example, with its Europeanness or Americanness in presenting its teachings to peoples of other cultures. On the other hand, it has had to relate to peoples of other cultures as they express Christianity in terms of their own indigenous life-styles and institutions. In its missionary outreach Christianity has had to face the revitalization of other major world religions and their often aggressive encounter not only with Christianity but with the same populations that are the missionary mandate of Christianity and Islam in the Middle East, Africa, parts of Asia, and the United States.

Because Christianity represents such a diversity of peoples and churches, it faces in its particular settings highly specific issues. The Roman Catholic Church struggles with its identity and relationship to liberation movements and to liberation theology promulgated by its scholars, especially in the developing nations where Roman Catholicism is the majority religion. Various Roman Catholic populations challenge the papacy's teachings on abortion and the ordination of women into the priesthood. Eastern orthodoxy for centuries has lived in the midst of a Muslim plurality in the Middle Eastern nations. It has struggled at times for its survival and at other times for the maintenance of its institutions.

American Christianity, through its variety of church organizations, has faced many social, economic, and political issues. During the last several decades American Christian organizations have been involved in the racial justice movements to end segregation, in the Vietnam War peace efforts, in world hunger and refugee relief, in the equal rights amendment and the role of women in society and in the church, especially in the ordination of women into clergy roles and in the moral majority emphasis. In these issues and certainly others, there have not always been consensus among the churches and among the various Christian groups.

One of the constant challenges to Christianity has been the interaction and attempts at solutions between its traditions and the changes which have confronted them. The forms of Christianity have been flexible and viable enough to preserve its inherent strengths and to be open to meaningful change. Its global approach has prepared it to be open to challenges and to seek solutions to them.

7

ISLAM

■   ■

One of the most recent religions of world significance is Islam. Born in the desert-oasis of the Arabian Peninsula in the early seventh century A.D., in a short 1,300 years it has spread to all parts of the globe and numbers some one billion followers. Its route of expansion began in Mecca in A.D. 622 (1 A.H., the first year of the Hegira, the flight to Medina). Islam then spread to Medina and rapidly to Palestine, North Africa, Spain, Persia, India, China, Africa, and North America, with stops in between. Islam has truly been a missionary religion.

Islam acknowledges its development out of Judaism and Christianity. It professes one God, Allah, who spoke to the prophet Muhammad. The revelation of Allah is written in the Muslim sacred scripture, the Qur'an. Islam accepts Jews and Christians as people of the book. It views the Jewish Torah and the Christian Gospel (Injil) as Allah's revelation to these pre-Islamic peoples. However, the Muslim believes that the Torah and Injil were misinterpreted by these peoples. The prophet Muhammad is the final prophet, and the Qur'an is the final revelation which clarifies and supersedes Allah's revelations prior to Islam.

Muslims practice their religion in a definite lifestyle. That lifestyle includes six specific responsibilities.

- The Muslim confesses one God, and the final prophet is Muhammad.

- Prayers are observed five times daily.

- There is a month of fasting.

- Certain percentages of one's income and properties are given for religious work.

111

• A pilgrimage to Mecca in Saudi Arabia is required.

• The Muslim is responsible to be a good spokesperson for the faith.

The law of Islam is all-inclusive for both the individual and the community. It governs the affairs of government as well as family and individual relations. There is no clear demarcation between religion and state. Islamic rulers, judges, scholars, clerics, and all the faithful look to the Qur'an for the principles and practices for all of life. The most visible institution of Islam is the Mosque, with its domed top and its spiraling minarets stretching into the sky. Muslims frequent the Mosque for prayers, sermons, social life, and general counsel from the trained specialists in Islamic law and ritual.

Although Islam is strongly unified around its beliefs and practices, there are divisions within the great body of believers. Just as Buddhists and Christians have their groupings, so do Muslims. The two major groups in Islam are the Sunni and the Shi'ite. One of their major differences is the interpretation of the successorship to the prophet Muhammad. Another influential group is the Sufi. The Sufi are the mystical movement within Islam, with their sheikh masters and brotherhoods.

Other Islamic groups include the Nation of Islam, nativistic to the United States, as well as the former American Muslim Mission. The stronghold of Islam is in its native region of the Middle East. However, because of its missionary zeal, there are sizable populations of Muslims in India, the former Soviet Union, China, and Indonesia. With their numbers above two billion and with their missionary emphasis, Islam and Christianity are among the most challenging global religions.

Allah and the Prophets

Islam is the third living monotheistic religion to emerge out of the Middle East. Its followers are called Muslims, and Muhammad is their prophet. Islam means submission, and Muslim means one who submits. Islam is based on the belief that Allah (the God) is the one supreme, all powerful, eternal God. Allah is creator, sustainer, and judge of all things. The Muslim confession is "There is no God but Allah, and Muhammad is his prophet." Allah revealed his righteous law to Muhammad, who spoke it to the people of the Arabian Peninsula. This law later became codified in the Muslim sacred scriptures, the Qur'an (Koran).

Islam, then, is a religion of absolute monotheism based on the God who is absolutely supreme, sovereign, and personal. The basic sin for a Muslim is idolatry (shirk), to give worship, service, or divinity to any except God. Islam has a problem with Christianity's emphasis on the doctrine of the Trinity and the claim that Jesus is both human and divine.

Perhaps Islam is the best example of a religion which places its great-est authority and confidence in a human individual without advocating in any sense his divinity. Muhammad was born of an Arabian tribal people who were practitioners of polytheism and animism. While a young man he spent long evenings in a desert cave outside the city of Mecca. In the cave Allah revealed messages to Muhammad and told him to recite them. His family ostracized him, and the Meccans threatened hostilities against him. When he was twenty-five, he married a wealthy caravan owner, Khadija. She was some fifteen years his elder. She, along with Ali, his cousin, became his first converts to the Islamic religion. In A.D. 622 he led his small band of followers to the city of Medina, where the city welcomed him as their leader. This migration is known as the flight to Medina, or the Hegira.

In Medina Muhammad attempted to negotiate peaceful relations among the tribal groups, including the Jews. Because of stubborn resis-tance, he formed his band of warriors to bring stability to the area. He built a mosque, and from its precincts he governed the people and coun-seled them in religious, economic, political, and social issues. By the time of his death in A.D. 632 he had become the prophet-statesman of that part of the Arabian Peninsula. Muhammad had formed a theocracy, gov-erning the people in the name and worship of Allah, and had launched Islam on the way to becoming a world religion.

Islam, like Christianity, has had its *mystics and saints*. Allah is the God with his law and prophet and disdain for idolatry. Traditional Islam tolerates no images of Allah. On the other hand tombs of saints and holy men and women dot the landscape and consciousness of Muslims. For the pious and mystics who rely on worship, prayer, and gifts at saints' tombs, religion is not only submission to God, but also friendship with him, leading to mystical union. Sufi Muslims represent this form of Islamic devotion. The popularity of saints has served as a means for the missionary expansion of Islam. Saints have been significant influential teachers whom their followers have imbued with something of divine grace. They have founded various religious orders and brotherhoods, and in their lifetimes they were known as sheikhs. Their tombs have become centers of pilgrimage and devotion.

After the prophet Muhammad's death, his religious community splin-tered into various groups, dividing over the issue of *leadership*. The Sunni Muslims followed their religious leaders, known as caliphs and muftis. The Shi'ite Muslims looked to their imams and ayatollahs. How-ever, all the groups maintained a tenacious belief in monotheism and prophethood as the ideal for their faith and practice. An interesting development occurred within the Shi'ite tradition. The Shi'ite adhered to a belief in the imam who was to follow the leadership of the prophet.

There were to be twelve imams. However, the twelfth imam disappeared in the ninth century A.D., and according to Shi'ite teachings he will return at some future time to deliver Muslims from the clutches of evil and restore an existence of righteousness and justice to them. This doctrine establishes an eschatological figure in Islamic belief who brings judgment and reform to the people. Among Iranian Shi'ite Muslims an ayatollah may rule or preside over the lives of people in the interim before the return of the twelfth imam.

One dimension of God which Islam also shares with Judaism and Christianity is *spirit*. Allah is a spiritual being and his spirit is present in the world. In fact, Islam asserts that Jesus has the spirit of Allah within him. Judaism also has the concept of the spirit of the Lord. Spirit, here, means the power and wisdom of Yahweh. The spirit is sent from Yahweh into the world to accomplish his purpose. The prophets have the spirit of the Lord that distinguishes Yahweh's presence with them.

Christianity fastens onto the Jewish concept. God is spirit according to the New Testament teaching. The Christian church's relationship to Jesus Christ adds another dimension to its understanding of spirit. The church relates the authority and power of Jesus with the work of the spirit of God. The doctrine of the Holy Spirit was understood by the church to be a channel of the knowledge of God. In all three religions the concept of spirit denotes the mystery of the divine-human encounter, which extends beyond what reason and words can describe. All three religions acknowledge the existence of angels who serve as messengers from God to specific people.

The three monotheistic religions have a view of deity that is transcendent and supreme. God is the one who takes the initiative to reveal his will and law to humankind. He is an ethical God who demands obedience to his will. He reveals his will to those he calls out, the prophets. Judaism portrays Yahweh in the Torah, yet continues to look for Yahweh's anointed one, the Messiah, to complete Yahweh's reign within history. Christianity acknowledges that Yahweh-God is the creator and redeemer of the world but looks to Jesus Christ as the Messiah who brings salvation and redemption to the world through his teachings, life, death, and resurrection. Islam asserts that Allah has revealed his law and will to the Jews and Christians, but holds that the perfect law of Allah was given to Muhammad.

Islam's Holy Book:
The Qur'an Road Map to Destiny

Of the scriptures of all the religions of the world, perhaps the Qur'an is looked upon by its followers as ideally and practically the most holy. Muslims believe that the Qur'an was revealed to their prophet, Muhammad, in the Arabic language, which is the very language spoken by Allah in heaven. Allah is the author of the Qur'an, and Muhammad is the channel of Allah's word to the people. Actually Qur'an means to recite. The Qur'an was written down soon after the prophet's death in the seventh century A.D.

Much information from the Bible is included in the Qur'an. Some twenty-eight prophets of the Bible are mentioned, and Muhammad, Abraham, and especially Jesus are singled out for special commemoration. Abraham is the friend of Allah and the very first Muslim. Jesus is born of a virgin and he is a miracle worker and a great teacher. Other terms used to describe Jesus are servant of Allah, spirit of Allah, and word of Allah.

The Qur'an is emphatic throughout in its statement about the oneness and sovereignty of Allah. Themes throughout the one hundred fourteen chapters (Suras) are creation of the world and humankind, religious principles and practices for life, judgment, punishment for the wicked and a paradise for the blessed, and the importance of the will of Allah. The Qur'an outlines explicitly the religious lifestyle, including prayer, fasting, and the pilgrimage to Mecca. The greatest sin named in the Qur'an is idolatry, and the greatest good is submission (Islam) to Allah.

Although the Qur'an is the supreme authority for Islam, there are other written traditions and means which play a significant part in religious life. The Hadith (Sunna) are the sayings of Muhammad which have been collected and transmitted by notable Muslim scholars. Sunna means the traditions of the prophet. Another source of authority is Ijma, the consensus of Islamic scholars (Ulama). When an interpretation of the Qur'an and/or the Hadith needs to be made, a group of scholars must agree on the interpretation for it to be valid. A fourth source of authority is Qiyas. Qiyas is the agreement of a Muslim community on an interpretation of the Qur'an and the Hadith.

Like all the major religions, Islam has developed theologians and philosophers through the centuries who have added voluminous writings. One may note that Sufism, a branch of Islam stressing mysticism, has a distinct literature with various mystical interpretations of the Qur'an and the Hadith.

The following selections come from the Qur'an. The first passage is the opening statement. It has been described as "The Lord's Prayer" of Islam. The very first phrase "In the Name of God, the Merciful, the Compassionate," opens every chapter (Sura) of the Qur'an. Other selections speak of the background of Islam in Judaism and Christianity, of a religious mandate of fasting, and of general teachings in Islam.

I

The Opening

In the name of God, the Merciful, the Compassionate

Praise belongs to God, the Lord of all Being,
The All-merciful, the All-compassionate,
The Master of the Day of Doom.
These only we serve; to Thee only we pray for succour.
Guide us in the straight path,
The path of those whom thou has blessed,
Nor of those against whom thou art wrathful,
Nor of those who are astray.[15]

II

The Cow

It is not piety, that you turn your faces to the
East and to the West
True piety is this:
to believe in God, and the Last Day,
the angels, the Book, and the Prophets,
to give of one's substance, however cherished,
to kinsmen, and orphans,
the needy, the traveller, beggars,
and to ransom the slave,
to perform the prayer, to pay the alms.
And they who fulfil their covenant
when they have engaged in a covenant,
and endure with fortitude
misfortune, hardship and peril,
these are they who are true in their faith,
these are the truly godfearing.
O believers, prescribed for you is
the Fast, even as it was prescribed for
those that were before you—haply you
will be godfearing—
for days numbered; and if any of you
be sick, or if he be on a journey,
then a number of other days; and for those
who are able to fast, a redemption
by feeding a poor man. Yet better
it is for him who volunteers good,
and that you should fast is better for you,

if you but know;
the month of Ramadan, wherein the Koran
was sent down to be a guidance
to the people, and as clear signs
of the Guidance and the Salvation.
So let those of you, who are present
at the month, fast it; and if any of you
be sick, or if he be on a journey,
then a number of other days; God desires
ease for you, and desires not hardship
for you; and that you fulfil the number, and
magnify God that He has guided you, and haply
you will be thankful.[16]

III

The House of Imran

He has sent down upon thee the Book
with the truth, confirming what was before it,
and He sent down the Torah and the Gospel
aforetime, as guidance to the people,
and He sent down the Salvation.[17]

III

The House of Imran

No; Abraham in truth was not a Jew,
neither a Christian; but he was a Muslim
and one pure of faith; certainly he was never
of the idolaters.
Surely the people standing closest to Abraham
are those who followed him, and this Prophet,
and those who believe; and God is the Protector
of the believers.[18]

V

The Table

And We sent, following
in their footsteps, Jesus
son of Mary, confirming
the Torah before him;
and We gave to him the
Gospel, wherein is

guidance and light,
and confirming the Torah
before it, as a guidance
and an admonition
unto the godfearing.
So let the People of the Gospel judge
according to what God has sent down
therein. Whosoever judges not
according to what God has sent down—
they are the ungodly.[19]

The Muslim Path:
A Straight Path from Prayer to Pilgrimage

Islam is a religion of submission to Allah, and a Muslim is one who submits. Of the major world religions, Islam may be the one that most emphasizes orthodox belief and uniform practice. Other religions may offer a variety of choices to their followers. Within Hinduism and Buddhism there are diverse beliefs in deities, paths to salvation, and ethical systems. A Japanese may be comfortable with dual loyalties to Shinto and Buddhist beliefs and ceremonies. However, Islam in theory and practice is very similar for an American, an Asian, and a Middle Eastern Muslim. Islam has its branches of Sunni, Shi'ite, and Sufi which differ on theological understandings and religious practices; but Islam is monolithic in terms of its unity and uniformity. In fact, Islam is so orthodox in its beliefs and practices that they can be numbered and discussed in a quite orderly fashion.

Muslim Beliefs

The major beliefs of Islam may be discussed in five specific categories. They are Allah, angels, sacred scriptures, prophets, and last things.

Allah

The name for God is Allah, which from the Arabic language means the god. The Muslim is a monotheist, and Allah is the only deity. Allah's uniqueness, sovereignty, and power are important. Nothing can be associated with Allah. In fact, the greatest sin in Islam is shirk, the giving to anybody or anything the smallest share of Allah's unique sovereignty. That is one reason why the Muslim cannot accept the Christian belief in the incarnation of God in Jesus. Allah's attributes are seen in creation, revelation, preservation, and predestination. Everything exists by the will of Allah, and his will is all law. There are ninety-nine names associated with Allah, including the compassionate and merciful one. The tasbih, a Muslim rosary, has ninety-nine beads on a string, which remind one of the beautifulness of Allah. Allah is a highly transcendent God who gives his law from a distance through an angel to his prophet. That law becomes codified into the sacred scripture, the Qur'an.

Angels

Angels are intermediaries between Allah and his prophet. There are various levels of angels, with specific duties. There are archangels like Gabriel, the angel of revelation sent by Allah to reveal his law to the prophet. There are ministering angels like Ridwan, the grand chamberlain of paradise. There are fallen angels like Iblis (Satan). Iblis refused to give homage to the first male and female created by Allah, and Allah deported him from heaven; he became the protagonist against Allah's elect. There are also various spirits called jinn. These jinn are both males and females and influence humans for good or for bad. For example, a Muslim believes that a mad person is jinn-possessed. Angels play an important role in the Islamic belief system.

Sacred Scriptures

Muslims are known as people of the book. The book is the Qur'an, often transliterated as Koran. The archetype of this sacred scripture is in heaven with Allah. Muslims believe without any change or interpretation the angel Gabriel transmitted the Qur'an from heaven to the prophet Muhammad. The Qur'an in the Arabic language is the perfect expression of Allah's law and will. The Islamic doctrine of scripture is consonant with Muhammad's conception of himself in the succession of the biblical prophets. Allah revealed his law to Moses in the Torah, and Allah gave Jesus the Injil (Gospel). Scripture is really one, and each successive book confirms or corrects those which precede it.

Prophets

Islam is a prophetic religion. The Qur'an names some twenty prophets stretching from Adam, Noah, Abraham, and Moses in the Torah to John and Jesus in the Injil. The final seal of the prophets is Muhammad, who received the revelation from Allah. Muhammad is referred to as rasul, which may be translated messenger or apostle. As Islam developed, it gave specific attention to six prophets. They are Adam the chosen of Allah, Noah the prophet of Allah, Abraham the friend of Allah, Moses the conversant of Allah, Jesus the spirit of Allah, and Muhammad the apostle of Allah. The Qur'an gives more honorific titles to Jesus, known as Isau, than to any other prophet. Jesus is referred to as messiah, servant, word, spirit, prophet, messenger, sign, witness, mercy, righteous, blessed, and near Allah. However, the Muslim view considers all the prophets as humans designated by Allah to be spokesmen. A prophet is not divine. It is interesting to note that while the Qur'an includes the view of the virgin birth of Jesus and Jesus as a miracle worker, it refutes the idea that He was the Son of God incarnate. The prophet, then, has an important function in Islam, and Muhammad himself was prophetic in denouncing the idols and idol worship of his day and preaching the will of Allah, brought religious and social change to the peoples of the day.

Last Things

The belief in last things, or eschatology, is very prominent in Islam. Islam's sense of history is very similar to Jewish and Christian views. From birth to death life is lived under the law and judgment of Allah. Beyond death there is the resurrection of the dead, the final judgment, and the rewards or punishments in paradise and hell. Muhammad preached that the final judgment was soon to come, but he gave no date for it. Islam is very explicit about the end time. At the judgment Allah opens up the book of deeds. Good and evil deeds are weighed and the balance determines one's destiny. Paradise is a garden of eternity while hell is described as a hot and beastly place. Islam's doctrine of last things is based on a view of the omnipotence and omniscience of Allah. The Qur'an indicates that Allah has written the entrance and exit of every soul and what it will meet. The Muslim believes that everything comes from Allah and that Allah leads astray whom he wills and guides rightly whom he wills. A favorite expression of Muslims is "if Allah wills."

Muslim Practices

Just as Muslims state a clear and concise set of beliefs, they also practice a highly stylized and visible religious life. Form and time are important in religious practices. The individual often becomes absorbed in community observances and rituals and becomes blurred in mass participation. Although Islam claims no ordained clergy, the Islamic religious scholars serve in various capacities as theologians, jurists, preachers, prayer leaders, counselors, and administrators of mosques and endowments. Many of the religious practices are led by religious leaders both in mosques and in homes. There are six basic practices or pillars of Islam, which involve both the individual and the community (unmah). They are the confession of faith, prayers, financial giving, fasting, pilgrimage, and missionary efforts.

The Confession

The confession of faith (shahada) is the creedal statement of Islam. In transliteration it is "la ilaha il Allah, Muhammad rasul Allah." It means, "There is no deity save Allah; Muhammad is the apostle of Allah." It expresses the Muslim belief in monotheism and the prophet as the agent of the revelation of Allah. The mere saying of it is an act of piety.

Prayer

Perhaps prayer (namaz) is the most conspicuous and constant practice among Muslims. The prayer ritual is a highly formalized pattern, and the prayers are said in the Arabic language. A good Muslim will pray five times daily: dawn, midday, afternoon, evening, and night. Traditionally the prayer leader of the community ascends the minaret of the mosque and sounds the call to prayer at the stated times. The individual may say prayers in the home or at the mosque or wherever it is convenient at the time. Prayers must be said facing the holy city of Mecca in Saudi Arabia. If one is praying in the mosque, there is a niche (mihrab) in the wall to line up toward Mecca. The individual states four times that Allah is great. Twice the Muslim says that there is no deity except Allah and that Muhammad is the apostle of Allah. There are various postures assumed during the ritual. There are genuflections, dramatized reading from the Qur'an, and listenings for the truths of Allah.

When prayers are said in the mosque, those who pray line up behind a leader known as the imam. Muslims also say informal prayers in their vernacular language in their homes and at various religious meetings. Prayer, then, claims much time and energy among Muslims. Some Muslims feel that it is best to say prayers in the mosque behind the imam; therefore, it takes time to leave work to go to the mosque. Every person must purify before praying, so water must be available to wash one's hands. The rituals of the prayers last fifteen to thirty minutes at each prayer time. Of all Muslim rituals the prayers are the most fastidious ones, observed seven days a week. Prayer is the lifeline of Muslim obedience to Allah. The Muslim holy day is Friday, and on that day at high noon Muslims go to the mosque not only to pray as a community but to listen to the Friday sermon by the Muslim preacher.

Fasting

Fasting is another stringent practice. It is observed during the month of Ramadan, the ninth month of the Muslim calendar. This is the same month in which Muhammad received the revelation of the Qur'an. A faithful Muslim abstains from food, drink, and pleasures from sunrise to sunset each day of Ramadan. The aged and pregnant women may be excused from fasting. Fasting is viewed as fostering a disciplined life and a healthy body. It is also a time when Muslims give to the poor the meals they give up during the season. After sunset and before dawn of each day, meals are eaten. Often when the month of Ramadan falls in the hot summer, the discipline of fasting becomes difficult and testy. A worker may be in the hot sun all day without water or food. Irritation becomes a temptation, and emotions may run high. At the end of the month a great celebration is held in the home and in the mosque signifying the breaking of the fast and obedience to Allah, who mandated its observance in the Qur'an.

Pilgrimage to Mecca

One of the Islamic practices most noticeable to the world is the annual pilgrimage (Haj) to Mecca in Saudi Arabia. Mecca is the birthplace of Muhammad. It also contains the ancient black stone, the ka'ba, where Muslims claim that Abraham was tempted to sacrifice his son Ishmael. It is around the precincts of the ka'ba that the great mosque of Mecca is built. The Qur'an requires the faithful Muslim to make a pilgrimage to Mecca once during one's lifetime. One may be excused if the financial means to do it are not available and if one's health prevents it. Several million pilgrims descend upon Mecca at the same time each year to accomplish the rituals. All must dress in a white garment to demonstrate their equality before Allah. Rituals include kissing the black stone of the ka'ba, circumambulating it, offering prayers before it, throwing stones at the devil near Mina, and making a trip to the city of Medina, where Muhammad is buried. At the conclusion sheep are sacrificed and the meat is given to the needy. The pilgrimage takes about two weeks to perform. One returns home to be called a Hajji and to become a celebrity and a religious elite. The dream of faithful Muslims is to make the Haj to Mecca; however, it is expensive and demanding. The Haj is a symbol of the global unity of Islam as people come from every corner of the earth. It is also a symbol of everyone's equality before Allah in terms of spirituality and religious practice.

Giving

Financial giving and religious taxation is a strong part of a Muslim's practice. The Qur'an designates that certain percentages of one's income, properties, herds, agricultural produce, and other possessions are to be given in praise and obedience to Allah. This financial obligation (Zadat) is interpreted and determined by the Ulama. Often the people will give monies to the Ulama. These monies are used to pay salaries of the Muslim clerics, to build and maintain mosques, seminaries, and schools, to provide scholarships for students, to maintain shrines, to produce literature, and to support Muslim missionaries. Endowments (Auqaf) are a big business in Islam. Large tracts of land or businesses are often left by pious and wealthy Muslims for the benefit of the Islamic community. These endowments may be tens of thousands of acres or often entire villages. Consequently, the Ulama have to be astute business people to wisely shepherd these investments. When one visits a market-place (bazaar) in a Muslim town, the shops around the environs of the mosque may be owned by the mosque, having been endowed by pious Muslims of generations past. Muslim finances and endowment, then, are an intricate and involved system of religious practice.

Holy War

Jihad has several meanings. It is the duty of every Muslim and the Islamic community to exert their energies for positive results. Therefore, every Muslim is a missionary on behalf of religion. Jihad, simply put, means holy efforts for Allah. In the beginning Muhammad declared Jihad or holy warfare against pagans and infidels. Muslim leaders throughout history have declared holy war against their adversaries. There have been certain qualifications about holy war. Only a top Muslim leader like a caliph or ayatollah can declare legal and proper holy war, and a holy war often is only justified in defense of the Islamic community. There is an understanding that Muslims should not consider holy war in countries where there is religious freedom. Yet the Jihad concept is much deeper than war. It means being a missionary. Islam has been a missionary religion since its inception. It moved out of the Arabian Peninsula to Africa and Asia largely through the missionary efforts of its merchants and clerics, who traveled to other lands to testify to Allah and to build mosques.

Muslim Groups

Muslim faith and practice is highly specific and community oriented. Although Islam presents a religion of unity and uniformity, there are divisions and various group identities. Three branches of Islam are particularly obvious. They are the Sunni, the Shi'ite, and the Sufi.

The *Sunni* are the traditionalists. They adhere to all the major beliefs and practices described. However, their key leaders have been the caliphs, who ruled over the vast Islamic empires from their office of the caliphate. The Sunni are the great majority of Muslims. Saudi Arabia is a Sunni nation.

The *Shi'ites* are predominant in Iran and Iraq. They also follow the major tenets and practices; however, the Shi'ites have key leaders called the imams or ayatollahs, whose office is the imamate. The Shi'ites have distinct rituals and shrines dedicated to members of the prophet Muhammad's family, like Ali, Fatima, Hasan, and Husain. The shrines are dedicated to these individuals who have actually become saints in Shi'ite ritual and theology. Shi'ites, then, include the same beliefs and practices as the Sunni, but they have parallel doctrines and rituals which emphasize the prophet's family, saint devotion, and an understanding of a community based on the leadership of the imam. The Shi'ites offer the little tradition in Islam.

The *Sufi* are the mystics and ascetics within Islam. They have their orders of brotherhoods with their leaders the sheikhs. The Sufi emphasize experience over ritual, feelings over thought, and the presence of God in the heart over the law of God given from a distance. The Sufi are prepared to speak more about the love of God than the law of God. God for them does not reside beyond the earth but comes to be present in the believer's heart. The Sufi recite both the Qur'an and poetry. They play musical instruments. The Sufi have brought the more legal and rigid approaches of Islam into a warm and emotional experience. Throughout the expansion of Islam, the Sufi were the vanguard of the missionary enterprise.

Islam projects a total way of life for its followers. Allah is the ruler, guide, and judge. The Qur'an contains all the essentials for a religious, social, economic, and political life for the individual and the community. Leaders of Muslim societies are to govern in the name of Allah according to the principles of the Qur'an. The Muslim family is to be educated in home and mosque concerning the beliefs and practices. A Muslim is to be a witness among others to the greatness and compassion of Allah. Of all the major religions perhaps Islam has most narrowed the choices of its followers according to beliefs and doctrines. There is an overriding emphasis on sameness and unity. The same confession is uttered numerous times each day. Prayers are said by hundreds of millions at approximately the same time each day using the same phrases. At the same two months each year, Muslims observe the fast and make the pilgrimage to Mecca. It may be said that Muslims are a large religious family that worship together, pray together, and pilgrim together.

The Mosque: Prayer, Sermon, Marching Orders

When the Prophet Muhammad fled from Mecca to Medina, one of his first orders of business was to build a mosque. At the mosque he led the people in prayer, preached sermons, taught the Qur'an, and gave general counsel to the people. Later, when he conquered Mecca and made it the pilgrim center for the Muslims, another mosque was built in the vicinity of the Ka'ba. Wherever Islam has expanded during its some fourteen hundred years of existence, a mosque has been built. Mosque (masjid) means place of prostration. Muslims pray five times daily, and the mosque is the structure in which they bow down in praise to Allah.

The Building

The architecture of mosques assumes various forms depending on the features of the culture; however, there are standard characteristics. One may associate six words beginning with the letter *m* with these characteristics. First, there is the word mosque. Second, there is the name of Muhammad, which is praised at each utterance of prayer, just as the name Allah. Third, there is the minaret, the slender and spiraling column which ascends from the mosque skyward. Inside, there is a stairway where the Muslim leader ascends to reach the open top to call the people to prayer at the daily stated times. Fourth, the mihrab is a notch in the wall of the mosque which directs the position of the Muslims in prayer to Mecca. Fifth, the mimbar is the elevated pulpit which the Muslim leader ascends to preach to the gathered people from the sacred Qur'an. Last, there is the mullah, the mosque leader, who is the Islamic scholar. He is trained in worship through leading prayers and giving sermons and general counsel to Muslims in family and domestic matters.

The mosque may be a simple one-room structure, or it may include a large prayer room with alcoves, offices, a library, a theological school, and residential quarters for students. A larger mosque has a courtyard with a pool. Every mosque has a water supply if possible, for the Muslim must ritually cleanse parts of the body before entering the mosque proper for prayer. Sand may be used in place of water. A shoe rack may be present at the entrance to the mosque, for Muslims must shed their shoes before entering the holy precincts for prayer. Qur'ans may be distributed around the floor or in racks for the worshiper's use. There are no seats inside the mosque; worshipers sit on carpets on the floor. There is little ornamentation inside because Muhammad forbade images. The main decorative art is the inscriptions of Qur'anic sentences on the walls, the mimbar, and the pillars.

The Activities

The activities surrounding mosques vary according to their location and status in the community. In the countryside a mosque may be built by a family in honor of the prophet Muhammad or other renowned figures of Islam. There may be no special Muslim leader or mullah at the small mosque, and meetings may be infrequent. A village mosque may have a resident mullah who leads daily prayers and gives a sermonette each day and the main sermon at noon prayers on Friday. A city mosque may have several resident mullahs who lead prayer, give sermons, and teach students.

Friday is the holy day in Islam. Of course, a Muslim offers prayers every day, and it is preferable to pray in the mosque. However, Friday is the community day at the mosque. At noon families gather at the mosque. Individuals wash their hands, elbows, and faces as purification rites as they gather in the courtyard around the pool filled with water. Men enter the mosque and sit in rows on the carpeted or bare floor and face the mimbar. Women with their children sit toward the rear of the alcoves or in the balcony. The mullah sounds the call to prayer from the minaret, and then he stands before the assembly with his back toward them and his face toward the mimbar and leads them through the prayer sayings and bowings. At noon the mullah ascends the mimbar, sits facing the assembly from his elevated position, and preaches the Friday sermon. Traditionally, the mullah preaches a sermon based on some teaching from the Qur'an and presents greetings from the king or supreme leader of the land. He preaches in a highly stylized form without notes. If the native language is not Arabic, he will sprinkle in Arabic sayings from the Qur'an.

At the conclusion of the sermon, the worshipers may drink tea or coffee, and mill about the mosque and the courtyard as families exchange greetings and visits with one another. In addition, gatherings at the mosque have always served social and civic purposes. Much socializing occurs in the mosque environs not only on Fridays but daily. Women gather in the courtyard to exchange gossip. Children play at the pool. Men conduct business deals as they huddle in small groups in the courtyard. Families may contract marriages for their children. At times hushed conversations may be politically volatile against the mayor of the town or even the king of the land. Constantly, the counsel for the mullah is sought on many matters dealing with law, business, family, Qur'anic interpretations, and politics. The mosque, then, is the focus of the Muslim community in the daily activities.

The mosque as a symbol of devotion and religious discipline flows over into the home and the marketplace. Muslims invite the mullah into their homes to conduct Qur'anic sessions, and the family and their invited friends will engage him in a discussion. This is usually a meeting for males. Women will have their own meeting gathered around a simple meal with prayers and Qur'anic interpretation led by a female mullah. Following the Islamic calendar various meetings will be held in both homes and mosques celebrating and commemorating the birthday of the prophet Muhammad, Ramadan, and haj, or the Shi'ite rituals associated with Husain (Muharram). During the season of Muharram there may be nightly services at the mosque for two weeks when a famous mullah preaches and narrates the tragic story of Husain. Families may invite renowned mullahs into their homes to recite the narrative of Husain. These occasions elicit emotional outbursts of crying in both mosque and home services. During Muharram, the marketplaces, which usually are strong Muslim quarters in predominant Muslim lands, finance ceremonies and parades in which the people go through the marketplace and the streets chanting the story of Husain and beating their chests.

Theological schools attached to mosque complexes train Muslim leadership for the varied responsibilities and functions of Islamic practices associated with the mosque. Islamic scholars write and publish pamphlets and books not only to edify Muslims but also to propagate the Muslim faith to outsiders. These writings may be found in and around the mosque precincts. The mosque is an institution with profound relations to the community and world surrounding it. The mosque both affirms the Muslim's faith and aids him or her in practicing it. It also sends the Muslim back into daily life to translate Islam into reality.

Religious Identity and Family, Rights, and Territories, Tradition and Change

Perhaps of all the major religions, Islam may be the one in the latter half of the twentieth century which will be tested the greatest in the areas of tradition and change. Since Napoleon came east at the end of the eighteenth century, the heartland of Islam in the Middle East has encountered western intrusions. The emergence of the state of Israel and the succeeding wars between it and the Muslim states have focused attention on religious identity and status and rights to territory. Islam had ruled the areas under the Ottoman caliphs through Islamic institutions and law for some four hundred years. Kemal Ataturk initiated a policy of secularization in Turkey, the center of the Ottoman Empire, after World War I. Islamic institutions and law were cast aside for western forms. Mosques, Muslim clergy, and Muslim seminaries were restricted and often eliminated. Reza Shah of Iran began some of the same kinds of secularization in the 1930s, modeled after Turkey. Islam began to face the same challenges, not only across the Middle East and North Africa but also in predominantly Muslim countries like Indonesia.

Islamic Law

At its inception in the seventh century A.D. Islam began with a community based on theocratic rule. The prophet Muhammad, as statesman, ruled over the Muslim community according to the law of Allah as revealed to him in the Qur'an. According to Islamic understanding, government is to be informed and guided by the Shariah, the law of Allah. In the twentieth century the rise of the modern nation-state among populations of Muslim predominance has brought conflict between modern leaders and traditional Muslim clerics. Whereas Kemal Ataturk basically succeeded in the secularization process, Reza Shah and his son, Mohammad Reza Shah Pahlavi, of Iran failed; the Ayatollah Khomeini chased the son from power and began the process of the restoration of Islamic values and institutions to Iranian society. When President Sadat of Egypt journeyed to Jerusalem and began making accommodations to the state of Israel, Muslim reactionaries initiated dissent which eventually led to Sadat's assassination. Syria has waged battle within its own country against Muslim reactionary forces. Islam, then, struggles with the ideals and realities of religion and politics not only with other nations but within her own body politic.

There are other areas of challenge to Islam besides the issue of theocracy and politics. A fundamental issue is the place of revelation and reason. This issue focuses on the interpretation of the Qur'an and the schools of law. Did revelation cease with the Qur'an? What part does modern scholarship have in the interpretation of the Qur'an? How are the differences resolved between the schools of law or between the qadis (judges) or between the ayatollahs in the interpretation of the Qur'an and the Shariah (Islamic law) and traditions?

A factor to be considered is that traditional Islam views Arabic as the theological language and the sacred language of Allah. Both language and hermeneutics have become problematic. Traditionally, Islamic scholars or clergy types (Ulama) have claimed authority to interpret the Qur'an and the law to the nation or community. Through mosque schools and through Islamic court systems, the Ulama implemented Muslim doctrines, values, and institutions. However, modern rulers have gradually placed education under the supervision of the government and the law courts under jurists trained under the influence of western law and practice. The struggle has ensued between religious traditionalists and modern secularizers.

As modern states emerge within Islamic populations other tensions surface. Traditional Islam has exerted influence and control over all the affairs of the community, including family matters, commercial relations, and criminal law. Islam has prohibited collecting interest on loans and payments. Since interest charges are a way of life with modern banking, there has been conflict over this issue. It is reported that over four hundred banks and their branches were burned at the time of the Iranian revolution, a symbol of protest against the modernizing policies of the Shah.

The Family

The Muslim family has faced the tensions of change. Traditional Islamic law has governed marriage and divorce, inheritance, and many religious duties. Under Islamic law a husband could normally divorce his wife by stating the fact in the presence of witnesses. Modern law in certain Islamic countries guarantees the rights of women to a legal proceeding in the courts of law. Divorce, then, becomes a matter of equal importance for both male and female. Extramarital relations, especially for the female, have been subject to extreme forms of punishment administered by the family members and/or the community. Under modern forms of law the courts hear the cases with both sides represented. Also, matters of family inheritance, traditionally under Muslim governance, have increasingly come under modern state judicial systems.

In the latter half of the twentieth century the influences on the Muslim family have progressively come from the government's control over the educational and social opportunities of the children and the students. Changes in dress, educational philosophy, opportunities for higher education, a myriad of social opportunities, training for vocations in technological society and a series of choices never before offered have given the younger generations new options. These changes have brought tensions between the old and the young, between parents and children, and between traditional religion and modern society. Embassies and their cultural centers, cinemas showing the latest American, Japanese, and European movies, hordes of international workers and their families mixing with the people have confronted the Muslim family with a different set of conditions for relationships. Muslim countries have sent tens of thousands of their young men and women for higher education to western and eastern nations. They, in turn, have returned with new ideas and values and social models to be tested with their traditional ones.

Criminal Justice

Islam has definite laws to apply to criminal matters as well as a definite way to administer them. As with other forms of domestic life, the role of religion in these areas has been supplanted by secular forces and secular interpretations of law. The conflict, then, continues between those trained in traditional Islamic theology, philosophy, and law, and those who have trained in the judicial and legal non-Islamic schools. The conflict is abetted by the modernizing tendencies encouraged by leadership in the varied life of the nation, especially the educational and social areas. The Muslim family, often caught in the transitions, experiences the struggles and tensions in the search for its identity, both religious and social.

Islam and Secularism

As Islam experiences a renewed struggle for its sense of identity amidst change, there is another issue. It is Islam's relationships with other religious neighbors. It is the question of religious pluralism and religious freedom. In most countries of the Middle East, Islam is the predominant religion. In other countries like India and France, it is a minority religion, though it has sizable numbers. In Indonesia it is the majority religion in a secular state that attempts to be equitable with all religious communities. Historically, Islam has guaranteed the rights and privileges of Jews and Christians, especially as people of the scriptural tradition, in terms of their religious freedoms. In modern nation-states where Islam is dominant, there are constitutional statements protecting religious communities and granting them religious freedom. As Islam faces the conflicts and dilemmas of shaping societies in the modern era, it will increasingly encounter religious pluralism and the question of religious freedom. Since Islam and Christianity are the two major missionary religions as well as the most populated ones, the question becomes critical between the two.

Judaism, Christianity, and Islam find themselves interdependent in many ways in the latter half of the twentieth century. Identity, status, and power as religious communities are at stake. In some ways it is land and territory. In some ways it is prestige and power. In other ways it is an attempt to relate to each other with the revelation, the truth, and the living community which each cherishes. These relationships are experienced not only in the arena of politics and power movements but also among the lives of Jewish, Christian, and Muslim families.

8

OTHER SELECT RELIGIOUS TRADITIONS

Hinduism, Buddhism, Confucianism, Judaism, Christianity, and Islam have long historical traditions with sacred written records. Their influences have been worldwide, and often they have impacted each other in their growth and development.

There are other significant religious traditions. Ancient Egypt, Mesopotamia, Greece, and Rome have offered their pantheon of deities and religious rituals. African Traditional Religion, with its high god, lesser spirits, ancestors, and ceremonies, is pervasive across Africa.

Zoroastrianism was a major religion of ancient Persia with its prophet, Zoroaster, its god, Ahura Mazda, and its scripture, the Avesta. *Jainism* became a religious tradition about the time of the Buddha in India, and was founded by Mahavira, who set out to reform Hinduism.

Sikhism was founded by Nanak in fifteenth century India. Nanak combined elements of Hinduism and Islam to form this new religious tradition. The *Baha'i* religion arose in Iran in the middle of the nineteenth century. Its prophet, Baha'ullah, especially drew upon the religions of Judaism, Christianity, and Islam.

Some of these select traditions are now remembered by their literature and monuments, and others are growing and vibrant traditions in both their native lands as well as across cultures. There are two patterns of beliefs and rituals which may have impact upon the religious traditions considered in this writing. They are animism and tribalism.

Animism is a pattern which has been prevalent among preliterate tribes in Australia, Oceania, and Africa with elaborate beliefs and practices which may include a spirit-filled world, ghosts, great and lesser spirits, ancestor veneration, and totem loyalties. Animistic patterns may include worship and veneration toward supernatural, human, family, animal, and nature spirits. These spirits may be held in awe or in fear. Special places, objects, or zones may be sacred places of residence or of meeting the spirits, and spirits may be benevolent or malevolent.

Belief in spirits is not restricted to preliterate societies. Major world religions also have their spirit worlds and systems to deal with spirits. Ancestor veneration remains a part of the traditions of Hinduism, Buddhism, and the Chinese and Japanese religions. Often, animism is blended with a major religious system. A Hindu god may be worshiped alongside an ancestor spirit. While Islam has a strong statement regarding monotheism, in the popular practice of Islam, there is the spirit world of the jinn, both good and evil spirits, which affect the daily lives of Muslims. Also, saint veneration is prevalent in Islam. Animism is a religious view of the spirit world and practice that cuts across many religions.

Tribal religion is a pattern of various peoples. Some tribes and clans among Africans and among Indians of the Americas, for example, worship a supreme deity among a hierarchy of deities of varying importance. The values associated with the high deity may be those of power over natural forces. Often, the deity will have military prowess which the warriors of the tribe exalt and emulate as they fight other tribes. Usually, in a tribal religion there are levels of service and rewards to which the followers respond.

Tribalism and animism may also share characteristics of the spirit world in which the spirits are categorized in hierarchies of importance. Both tribalism and animism are prevalent among peoples who communicate through oral traditions rather than written ones.

Ancient Egypt, Mesopotamia, Greece, and Rome

The ancient world surrounding the Mediterranean gave rise to Egyptian civilization, Mesopotamian culture, and Greek and Roman culture and religions. From the fourth millennium B.C. to the early centuries of the Christian era, religious traditions of these areas made their impacts. Although some of the elements of these religious traditions make little impact on current cultures, the traditions are rich in history and provide engaging backgrounds for world cultures today.

Egypt

· Egypt was united, with few exceptions, under a series of dynasties and kingdoms from 2300 B.C. to the conquest of Alexander the Great in the fourth century B.C. Among the patterns of Egyptian religion, several were prominent. They included the status of the Pharaoh, elaborate ritu-als associated with the dead, and the cult of the sun god.

The Divine Being

The city-states throughout Egypt each had their own protective dei-ties. Each deity had its own family. With the merger of city-states deities often merged. An early god, Horus, known as the falcon god, was asso-ciated with the king. The king became a divine-king, the linkage between humans and god, between earth and heaven. In later history Horus was replaced by or identified with the sun god, Re. When the city of Thebes became powerful, its god, Amon, was fused with Re to become Amon-Re. Despite other changes in the pantheon of deities, Amon-Re and the Pharaohs associated with him served in the role of God-king with a priesthood and rituals. The Pharaoh represented the rays and power of the shining sun.

The Pharaoh as divine-king represented religious, political, economic, and social stability among the Egyptians. He was the hub of the cosmic order, assuring harmony in the city as well as peace with the god. The god of the sun whom he represented brought energy and fertility to the people and to the land.

Cult of the Dead

A great symbol of the cult of the dead was the pyramid. The pyramids contained the mummified bodies of the Pharaohs, their families, and their entourages. The Pharaoh was the intermediary between earth and heaven, and at death the body was to be preserved for the journey heav-enward. The status of the divine kingship was the focus of the cosmic order, and a part of that focus included fertility of the crops and the pros-perity of the people. Divine kingship became associated with the vegeta-tion deity who was Osiris.

Osiris was the deity related to the cycle of the seasons and the crops. He symbolized the decay and the renewal of life; he was associated with the patterns of death and resurrection. The Egyptian *Book of the Dead* provided information and directions to the afterlife. Especially significant was moral judgment. Judges decided the fate of the deceased in the pres-ence of Osiris based on qualities of honesty, justice, family life, and benevolences which reflected the social ethic of Egyptian society. The deceased had to be declared worthy to enter the land of Osiris.

As the cult of the dead, with mummification and preparations for the afterlife spread through the population, more attention was given to the cult of Osiris and Isis. They represented restored life and immortality after death. The myth of Osiris continued after the age of the Pharaohs and influenced other cultures surrounding Egypt.

Mesopotamia

The religion of Mesopotamia focused on the deities of Sumeria, Babylon, and Assyria. The many deities were organized according to cosmic spaces, geography, cities, families, and functions. There were connections between the status and power of the gods in the heavens and the rulers of the city-states.

Among the deities was Anu, known as the Sky God with supreme power. Enlil was the Storm God, who was also known as the protector. Enki was the Lord of the Earth. Enki's son was Marduk. An assortment of star gods were Sin the Moon God, Shamash the Sun God, and Hadad, another Storm God. An important star goddess was Ishtar.

The cult of Mesopotamian religion centered on the gods, and the focus for ceremony and ritual was on the temple complex which featured the ziggurat. The ziggurat, a tower reached by a series of steps and platforms, was the focal point for the housing of images of the deities. The priest cared for the deities, and the people offered their gifts to them. In the festivals and ceremonies the king represented the god to the people, and the priests assisted the king.

Besides the greater deities of the cosmos and the earth, there were lesser deities to whom people looked for daily assistance. Religion also was expressed in divination and astrology. Through incantations and spells, demons were warded off. Through divination and omens people sought to come into contact with the power of the gods and to learn the signs and symptoms of the will of the gods. Various levels of priests assisted in these endeavors.

Astrology was also important. It focused on the arrangement of the stars and other cosmic bodies to the earth in interpreting and predicting the destiny of the people. Later Babylonian deities were associated with the planets, including Jupiter-Marduk, Venus-Ishtar, Saturn-Ninib, Mercury-Nebo, and Mars-Nergal. Astrology was developed further by the Greeks with the Zodiac.

Life in Mesopotamia was lived under the rule of the gods through the divine king with the assistance of the priests. The kingship was a divine institution, and the king held responsibility for the welfare of the state and the people. The Code of Hammurabi, the Babylonian ruler of 1700 B.C., focused on the king's divine power through law to rule the people and expect their obedience to him and thus to the deity. Various kinds of social and business relationships were governed by the Code.

Within Mesopotamian religion was the *Epic of Gilgamesh*, the story of the search for immortality. Also, the *Epic of Creation* depicted the great god, Marduk, associated with both the sun and vegetation, in his creative functions of heaven and earth.

Mesopotamian religion faded with the conquest of the Persians in 539 B.C. The deities lost their power, the divine kings and their rule became history, and other religious and political shapes occurred. However, Mesopotamian religion continued to have its influences beyond its geographical area.

Greece

The religion of Greece portrayed many gods and goddesses who were very human in their thinking and behaving. The Greek writers Homer and Hesiod were the informers of the characteristics of the deities. In general the deities may be classified into two broad groups according to their birthplace and their abode. The first were the deities of the sky or heaven; they were the Olympians of Homer with their home in Mount Olympus in northern Greece. The other group was from the Mediterranean regions with emphasis on the earth and its fertility.

The saga of the Greek deities portrayed their immortality, morality, or amorality, and their successes and failures. Zeus was the sky god, the bright one from the word "to shine." He was supreme, being ruler, father, and lord of wisdom. Born to Rhea and Cronus, he also had brothers, Poseidon, who was lord of water and seas, and Hades of earth.

Apollo was identified with art, poetry, and music, as well as medicine, order, and harmony. He was associated with the Delphic sanctuary and the Delphic Oracle. In contrast to Apollo, there was Dionysus, the god of vegetation, emotion, ecstasy, and wine. Other deities were Aphrodite the goddess of love, Athena the Patroness of Athens, Hermes the messenger of the deities, and Artemis the all-Mother or Earth-Goddess.

Besides the Olympian pantheon of deities, there were the mystery religions associated with the Dionysian, Orphic, and Eleusinian mysteries. These cults appealed to personal religion. The Dionysian mystery cult centered around the god Dionysus. Rituals were held in more remote areas and emphasized wild dancing, music, and wine. Also, there was the eating of a wild animal identified with Dionysus. The cult followers felt one with Bacchus, another name of Dionysus, which meant lord of the vine. Many of the participants were women.

The Orphic mysteries focused on ascetic practices which would enable one to be liberated from bodily entanglements and to achieve immortality. A central belief was the division of the body from the soul. The soul could be reincarnated into immortality. Thus, for the Orphic devotee, this life was evil, and the goal was to pursue the next world by overcoming the evil in the present one. The Orphic idea of the immortality of the soul influenced Pythagoras, who in turn influenced Plato in his idea of the immortality of the soul in the *Phaedo*.

The Eleusinian mysteries focused on Demeter, the deity of vegetation, or corn mother. The theme around Demeter was that of death and rising again to life. The follower of Demeter through identification with the deity in the ritual was able to share a new and risen life.

Rome

The Romans conquered Greece in the second century B.C. The Greek and Roman religions mingled, and Greek philosophy impacted Roman ways. However, Hellenistic religion continued to make its contribution to other religions, including Judaism and Christianity.

Roman religion included both native as well as imported *deities*. Religion served the Roman Empire whether born within or brought from without. Early Roman religion focused on the numina, the power of the gods. The early deities were related to home and family. An example is Vesta, goddess of the family and domestic life. She was the spirit of the fire on the hearth.

Other gods were Janus, Jupiter, Mars, and Quirinus. Janus was a foundational deity like Vesta in the rituals of home worship. Jupiter was the supreme god, the sky god, whose temple became the center of state occasions. Jupiter also became the war god. Mars was the god of war and of agriculture. Quirinus was associated with Mars but had his own temples and festivals.

Roman religion adopted new gods from other lands as well as giving old gods new names. Diana was the forest goddess who aided women and later became associated with Artemis. Other Greek goddesses were Minerva, Tyche, and Venus. Also from Greece came Hercules and Apollo. Apollo was the inspirer of the Sibyls, women oracles.

In the Second Punic War (218-201 B.C.), the sacred stone of the Great Mother Goddess, Cybele, was brought from Phrygia in Asia Minor. The temple of the Great Mother was built to house the stone. Later, Dionysus was worshiped in the Bacchus cult. Roman religion also received the Isis-Serapis-Osiris worship from Egypt which emphasized fertility and immortality.

Religious life centered around the temples of the deities, rituals, festivities, and calendars. Rituals included the offering of sacrifices, first fruits and animals, to the alter of the deity. It was Emperor Caesar Augustus who had eighty-two temples rebuilt during the decline of faith in the Roman gods. He installed Emperor worship. His predecessor, Julius Caesar, had been given divine attributes by the Roman senate.

There was never a priesthood or priestly caste in Roman religion. The state had colleges of priests. They interpreted the omens of the deities. Roman religion tied together diverse peoples to the Empire and the Emperor, to the family, and to the home.

Roman culture also included the *philosophical religions* of Epicureanism, Stoicism, and Neo-Platonism, influences which had come from Greece. Lucretius wrote *De Rerum Natura* in the first century B.C., strongly attacking superstition and traditional religion. Epicureanism emphasized moderation in life in pursuit of pleasure. Stoicism offered the Romans a combination of self sufficiency and reliance upon religion. The supreme being of Stoicism was identified with the reason and order of the cosmos, and the deities were emanations from the one supreme being. Marcus Aurelius, the Roman Emperor who died in A.D. 180, was the last eminent Stoic. He taught the core of Stoicism, individual self control, and responsibility as a citizen in the order of cosmic government.

Neo-Platonism was taught by Plotinus, a successor of Platonic thought, who settled in Rome in the third century A.D. He taught the Divine Being was the eternal one. From the Divine Being flowed good, intelligence, and the world soul. The material world was far away from the One, and the individual soul in the material world needed to follow the path back to the Divine Being or the One.

Another feature of Roman religion was *Mithraism*. The cult of Mithra was brought from Persia and Mesopotamia by the Roman legionaries. Mithra had been a part of the solar deity of the ancient Iranians. He won the battle between good and evil, and sacrificed a great bull to symbolize his victory. A part of the cult of Mithraism was the ritual slaughter of a bull, in which the followers were baptized in its blood. Thus, the cult expressed symbols of the light and energy of the sun, of sacrifice of death and renewal in the blood, and of the courage, success, self control, and confidence of the soldier who followed Mithra. Mithra brought light and immortality. Mithraism was only open to males.

Only a few of the religious patterns of the Mediterranean area have been observed. These patterns indicate local deities and spirits, state, national, and empire gods and goddesses, and a liberal borrowing of traits of deities among various populations. There was official religion, and there was popular and folk religion. There was the rise of religion, and there was the fall of it.

Jainism and Sikhism

Four major religious traditions emerged in India. They were Hinduism, Buddhism, Jainism, and Sikhism. Jainism arose within the dominant Hinduism of India of the sixth century B.C. in close proximity to the time of the Buddha. Sikhism developed in the sixteenth century A.D.; at this time both Christianity and Islam had already appeared in India.

Jainism

The founder of the Jain religion was Mahavira (ca. 599-527 B.C.). Mahavira means great hero, and Jina or Jaina means victor. Tradition holds that Mahavira was born miraculously of a royal family of pure lineage. He lived in luxury and married a princess.

Mahavira renounced his family life and joined an ascetic order with ties to the teacher-saint of several centuries earlier known as Parsva. He reacted against the Hinduism of his day, rejecting some of the Vedic teachings, the animism and polytheism in Indian culture, the caste system, and the priestly religion. His was a reformist movement of Hinduism.

He traveled with an ascetic order for some twelve years. In nakedness and without possessions, he practiced non-violence and fasted. Mahavira, then, left the order and established his own, known as the Jains. He established the five vows of

- Sexual continence or chastity,

- Non-violence or ahimsa,

- Truth telling or no lies,

- Rejection of materialism, and

- Non-stealing.

He stressed vegetarianism and mathematical concepts.

His organization included monks and nuns as well as laymen and laywomen. His teachings were incorporated into the *Agamas*, known as precepts. There was no need for deities either in creation or in living. His metaphysics included two kinds of entities, soul and matter. The soul is the life-monad or jiva, and non-living matter is ajiva. The life-monads are infinite and omniscient, but they are caught up and obscured in matter. Mahavira taught that karma (actions), even good karma, bound the individual to the cycle of rebirth. Thus, he taught a complete withdrawal from the world, involving withdrawal from worldly affairs and the practice of severe austerities.

The monastic life became the way to liberation from karmic activity and continual reincarnations. Ahimsa, or non-violence, became the supreme ethical pursuit for the monks. Every form of life became sacrosanct. Monks strained water before drinking and placed gauze masks over their months to prevent the taking or inhaling of any insect. Monks swept the ground before them to avoid crushing any life-monad. Thus, they practiced extreme measures of asceticism and non-violence.

Laypersons could not follow the strict codes of the monks. Nevertheless, they were forbidden to engage in vocations which took life, such as butchers or soldiers. Many Jains pursued business and professional interests. They, too, were vegetarians and had to refrain from unchastity, intoxicants, lying, and stealing.

Jainism later developed temple complexes with images of Mahavira and other teachers of the order for veneration. In the first century A.D. the Jains split into two sects over the issue of nudity: the Sky-Clad believed in nudity as a symbol of the complete renunciation of world goods; the White-Clad also believed in renunciation but wore white robes.

Jainism has remained a minority religion in India. Its pessimistic view of life and the direction of history has not made it of great appeal to the masses, nor has it become a missionary religion. Jains have quietly made their place in the Hindu caste system and social order and have preserved their religion for over two millennia.

Sikhism

The religion of the Sikhs was founded by Nanak (A.D. 1469-1539) in India. He was born of Hindu parents near Lahore, where a Muslim nobleman governed the province. Nanak became a disciple of Kabir, the Muslim follower of Ramananda. Sikhism combines the Sufi and monotheistic expressions of Islam with the Bhakti themes of Hinduism.

Nanak emphasized the uniqueness and personality of God from the Islamic view. God was sovereign, and the attributes of love and mercy were primary. The True Name of God was personal. Sikhism rejected the avatars or divine incarnations of Hinduism. From the Hindu view, Nanak held to karma and rebirth and the cycles of samsara. Karma was the inexorable moral law of human behavior. The concept of Nirvana was absorbed into God. He preached that to worship the True Name of God would break the cycles of rebirth, and one with good karma would be with God.

Nanak had had a spiritual experience in which the True Name had been revealed to him. God to him was in the world and in his heart. His experience taught him to become neither a Hindu nor a Muslim, but only a disciple of the True Name. Sikh means disciple. The teachings of Sikhism are compiled in the *Adi Granth*, which means book in Sanskrit. It became known as the *Granth Sahib*.

After his death in A.D. 1539, nine other teachers or gurus followed him. The tenth follower, Govind Singh (A.D. 1675-1708), preached against the caste system and instituted the Khalsa. The Khalsa, meaning pure, became a tightly knit military community. The initiation rites included the drinking of nectar and pouring it over the devotee's head, as well as the baptism of the sword. Their slogan became "The Pure are of God and victory belongs to God."

Sikhs adopted the surname Singh, meaning lion, and assumed a dress code. The five *k's* distinguish the Sikh warrior.

- Kangha is the comb to hold the hair in place and denotes spirituality.

- Kara is the steel bracelet worn on the right arm to denote unity.

- Kesa is uncut hair which is the sign of a holy man.

- Kirpan is a doubled-edge sword to symbolize the warrior's protection of the weak.

- Kacch is knee-length trousers worn to express modesty and oral restraint.

After Govind Singh, it was decreed that there be no more gurus. The Sikh scriptures were placed in the holy temple at Amritsar. The Golden Temple at Amritsar is the most sacred place for Sikhs. It houses the Granth Sahib and relics of the gurus, and it serves as the administrative center of Sikhism.

Nanak sought out what he considered to be the best elements in the two religions of Hinduism and Islam to establish the Sikh religion. Later the Sikhs were to face the social, political, and religious upheavals of both Hindus and Muslims, as well as the British colonialism in India. They were to leave their earlier ways of non-violence to seek land in Punjab for their religion to be secure and to grow. As the British came to India, Sikhs served as soldiers under British command in places like Hong Kong and Shanghai.

Sikhism, thus, became another religion in the mix of Hinduism, Buddhism, and Islam in India. It called attention to the one God, known as the True One, compassionate and free from fear and hate. The True One was in the beginning, in the distant past, in the present, and will be in the future.

Zoroastrianism

Zoroastrianism was born as a religion under the influence of Zarathustra Spitama, known in Greek as Zoroaster. Scholars differ on the prophet's dates and birth. Perhaps he was born around 600 B.C. in northeastern Iran. The meaning of the name Zarathustra is "Mr. Old Camel," indicating a livelihood of animal husbandry. Spitama means white; Zoator means to pour. The meanings of white and pour may indicate his association with the priesthood and social status.

It is uncertain if King Cyrus of Persia knew of the prophet's teachings. However, it is believed that the Persian King Darius I (522-486 B.C.) knew of Zarathustra's belief in the god, Ahura Mazda, from references on the sculpture at Persepolis. Zoroastrianism became the state religion under the Achaemenid dynasty. Fire temples became the center of worship, and the Magic became the priests.

The sacred book is the Avesta. The five portions of it are the Yasna, Visparad, Yashts, Vendidad, and Khordeh Avesta. They contain various poems, hymns, and treatises. The Yasna contains the most important texts called the Gathas, which may go back to Zarathustra.

Zarathustra spoke out against the polytheism of the gods or daevas of his day. He preached that *Ahura Mazda*, the Wise Lord, was the creator and preserver of all that was good. He was the supreme god, all knowing and full of light and truth. Ahura Mazda had attributes or spiritual forces which aided in fostering good in the earth. Sometimes called the "Immortal Holy Ones," they included Vohu Manu (good thought), Spenta Armaiti (piety), and Ameretat (immortality). These forces assisted the good earth of cattle, fire, metal, good men, water, and crops.

Although Zarathustra did not attribute evil to Ahura Mazda, he preached that there was an evil spirit in the earth. Its name was Angra Mainyu or Ahriman. It is unclear of the origin of Angra Mainyu, but the evil spirit's opposition to God is the great theme of the prophet's pronouncements. Angra Mainyu had diabolic forces or demons in the earth. Bad thought counter-attacked Vohu Manu; the demon of arrogance was against piety; and the demon of destruction went against immortality. The wolf opposed cattle; rust opposed metal; bad men were against good men; drought was the opposite of water; and crop failure and sterility was the nemesis of good crops.

The *dualism* in Zoroastrian thought was the battle between good and evil, between truth and falsehood, and between righteousness and wickedness. Ahura Mazda was the Wise Lord in battle against the evil spirit Angra Mainyu. To Zarathustra there was a clear choice of belief and practice.

The *cosmology* of Zarathustra was based on spiritual warfare between the good forces of Ahura Mazda and the evil demons of Angra Mainyu. Judgment followed death. In the resurrection people would approach the Chinvat Bridge. If they had lived good lives, they crossed over to paradise. Otherwise, they fell into the punishment of hell. The cosmology included savior types to assist the people in the resurrection and judgment.

The *rituals and ceremonies* of the religion included temples, towers, priesthood, and initiation rites. The fire temple was a place of worship and of the reading of the Avesta. Zoroastrians did not worship fire; fire was a symbol of the light and purity of Ahura Mazda. Sandalwood was used for the fire, which was considered eternal. Ashes from the fire were applied to the forehead.

The Tower of Silence was an elevation over a pit for exposing the dead so they would not bring pollution to the earth. Bodies were placed so the vultures could clean them to the bones, which would then fall into the pit. Then the bones would be buried. A symbol of Zoroastrianism is the form of the winged Achaemenid representing Ahura Mazda, which was placed over the entrance of the cemeteries.

The *priests* of Zoroastrianism, known in their various statuses as Dastur, Mobed, and Ervad, were hereditary positions. They tended the fires of the temple; they recited portions of the Gathas; they presided over the various ceremonies of initiation rites, marriages, and funerals.

The height of Zoroastrian influence in Iran was in the Sassanian era from A.D. 226 until the Islamic invasion of A.D. 651. It was a state religion for everyone with an official priesthood. Unable to grow under the dominance of Islam, Zoroastrians migrated to India to form a community in and around Bombay. They were known as the Parsees. They became for the most part a solid community of business and professional people. They currently number some one hundred thousand. In Iran, Zoroastrians number only several thousand.

Although this ancient religion has few followers, it made a significant impact on other religions. Its ideas spread through the conquest of Alexander the Great and through the Roman armies throughout the Mediterranean areas. Its influences were also upon the Jews in the Diaspora. Some scholars assert that it influenced Judaism and other religions with the concepts of Satan or devil, the prince of light and the prince of darkness, last judgment, resurrection, Son of Man, and savior.

Zoroastrianism is an ancient religion with few living adherents, that has contributed much to the religious history and experience of humankind. A summary statement frequently used to describe the religion is "good thought, good word, good deed."

African Traditional Religions

Africa is a continent rich in religious traditions. Oral history among Africans has kept alive Africa's religious heritage and mosaic. More recently, its own scholars have reported the deep roots of its religious traditions. Beliefs and practices vary widely across Africa. However, there is a general frame of reference for traditional religion in which a broad typology emerges.

Christianity and Islam stand beside traditional religions across the countries. In its early years Christianity spread to North Africa and to Ethiopia. Christian scholars and churchmen including Origin, Tertullian, Cyprian, Arius, and Athanasius, were leaders of the early church in North Africa. Christianity's spread to sub-sahara Africa was diminished by the Arab-Muslim conquest of North Africa in the seventh century

A.D. Not until the fifteenth century A.D. was Christianity brought to subsahara Africa by Portugese traders. In the nineteenth and twentieth centuries in particular, missionaries from the Roman Catholic Church and Protestant churches in Europe and North America came. They brought western medical technology, education, and evangelists. Churches were built across the African landscape.

Islam was introduced to North Africa within one hundred years after the death of Muhammad, in A.D. 632. In later centuries, Muslim traders brought their religion southward to affect several African tribes and empires. The twentieth century has seen great advances into both West Africa and East Africa by Islam.

Africa, then, has several prominent religious traditions. African traditional religions have been the targets of missionary advance by Christianity and Islam. Other religions are represented in Africa, including Jews in Ethiopia and Hindus in East Africa.

The traditional religion of Africa provides glimpses into an African world view, general customs, family life, death, and an after life. While there is no "African traditional religion" as such, there are general concepts and practices which may serve as a typology. The following will be considered: the High God or Supreme God; lesser spirits or divinities; humans and ancestors; rituals and rites of passage; divination, medicine, and leadership.

The Supreme God

The High God is supreme, above all spirits and humans. God created the world and then withdrew from it, either because humans offended God or because God tired of the mundane affairs of the world. In any event God has little contact or participation with the world. Humans depend on lesser divinities, spirits, or ancestors.

As an example, the traditional religion of the *Yoruba* of West Africa has a Supreme God, Olodumare. Its meaning focuses on greatness, on incomparable majesty, and on excellence in attributes. Another name for the Yoruba Supreme God is Olorun. It means the owner or Lord of Heaven. Both names, Olodumare and Olorun, refer to the Supreme God and to no other divinities or lesser spirits.

Olodumare has many attributes. These are described in conversations, prayers, music, and art. He is called creator, the origin and owner of life. He is king, with absolute authority and power. He is perfect in wisdom, knowledge, and understanding. Other lesser ones are fallible, but Olodumare is infallible. He is judge and controls the destiny of all. He is changeless and immortal in the midst of a world of change and death. Olodumare is also the invisible and unsearchable king.

Another High God concept is that of the *Zulus* of the Republic of South Africa. They have their God of the Sky (Inkosi Yezulu). He is associated with creation and with origins. The God of the Sky appears to be a twin to the Earth, albeit the first of twins. His major attribute is power. He is in control of the weather, wind, and rain. Since the Zulus raise cattle, they need rain for their grazing lands, and the God of the Sky affects storms, lightning, thunder, and rain. However, the Zulus work through the special assistants of the God of the Sky for their requests. It appears that in everyday life the God of the Sky is mostly removed and his assistants are called upon by the intermediaries.

Divinities and Lesser Spirits

The Supreme God tops the hierarchy in traditional religion. Beneath are the divinities and lesser spirits. The universe is peopled with spirits, like spiritual life forces. The earth, sea, and sky, as well as mountains, forests, trees, animals, sun, moon, storm, and thunder, are associated with these forces.

These forces can be beneficial or harmful. They are subject to flattery and appeasement. They assist in everyday matters, including fertility for crops and for human conception and birth, and in rites of passage. Since the Supreme God is distant to everyday life, people turn to divinities and lesser spirits for assistance in personal and community matters. Often, these divinities are given a cult status in terms of worship or veneration, with a sacred place and ritual leader.

The Yoruba have divinities and spirits. Divinities are called Orisa. The Orisa carry out the will of the Supreme God, Olodumare. They act as ministers or intermediaries of Olodumare. Each divinity functions in a particular area of the world of experience. Each divinity is assigned a symbol expressive of its function in Yoruba society. Since abstract religion is not very meaningful to the Yoruba, the divinities are seen as functional and immediate presences of a more distant Supreme God. For example, Orisa-nla is Olodumare's representative on earth for creative functions. Orunmila is representative for matters of wisdom and knowledge. Whatever the number of divinities, their authority and power are completely dependent upon Olodumare.

In the Yoruba hierarchy, the lesser spirits are immaterial entities who may take human shape or other expressions. They can reside in trees, rivers, mountains and other phenomena. A guardian spirit is a person's double, whose well-being affects a person's destiny. It may also affect one adversely. Ghost spirits are wandering spirits whose dead bodies were not properly buried or not buried at all. They are similar to outcasts who may bring one mischief. Witches also have spirits that may leave their bodies, especially at night, and bring harm to others. The Yoruba often employ ritual leaders to offer sacrifices to appease the spirits.

The Zulu God of the Sky has assistants who relate to the people. These spirits are strongly believed by the Zulus to aid them, since the God of the Sky is distanced from their ordinary lives. The spirits are called upon during the significant rites of passage like birth, puberty, marriage, and death. These are critical times in the lives of humans, and they seek help from spirits to ward off harm and disaster.

Humans and Ancestors

African traditional religion demonstrates a unity or correlation of the living world with the world of the dead and of the material world with the spiritual world through its relationship with ancestors. Ancestors belong to a wider population of spirits with a link between the past, present, and future. It is said that ancestors are the most commonly recognized spiritual forces in African religion.

Departed ancestors relate to the living for help and for harm. They may bring prosperity to individuals, families, and tribes in times of planting, war, and child birth. They may also cause sickness, death, and drought. Ancestors elicit attitudes of both awe and dread.

The Yoruba view ancestors as a part of their community. Death is an extension of life, and the dead become a part of their ancestors in the spirit world. It is important in order to become an ancestor to have left offspring in the world. Ancestors, then, are a connecting point of communion and communication between the living and the dead.

Zulus believe that ancestors are deceased family members who are present to the family in good times as well as bad. Ancestors are present at particular places in and near the home and village and assist the living. A headman serves as an intermediary between family and village and ancestors. In the Zulu patrilineal society, the male ancestor is given special status.

Rituals and Rites of Passage

Traditional religion has many rituals and ceremonies which function to appease the spirits and ancestors and to assist in all critical junctures of life to ensure good results. These rituals include sacrifices of animals with use of their meat or blood, libations of food and drink, the use of special artifacts, incantations, and possessions or trances. Many of the rituals employ a specialist who has knowledge and experience to perform the ritual and accomplish a successful end.

Peoples whose livelihood depends on hunting and farming have rituals and specialists to call on spirits and ancestors for abundance of animals and herds and for rain and fertility of crops. Four significant rites of passage are birth, puberty, marriage, and death. Children are a great blessing, while childlessness is a great curse. Thus, there are rituals associated around conception, fertility, and naming of the new born.

In puberty young men and women learn about their adult and sexual roles. There is circumcision for males and clitorectomy for females. Rituals of marriage revolve around fertility, family, and social alliances. In rituals of death the dead are made comfortable so as to join the ancestral spirit world and bring good things to the living. Traditional religion has rituals and specialists surrounding events associated with health, sickness, disaster and tragedy, both human and natural, and death.

Divination, Medicine, Leadership

In *Yoruba* religion there is a close association between religion and health care and medicine. The traditional doctor or "medicine man," called a Babalawo, is a priest of Ifa, a method of divination or oracle divinity. The Babalawo has a dual function as doctor and priest. Since it is believed that religion and medicine are results of the Supreme God Olodumare, through his divinities, then the Babalawo not only shares the knowledge or secrets of Olodumare with the people, but he also prepares medicinal herbs and other medications and administers them to the people for healing.

Traditional doctors are believed to be taught medicine by the divinities and ancestors. They learn their craft through dreams, trances, and living close to nature. Rituals are performed by the doctors to consecrate the medicine and to enable it to be effective in its cure, as well as to prepare the sick or distressed to receive it. Some medicines are prescribed to be taken under certain conditions in special places using specific incantations. Often, it is unknown by the recipient whether healing occurs from the effects of the medicine or the ceremony.

Zulu traditional religion has several specialists to assist the people in rituals and ceremonies. An important specialist is the headman-priest, who represents the family or the village to their ancestors. The headman seeks the blessings of the ancestors for the family, as well as attempts to ward off the ancestor's ill feelings.

There are other specialists or intermediaries, sometimes called power brokers. Zulus desire to maintain harmony in both family and village life. When events happen or are anticipated which will bring imbalance or disharmony, even misfortune, sickness, or death, people turn to the rituals of the power brokers.

Diviners serve as specialists among the Zulus. Often diviners are women who have received the "vocation" through dreams or visions or approval of ancestors. They serve like counselors, providing information to victims or potential victims about the causes of illness, harm, and death. The Zulu world is filled with harmful entities, and diviners have powers to frustrate and prevent harm.

Sorcerers also are power brokers. They have learned their trade of black magic from other sorcerers. Through black magic they get rid of the malevolent entity. Witches, too, have status among the Zulus. They are said to have the ability to fly and to become invisible. Witches, through their craft, may use evil against good, and therefore become a part of the harm to others. They operate in a domain different from that of the God of the Sky and of ancestors.

Traditional religion across Africa includes a variety of rituals and specialists to assist in rituals. Generally, there is no priesthood or temple worship, but in some parts of Africa there are temples and altars dedicated to certain spirits. Associated with these are "priest" types who are sanctioned to perform ceremonies. Basically, the African world view sees disease and death as a result of the spirit world, not from natural causes. Often, medicine men or traditional doctors combine the traditional practices associated with magic, incantations, and herbs with western forms of medical practice.

The role of a chief-king may be one of special status. He may be the central figure to relate the people to the spirit world and to ancestors. He may be an object of taboo. With the coming of Christianity and Islam to Africa, a prophet type has arisen who speaks the words of God. Cargo cults are associated with the charismatic prophet.

Traditional religion in Africa is expressed in numerous diversities. Despite the varieties of expressions, there are several general concepts and practices which appear to be similar. A concept of a high god or being is present. This being is usually given reverence or deference, but there is no vital connection of this god to the daily and mundane lives of the people. There is a world of spirits or entities below this god who function in various capacities which affect the daily lives of people. There are specialists among the people who are "called" or set aside to act as intermediaries or power brokers between the spirit world and the people. Through various rituals and ceremonies there are attempts to affect change for the good, and sometimes for the bad.

A major concern within African traditional religion is the preservation of harmony and balance within the individual, family, village, tribe, and nation. Since family is central, ancestors are looked after and their counsel and protection is sought. Places and objects take on a sacred or special significance for interaction with the spirit and ancestor worlds. These places and objects are used by specialists to affect a harmonious balance for the people.

Baha'i

The Baha'i religion arose in nineteenth century Iran in the midst of Iranian Shi'ite Islam. A doctrine in Shi'ite Islam anticipated the return and appearance of the twelfth imam to bring justice and righteousness to the world. In the milieu of this teaching and expectation there came a prophet named Baha'ullah. Consequently, the Baha'i religion was established with its own sacred scriptures, its own laws, its own administrative institutions, and its own holy places. It has become a global religion.

Leaders

There are *four major figures* in the religion with which its history and development are associated. They are the Bab, Baha'ullah, Abdul Baha, and Shoghi Effendi. The Bab's name was Mirza Ali Muhammad, and he was born in Shiraz, Iran. In 1844 he prophesied that a greater prophet was to follow who would bring a new age of peace for all peoples. Because of his preaching he was persecuted by Muslim officials. He was imprisoned, and in 1850 in Tabriz he was executed by the government. His followers were known as the Babis, and many lost their lives for their faith.

The Baha'i religion was founded by Mirza Husayn Ali (1817-1892) who came to be known as Baha'ullah which means "Glory of God." He was born in Tehran. The word *Baha'i* comes from Baha which means glory or splendor. Baha'ullah had been an early disciple of the Bab. He was imprisoned in 1852 in Tehran when followers of the Bab attempted to assassinate the Shah of Iran. Although he knew nothing of the attempt, he was implicated in it. While in prison, he became aware of his mission as a prophet.

He was exiled to Baghdad, where he announced his prophetic mission. From there he was transferred by the Ottoman authorities to Constantinople and to Andrianople. He wrote letters of his mission to rulers in Turkey, Iran, Russia, Prussia, Austria, and Great Britain. His last exile was to Akka (Acre) in Palestine, where he died in 1892.

Baha'ullah appointed his oldest son, Abdul Baha (1844-1921), to be the leader of the Baha'i community and to be the interpreter of his teachings. Abdul Baha means "Servant of the Glory." Abdul Baha both administered the religion from Palestine as well as spread the faith. He traveled in Africa, Europe, and America. Baha'i communities were established in North Africa, the Far East, Australia, and the United States. In 1912 he spent eight months in the United States speaking in churches, synagogues, and universities.

Abdul Baha appointed his oldest grandson, Shoghi Effendi (1896-1957), to succeed him. He was "Guardian of the Cause," the authorized interpreter of the teachings of Baha'ullah. Shoghi Effendi developed the administrative order of the religion and laid the groundwork for the Universal House of Justice. After his death the leadership of the Baha'i religion was assumed by the supreme administrative body, which became the Universal House of Justice in 1963 and was located on Mount Carmel in Haifa, Israel.

Scriptures

The sacred *scriptures* include the writings of Baha'ullah, the Bab, and Abdul Baha. There are also important commentaries and explanations written by Shoghi Effendi. Baha'ullah wrote more than one hundred volumes or tablets including Kitab-i-Aqdas (The Most Holy Book), containing many of the laws and statements of the religion; Kitab-i-Iqan (Book of Certitude), which explains the unity of religion; and The Hidden Words, which presents all the revealed truth about all religions.

The Bab's writings consist mainly of the telling of the coming of Baha-ullah. The writings of Abdul Baha include the Will and Testament in which he appoints Shoghi Effendi as the guardian of the faith, and many letters. Shoghi Effendi wrote The World Order of Baha'ullah and numerous letters to Baha'is throughout the world.

Teachings

The religion emphasizes the oneness of God, the oneness of religion, and the oneness of humankind. Although God, in essence, is unknowable, God has revealed his Word in each period of history through chosen *messengers*, sometimes called prophets, and titled by the Baha'is "Manifestation of God." They include Abraham, Moses, Buddha, Zoroaster, Christ, Muhammad, the Bab, and Baha'ullah. God is one although humankind has called God by various names.

Unity is a common concept in the religion, especially in its teachings on God, religion, and humankind. Each age should search for truth, unhindered by superstition and tradition. Worship to God is important, and work performed in the spirit of service is worship to God. All forms of prejudice, whether religious, racial, class, or national are condemned.

The *equality of men and women* is foundational to their belief and practice. They work toward the adoption of a universal auxiliary language, of compulsory education, of a world tribunal to bring justice and peace between nations, and of the abolition of the extremes of poverty and wealth. Thus the unity of humankind, world peace, and world order are special goals of the Baha'i community. The development of spiritual qualities such as honesty, compassion, and justice all occur within the worship of God.

Great emphasis is placed upon *good character and deeds*. Monogamous marriages and devoted family life are expected. Divorce is strongly condemned and is sought only as a last remedy after a year of examination. Baha'ullah forbade the consumption of intoxicating drinks and narcotics. Baha'is respect and obey the laws of the land of the citizenry, while they promote a universal patriotism to the planet. Baha'ullah said that the earth is one country and humankind is its citizens. The Baha'i International Community is accredited with several programs of the United Nations, including the United Nations Children's Fund (UNICEF) and the United Nations Economic and Social Council (ECOSOC). It has representatives with the United Nations in New York, Geneva, and Nairobi.

The spiritual life and the *administrative orders* of the Baha'is are committed to unity and order. Baha'is are organized into the Local Spiritual Assembly, the National Spiritual Assembly, and the Universal House of Justice. The Local Spiritual Assembly is composed of a nine member administrative body elected annually in every town, city, or district where nine or more adult Baha'is live. There are over 25,000 local assemblies worldwide.

The National Spiritual Assembly is a nine member body elected annually by delegates to the National Baha'i Convention. They are elected by delegates from local assemblies. There are over 130 national assemblies. The Universal House of Justice is a nine member body elected once every five years by the delegates of the national assemblies. It has legislative powers on matters not expressly revealed in the Baha'i scriptures. It is located on Mount Carmel in Haifa, Israel. The headquarters of the National Assembly of the United States is located in Wilmette, Illinois.

Prayer, scripture readings, meditations, and lectures are prominent functions in the assemblies. The scriptures of the major religions are used in the worship services, as well as a capella music. The Baha'i calendar is based on the solar year, and it consists of nineteen months with nineteen days in each month. On the first day of each month Baha'is meet for the nineteen-day feast. Its purpose is worship, fellowship, and community consultation.

Major houses of worship are located in Wilmette, Illinois, U.S.A.; Frankfurt, West Germany; Kampala, Uganda; Sydney, Australia; and Panama City, Panama. The only architectural requirement is that all houses of worship be nine-sided and surrounded by a dome. Baha'is also observe a fast from March 2-20 each year in which no food or drink is consumed during daylight hours. There are no clergy in the community.

On Mount Carmel are located not only the Universal House of Justice, but also the golden-domed Shrine of the Bab, the tomb of the Bab, and the burial place of Abdul Baha. Baha'ullah is buried near Haifa at Bahji, where there is a shrine surrounded by beautiful gardens.

In the United States Baha'ullah was mentioned for the first time in 1893 at the World Parliament of Religions in Chicago. The first Baha'i group was formed in Chicago in 1894. Abdul Baha visited the United States in 1912 and laid the cornerstone for the Baha'i House of Worship in Wilmette, Illinois, which was begun in 1920. It was dedicated in 1953. The first National Spiritual Assembly was organized in America in 1925.

The Baha'i Publishing Trust publishes and handles the sale of authorized literature, pamphlets, study courses, and audiovisuals. Publications include the *Baha'i News*, *National Baha'i Review*, and *World Order*. Baha'is also operate a home for the aging, service for the blind, summer schools, and an office for human rights.

Baha'is assert that they are the custodians of the most recent revelation of God. That revelation completes the essential knowledge, religious values, and institutional arrangements needed to bring spiritual and social unities to the world population. Their appeal reaches to all segments of society, especially to women and minorities. Their teachings appear to be translated easily across cultures. People who gravitate to the Baha'i religion have a keen interest in education, global issues, and an appreciation for various religious philosophies and teachings exemplified in the major world religions. Literature is abundant and willingly shared. Although membership figures are general, it is estimated that there are over five million worldwide, with over one hundred thousand in the United States.

In its native Iran, the Baha'i religion has always been affected by the dominant religion Islam. Its history has been filled with instability and persecution in the ebb and flow of religion and politics between the shahs in Iran and the ayatollahs. Since the Iranian Revolution of 1979 under Ayatollah Khomeini, the Baha'is have suffered much persecution and disadvantage.

Membership is open to all who accept the tenets of the Baha'i faith, recognize its prophets and leaders, and accept the writings and administrative orders. Since there is no clergy, the responsibility for teaching and spreading the religion rests with the individual. Volunteers known as pioneers may take up residence in areas where there are no Baha'is, assume jobs, and spread their faith.

9

RELIGIONS IN ACTION:
A CASE STUDY OF
THE MIDDLE EAST AND IRAN

■   ■

From 1968 through 1978 I lived and traveled in Iran and throughout the Middle East. During those years Teheran experienced the building of more movie houses than Muslim mosques, and it became the battleground between the modernization programs of the Shah and the traditional religious forces of the Ayatollahs. Beirut changed from the beautiful port city on the Mediterranean Sea where east met west, especially at the American University, to the battleground of dissident religious and political forces which decimated its population and its city life.

Cairo saw Russians one day and Americans the next vying for international favor. Cairo also saw soldiers march off to war as Arab Muslims to fight Israeli Jews during one season, and at another season Cairo's president, a devoted Muslim, flew off to Jerusalem to talk peace and reparation of lands, to the chagrin of his Arab Muslim neighbors.

Amman experienced the shock waves of warring with Palestinian Muslims, itself being a Muslim city, and celebrated the wedding of its king with an American wife. Damascus sent Muslim armies into Lebanon to keep the peace among the Muslim and Christian populations, as well as to fend off any intrusions into Lebanon by Jewish neighbors.

Jerusalem witnessed the skirmishes of war with Arab nations and Palestinian dissidents within sight of Judaism's temple wall of King Solomon, of Islam's proud Dome of the Rock, and of Christianity's places of the crucifixion and resurrection of Jesus Christ.

In the shadows of some of these same cities there were other occurrences. In Teheran an Ayatollah and his board of directors of the Mosque visited in the living room of a Christian to discuss mutual concerns of Christianity and Islam. In Lebanon, the Beirut Baptist School, an elementary and high school of several hundreds of Christian and Muslim students about equally divided religiously, continued to meet daily amidst the conflicts between the Muslim and Christian populations. Outside Jerusalem a Christian visited the home of a Muslim family in bereavement over the death of its young son. The son was the playmate of the Christian's son and had been run over by a vehicle. The Christian prayed with the Muslim family on that day.

The Middle East is a complex mosaic of peoples, religions, politics, and conflicts. The people deeply desire stability. They shout out from many kinds of disenchantment. Territorial boundaries are problematic for them, as well as foreign intrusions. Yet they have been a tenacious religious people since the recording of history. The themes of theocracy, religious pluralism, religious freedom, and the tensions between religion and politics have appeared to be constants in the fabric of Middle Eastern life. They have been the seeds of power struggles, wars, international intervention, and even friendships between the peoples, but the people of the Middle East are not alone in their struggles with these themes.

Theocracy, religious pluralism and freedom, and the tensions between church and state have been ingredients in the history of the United States, and they continue to be alive today. The American heritage is just two hundred years old, as compared to the millennia of the Middle East. The founding fathers and mothers of America had dreams of establishing a church-community ruled over by God through its elected leaders. Religion and politics merged into a unity in which there was to be no distinction between church and state, between church membership and commonwealth membership. Those who criticized this arrangement and who raised the questions of its meaning for religious liberty and freedom of conscience were exiled or had to flee for their lives. The Massachusetts Bay Colony and Roger Williams are examples of these tensions and patterns in seventeenth-century America.

By 1791 the first amendment to the constitution guaranteed that Congress would make no law regarding the establishment of religion or prohibit the free exercise of it. A multiplicity of reasons existed for the separation of church and state, including the dominant values of liberalism, pluralism, freedom of choice, individual responsibility, and voluntarism which had emerged in society. However, the lines of relationship between church and state have been obscure and problematic at times. The state often decides what religion is. It has stated that Scientology is not a religion while Scientology itself claims to be a religion. On the other hand, the state has declared that Transcendental Meditation is a religion while the TM movement claims to be a science. The Nation of Islam (Black Muslims) at times has been considered by the state to be more political than religious. Muhammad Ali, the heavyweight boxing champion, was denied the status of conscientious objector in 1968, but this ruling was overturned in 1971. Matters of taxation, armed service chaplains, and prayer in public schools are among the problem areas within the relationship of church and state.

It is evident that the state has seen religion in general as a valuable ally in sustaining the dominant values of American society and in maintaining the social order. On the other hand, the church has used its traditional ties to the state to gain favorable status for itself in protecting its own interests. Religion and politics in the American tradition have seen both peaceful and stormy relationships. Battles have been fought and continue to be fought over the belief and practice of religious liberty and freedom. The continuing relationship between church and state and the interfacing of religion and politics occur in a society shaped by the patterns of belief and practice based upon the Hebraic-Christian tradition. Even the American civil religion, as interpreted by Robert Bellah, cushions itself on the bedrock of Hebraic-Christian symbols and values as it adds another dimension to religion and politics in America.

American society, like the Middle East, has dealt with themes from theocracy to religious freedom in varying patterns and intensities. Protestantism, Roman Catholicism, and Judaism, as well as other religious communities in other nations also face the challenges of these issues. However, the Middle East, with its "crazy quilt of religions and politics" serves as a prime example of religions in action in the complexities of life in the latter part of the twentieth century.

The Middle East

From Morocco to Pakistan the mosaic of the Middle East is like a finely woven Persian tapestry, colorful, tightly knotted, intricate in detail and design, and reminiscent of a long and proud historical consciousness. Great civilizations have risen and fallen and remain in the area. The pyramids and sphinx are reminders of the great Egyptian dynasties, when pharaohs ruled as divine kings. The scars and coatings of Alexander the Great's march remain through Egypt to India. The struggles between the Byzantine Christians, with their empire spilling over from Constantinople, and the Persian Zoroastrians are still remembered. Judaism, Christianity, and Islam all developed in close proximity to one another with their intricate involvement in and around the city of Jerusalem. The rise of Islam from the desert-oasis of Arabia and its rapid spread in one hundred years to dominate Mesopotamia, Palestine, North Africa, Spain, Persia, and India, and even its faraway arrival to China, remains a phenomenal and intriguing explosion and advancement on the world scene.

There are several movements sweeping across the contemporary Middle East which are greatly affecting the religions of the area. These movements are secularization, geopolitics, and the resurgence of ethnic, national, and religious identities. The outstanding example of secularization occurred in Turkey after World War I.

Secularization

Turkey had served as the base of the Ottoman Empire that ruled over the Middle East for four hundred years, with the pattern of an Islamic theocratic caliphate. In 1925 Kemal Ataturk came to power in Turkey, completed the dismantling of the empire, and headed the country in the direction of a secular state. Ataturk closed the mosques, muzzled the preaching of the Muslim clerics, and instigated western concepts and practices of education, law, and courts, which supplanted the Islamic institutions. The wearing of the veil by women and the fez by men was prohibited, and western dress styles were encouraged. The script of the Turkish language was reinstituted to take the place of Arabic, which was the language of Islam.

Thus, an Islamic theocracy was turned into an emerging modern secular state. Religion was suppressed, and anti-clericalism and anti-religious establishment became the ideal and practice of the new politics. The last decade has seen a revival of Islam in Turkey, but the secular state continues to be firmly in control of the social and religious life of the nation.

Another obvious example of secularization in the Middle East occurred under the reign of Reza Shah the Great of *Iran* at the time of Ataturk's experiment in Turkey. Reza Shah went for the jugular of Islam. He antagonized Islamic Ayatollahs, confiscated Islamic endowments of lands and monies, and supplanted Islamic education and law by bringing elementary and high school education and law courts under the supervision of the government, and thus, secular influences. He forbade women to wear the traditional veil. He established the University of Teheran which included a Faculty of Islamic Theology. In this Faculty the Shah hoped to foster a more enlightened understanding of Islam.

The secularization process in Iran also included sending students abroad for western technological and scientific training, establishing armed forces based on western models, and importing western consultants to advise and assist in helping Iran to modernize industry, agriculture, education, and other areas of social life. Turkey and Iran stand out as arenas in the Middle East where political leaders encouraged secularization as a process to storm the bastions of Islamic religion. Turkey continues to be a secular state. Iran under Mohammad Reza Shah Pahlavi reached a point in the secularization process where Islamic forces exploded under the leadership of the Ayatollah Khomeini. This process will be described later.

Geopolitics

Western nations have used the Middle East as a buffer zone to prevent the spread of communistic influences into the Persian Gulf and the Mediterranean basin, to establish the security of religious sectarianism within the boundaries of countries, and to protect the flow of oil resources vital to the industries and economies of the world.

After World War I, under French auspices, *Lebanon* was structured to be distinct from Syria, to protect the Christian population within a Muslim majority area, and to give the French leverage in the area. The constitution of Lebanon declares that the president shall be a Christian and that the prime minister shall be a Muslim. In this way religious pluralism is acknowledged in the legal structures of the nation. In recent times Lebanon's population has shifted to a majority of Muslims, and Muslims have their eyes on a constitutional change which will favor them with higher representation in government. Also, the periodic wars and running battles in Lebanon between Christians and Muslims, as well as between Muslims, reflect a complex mix of religion, political rivalry, lands controlled by religious communities and international intrigue.

The state of *Israel* was nurtured into existence with the assistance of western powers. Its intention was the founding of a homeland for the Jewish people. It occurred in the background of the ghettoizing of Jews and anti-Semitism, especially with the Nazi attempt at the extermination of the Jewish people. This challenge to the very life of Jews as a people occurred in the heartland of Christendom, albeit a Christendom with secularization at its heels. The state of Israel developed in the midst of Christian and Muslim Arabs in Palestine. This development initiated violent tensions within the religious communities of the area.

Palestinian Arab Muslims and Arab Christians fought against Israeli Jews. Arab Muslims of Egypt, Syria, Jordan, Lebanon, and Iraq also fought against the state of Israel. The Arab-Israeli wars of 1948, 1956, 1967, and 1973 saw not only the geo-politics of area nations but also the geopolitics of the United States, European nations, and the former Soviet Union. The city of Jerusalem became the symbol of religious rights and privileges, especially between Jews and Muslims. Jerusalem became the capital of the state of Israel, and the nations debated that it should be an international city, controlled by an agency that would guarantee the sacred sanctuaries of the major religious communities.

From time to time the orthodox rabbis in the state of Israel, as well as religious political parties, have pressured the Israeli leadership toward tendencies of a theocracy based on the Torah. The Israeli parliament, the Knesset, enacted laws restricting the activities of religious minorities which raised serious questions about the state's intentions toward religious liberties and the continuation of favor upon religious pluralism. This parliament's action prompted much protest from religious communities within the state of Israel. Also, the president of the Southern Baptist Convention, which has deep relationships with religious institutions and peoples in Israel, visited Israel specifically to discuss with Israeli leaders the parliamentary actions. Thus, the nation of Israel represents a complexity of religious communities, an involvement of international powers, and the politics of rights and privileges based on sacred sanctuaries and lands.

Resurgent Identities

The resurgence of ethnic, national, and religious identities also affects religions. The status of the Kurdish tribal peoples within and along the borders of Iran, Iraq, and Turkey demonstrates the interrelationships between geopolitics and national and religious identities. The *Kurds* are Sunni Muslims, numbering over fourteen million. For years they have fought against the government of Iraq, a nation which is also Sunni Muslim. At one time Iran, a Shi'ite Muslim nation, supplied the Kurds with arms with American aid to fight for their freedom against Iraq. At another time Iran abruptly abandoned the Kurds in their struggle against the Iraq regime.

In the Khomeini revolution in Iran, the Kurds fought against Iran for territorial rights and their freedom to live independently within Iran as an ethnic-religious community. Iraq itself has a majority population of Shi'ite Muslims who are restive against the policies of discrimination by the Sunni leadership in the government. Iraq's relations with Iran have varied from hostile to peaceful. Iran under Ayatollah Khomeini fought Iraq under President Saddam Hussein. In the Persian Gulf War when Iraq invaded Kuwait, Muslim Arab nations under the United Nations mandate fought Iraq. Both the Kurds and the Shi'ites in Iraq continue to struggle with the government of President Hussein.

Iran serves as an outstanding example of a nation of religions which have served in minority positions. Although Iran is a Shi'ite Muslim plurality, the Shi'ite Muslims throughout their history have been a minority movement within greater Islam. The Sunni have been the overwhelming majority of Muslims, not only in the Middle East but worldwide. Zoroastrianism, Judaism, Christianity, and the Baha'i religion have also had minority standing in Iran under the predominance of Shi'ite Islam. These religions have learned to co-exist, although the Baha'i religion has undergone, more than others, difficult times of restraint and persecution.

As the modern state concept has emerged in the Middle East, governments have often sought to explore and to express their national roots and cultural heritage. *Egypt* has sought to express its Egyptian roots to the ages before the Arab and Islamic conquests. Iran under the late shahs attempted to revitalize Persian cultural contributions during the Zoroastrian dynasties before the Islamic conquest. In Egypt the Coptic Christians trace their descendants to the native Egyptians. The Coptic Christians represent some ten percent of the population, which is predominantly Sunni Muslim. These nationalistic explorations and praise of cultural meanings which extend beyond the time of the beginning of Arab culture and Islam often have ambivalent meanings for the minority religious communities, like Zoroastrians, Christians, and Jews. Political leaders voice policies of religious freedom for the minorities, and sometimes leaders manipulate the minorities against the majority religious community. Mohammad Reza Shah Pahlavi used to praise the Zoroastrians of Iran as hard working, honest, trustworthy people. This statement may have been true, nevertheless, it was a throw off on his enemies within the Shi'ite Muslim Community.

Saudi Arabia has long claimed to be the guardian of the Islamic shrines in the cities of Mecca, where the ka'ba is located, and in Medina, where the prophet Muhammad is buried. Millions of devoted Muslims from all parts of the world make pilgrimages to these shrines each year. Saudi Arabia also presides over one of the greatest oil deposits and reaps billions of petro dollars each year, which helps it to influence geopolitical decisions in the area, as well as among the powerful nations.

This nation in its recent history has executed a royal couple by beheading, which claimed the attention of the world's press, and it executed tens of Muslim dissidents who stormed the sacred precincts of Mecca and held it until Saudi troops retook it. In the recent Persian Gulf War, Saudi Arabia took a harsh stand against its neighbor Iraq and allowed the United Nations forces to use its soil as a staging area for the assault against Iraq. The nation now rushes rapidly into modernization in the midst of a very traditional society, socially as well as religiously.

There are several unknowns. How will orthodox Islam, basically of the Wahabbi sect, relate to the modernizing influences of tens of thousands of internationals building the new society on her soil? How will secularization affect its leadership? What role will it continue to play among Arab Muslim nations? Will there be accommodation and synthesis between the old and the new, or will there be conflict?

Iran

Iran's rich religious history covers millennia of civilizations. King Cyrus of Persian Empire fame, in the time of the Magi religion, freed the Jews from the Babylonian captivity in the sixth century B.C. He brought the Jews to Persia, where they established a stable religious community. Later, Persian kings like Darius encouraged the Jews to return to Palestine to rebuild the temple in Jerusalem. Esther, of Jewish lineage, married a Persian king. The Jewish community has lived with relative religious freedom and social and economic stability in Iran for some two thousand five hundred years.

Religious Composition

Zoroastrianism was the dominant religion in Iran from the time of King Cyrus to the Islamic invasion. Its zenith was during the reign of the Sassanian kings from A.D. 220 to 651. Nestorian Christians entered Iran during the fourth century. Since that time Christian communities of Assyrians, Armenians, Eastern Orthodox, Roman Catholic, and Protestants have founded their churches. Jews, Zoroastrians, and Christians have been considered by Muslims as people of the book, that is, of the same divine revelation of God. When Islam has been the predominant religion of a nation, Jews, Christians, and Zoroastrians, usually have been given official recognition and religious freedom. In fact, under the reign of the late Shah of Iran, these religious minorities were allowed to elect from their own religious communities representatives to the Iranian parliament.

In the seventh century A.D. Arab *Muslims* from the Arabian peninsula penetrated Iran and established Islam as the major religion. By the sixteenth century the form of Islam known as Shi'ite had become dominant in Iran, as distinct from the Sunni branch. Under the Iranian monarch, Shah Abbas, Armenian Christians from Turkey were brought to Iran to become the great artisans of the city of Isfahan, which rivaled the grandeur of London in the sixteenth century. Zoroastrians migrated to India to settle around the city of Bombay during the early beginnings of Islam in Iran. Some remained in Iran to maintain their fire temples and communities. However, in recent times they have decreased in numbers to less than fifty thousand.

The *Baha'i* religion arose in Iran in the mid-nineteenth century. Its prophet, Baha'ullah, grew up in the tradition of Shi'ite Islam and spoke of himself in the line of the Shi'ite imams. The Baha'i religion was officially considered a heresy and a political threat to the Iranian authorities. Its leadership was exiled, and its communities were threatened. The Baha'i religion never enjoyed the religious freedom and security which the people of the book were officially granted. Under Mohammad Reza Shah Pahlavi, the Baha'i communities were given some favors and protection as all religious minorities were. However, during the Iranian revolution the Baha'i people were at the vanguard of persecution.

Although Iran is about ninety-eight percent Muslim, some eight to ten percent are of the Sunni branch. The *Sunni Muslims* include the Kurdish peoples in the northwest and southwest. Mention has been made of their instability over national identity and their aspirations for a land and nationhood of their own. The tribal peoples of Baluchestan in southeastern Iran are Sunni Muslim who also have had their dreams of territory. Another large group of Sunni Muslims is found in southern Iran at the Persian Gulf and the Iraqi border, a region known as Khuzistan. All of these Sunni Muslims have lived under the rule of the Persian nation. However, from time to time they have been influenced both internally as well as internationally to agitate against Iranian authorities.

Iran, then, offers a rich mosaic of the history of the major religions of the Middle East in interaction and co-existence with one another. With this brief historical overview attention will be given to contemporary Iran, especially from World War II to the Iranian Revolution, with special emphasis on the monarchy of Mohammad Reza Shah Pahlavi and the challenges of traditional Shi'ite Islam, religious minorities and religious freedom, and the process of modernization.

The Iran of the Shahs

The constitution of Iran implemented in 1907 defined Jafarite Ithna 'Ashari Shi'ism, as the state religion which the ruling Shah should profess and propagate and which the majority of the people would practice. It stipulated that parliament could not contradict the holy Islamic prescriptions or laws made by the prophet Muhammad. It required that the Shah take an oath upon the Qur'an to propagate the Shi'ite faith. The constitution also required that a committee of the most learned ayatollahs, selected by the parliament and given full and equal rights as parliament members, should oversee all laws passed by that body to make sure they were in accord with Islamic law and teachings. The religious freedom of minorities was also guaranteed. Thus, the state was set for the classic struggle between the traditional ayatollahs and the secularizing shahs, or more specifically between Mohammad Reza Shah Pahlavi and Ayatollah Khomeini.

Since 1925 there had been a clash between the *Pahlavi dynasty* established by Reza Shah and continued by his son, Mohammad Reza Shah Pahlavi, and the ayatollahs. Reza Shah (1925-1941), a colonel in the militia without royal lineage, crowned himself shah in the long tradition of Persian kings like Cyrus, Darius, Artaxerxes, and Shah Abbas. As already indicated, he launched a vast program of reform which influenced an attack upon a rearrangement of the powers and structures of Islam, including the weakening of the roles of the ayatollahs.

Reza Shah placed the enormous wealth in monies and lands of the Islamic religious endowments under government control. He subsumed Islamic education under the auspices·of a secularizing government bureaucracy, thus withdrawing students from the tutelage of the vast network of schools presided over by the ayatollahs. Law, courts, dress, and forms of government were westernized. Industrialization was begun, and a modern, equipped army was instituted to back the implementation of his modernization policies. The power of the ayatollahs was curtailed, and deep resentment grew within the traditional religious communities against the shah.

Mohammad Reza Shah Pahlavi, who ruled from 1941-1979, inherited the Peacock throne from his father in 1941. In the first decade of his rule the young shah faced the crises and intrigues of communism, nationalism under Prime Minister Mossadeq, the influence of international powers, and the religious dissatisfaction of the ayatollahs. The shah made accommodations with the ayatollahs and overcame the difficulties of internal politics through shrewd dealings with other nations, including the United States. By the early 1960s the shah had a stable control in governing the diverse population. He developed proficient armed forces and a powerful secret police (Savak) that reinforced his power throughout the country, including the territories populated by the minorities. He had also chosen by this time to ally his fortunes with the United States and contracted billions of dollars to rapidly modernize his nation. Technology, armaments, and advisors from the United States as well as other nations were brought to Iran in enormous amounts and numbers to saturate the country with internationalism.

The shah rallied as many of his compatriots around him as possible. The ethnic-religious minorities especially prospered under his reign. Indigenous Jews, Zoroastrians, and Christians felt secure as religious minorities. Jews were prominent in the marketplaces as business entrepreneurs. Synagogues were well attended. The Jews as an ethnic community had one representative to parliament. Although there was no embassy of the state of Israel in Iran, the shah allowed a consulate of Israel. During the oil embargo of 1973 the shah allowed shipments of Iranian oil to the state of Israel. Judaism as a religion and the Jews as a people experienced a basic stability under the reign of the shah. There were immigrations of Iranian Jews to the state of Israel, and there were periodic harassments of Jews within Iran, but overall the religious freedom of the Jews was preserved.

The Zoroastrian community had received new life under the reign of the shah. He had invited the Zoroastrian Parsees, whose ancestors had fled to India at the time of the entry of Islam, to return to Iran with full citizenship. Often in his addresses he spoke highly of the character of the contribution of the Zoroastrians. His attempts to focus Iranian culture on its roots to pre-Islamic times when Zoroastrianism flourished encouraged Zoroastrians.

Christian communities also experienced stability and at times growth during the Pahlavi era. While Zoroastrians numbered less than fifty thousand and Jews around one hundred thousand, Christians claimed some two hundred thousand, representing a variety of church families. The Armenian Apostolic Church, the Armenian Catholic Church, the Assyrian Church of the East, the Chaldean Catholic Church, the Roman Catholic Church, the Episcopal Church, and a host of Protestant churches composed the main Christian communities at the time of the shah. The Armenian Apostolic church was by far the largest Christian community. Thirteen of its two dozen churches which were constructed during the time of Shah Abbas in the sixteenth century were still standing in New Julfa, next to the city Isfahan. Its archdiocese in Teheran claimed over one hundred thousand communicants, with some twenty-one ordained priests.

Both Roman Catholic and Protestant missions flourished in Iran during the reign of the Pahlavi shahs. Mission schools, hospitals and nursing schools, book stores, Bible translation works, orphanages, and congregations grew. At one time there were five Christian hospitals throughout Iran, including Teheran, Meshad, Tabriz, and Hamadan.

The Anglican Church and the Presbyterian mission were instrumental in establishing missionary work. During the decade of the seventies, with the influx of tens of thousands of internationals, English language churches cropped up in key cities, especially Teheran, Isfahan, Shiraz, Ahwaz, and Abadan. Southern Baptists exerted a key role in leadership among these churches. The Community Church of Teheran had long been an English speaking church appealing to internationals as well as to English speaking Iranians. The Presbyterian Mission began a language and cultural center in Teheran opposite the main campus of the University of Teheran, which enrolled some six hundred students at a time. Southern Baptists placed a professor on the Faculty of Islamic Theology of the University of Teheran.

Thus, there was growth among the various Christian communities during the Pahlavi shahs from 1925 to 1979. Not only did the ancient ethnic-religious communities like the Armenians and the Assyrians have high visibility in church ministries and programs, but also missionaries and personnel from western churches, especially Europe and the United

States, were granted opportunities to work in Iran. From these western missions, Iranian churches arose, with their own pastors and church ministries. In terms, then, of religious pluralism and religious freedom, Christianity, as well as Judaism and Zoroastrianism, had a relatively good standing and experience. In the midst of a nation overwhelmingly Muslim, Christians had high visibility and stable communities.

In the 1960s, as Mohammad Reza Shah Pahlavi gained firmer control in Iran, he initiated programs and social reforms which were intended to improve the life of the people but which alienated the Shi'ite leadership. A continuing struggle, then, ensued between the shah and the ayatollahs. Ironically, the shah courted and favored various constituencies, including the minority religious communities, but he alienated the religious leaders who commanded the attention and loyalties of the millions of Iranians. The shah laid claim to the powerful and dynamic symbols of Shi'ite Islam in order to legitimate his rule and authority among the masses. In his autobiography he referred to his dreams of Allah's claims upon him, of Allah's protection of him from assassination attempts. He said that his father named him after the eighth imam, Imam Reza. The shah referred to his White Revolution as inspired by the Qur'an.

The lands and monies which pious Muslims donated to their religious organizations under the authority of the ayatollahs were confiscated by the shah's government and placed under the control of the Endowments Organization. This organization became the second wealthiest institution in Iran, next to the National Iranian Oil Company. The Endowments Organization controlled and regulated the building and reconstruction of mosques; it undertook the training of young clerics; it oversaw, together with the secret police, the activities that occurred in the mosques as well as the messages preached by the Muslim clerics and the pronouncements of the ayatollahs. This organization also published books and pamphlets describing the shah and his family as good Shi'ites.

The shah patronized several Muslim seminaries, including the Faculty of Islamic Theology of the University of Teheran. One of the most poignant attempts of the shah to identity himself with religious legitimacy was the sending of several Muslim clerics to the tomb of his father just outside Teheran to perform prayers. The shah's father had died in exile in South Africa and had been brought back to be placed in a tomb amidst other Islamic shrines near the capital. The shah had annexed the title, "Great" to his father's name. The young Muslim clerics performed a weekly prayer ritual at the tomb.

The Iran of the Ayatollahs

In the 1960s and 1970s a deep struggle surfaced between the shah and the ayatollahs. The 1963-64 uprisings led by the ayatollahs brought bloody riots to the streets of Teheran and Qum, the stronghold of traditional Islam. The issues of conflict between the shah and the ayatollahs as voiced by Ayatollah Kohmeini in 1963 were the following: land reforms which deprived the mosques and religious communities of their wealth and influence; dependency on the "imperialistic" forces of the U.S.; and the granting of voting rights to women. One of the leading ayatollahs of the day said to the shah, "It is not you who decides what is right; it is I and the ulema (ayatollahs)." Another ayatollah protested, "National interests are threatened and violated by the corrupt Ruling Body."

In the riots that followed thousands were killed, and Ayatollah Khomeini was exiled. Through house arrests and imprisonment of Muslim clergy, through the prohibition of the clerics to speak uncensored in the mosques, and through travel restrictions upon them and censorship of their writings and publications, the government began a process of embattlement with the ayatollahs and their mass following which was to last until the Iranian revolution. In his frantic effort to modernize Iran, the Shah had unleashed the powerful forces of secularization interpreted by the ayatollahs in certain most visible ways: movie houses with marquees depicting violence and sex overshadowed the mosques in towns and cities; young women wearing hot pants beneath their veils; automobile and steel industries supplanting emphasis on agriculture; billions spent on arms and weapons; and western values and institutions implemented into the fabric of the nation at the expense of Islamic teachings and ways of life.

At the time of the Iranian revolution of 1978-79, the shah had built an armed forces of staggering proportions in numbers of personnel, sophisticated weaponry on land, sea, and air, and an industrial-military complex to service the enterprise. The shah had also imported tens of thousands of internationals to build and manage his emerging new society and to train Iranians in the same arts of construction and management.

The shah had also alienated himself and his policies from the traditional Shi'ite communities under the leadership of ayatollahs, as well as other segments of Iranian society. During 1978-79 millions of people marched in the streets of the country demanding the end of the shah's rule. Oil production, the lifeline of the nation, was disrupted. Schools and universities were closed, as well as marketplaces and banks. The central government and the armed forces became disarrayed. The shah was forced to flee the country, and Ayatollah Khomeini was welcomed from exile to establish an Islamic republic. During the immediate days of the revolution and in transition from rule under the shah to the inauguration of a new constitution and government, there were battles, deaths, executions, imprisonments, and mass instability across the country. Ethnic-religious communities like the Kurds battled the central authorities of the transition government, raising the issue of their rights to autonomy and territory. Reports of persecution among the religious minorities, especially the Jews, Christians, and Baha'is, surfaced. Ayatollah Khomeini stated that Iran would protect the rights of all the people, including the religious minorities.

The Iran-Iraq War under the leadership of Ayatollah Khomeini (1979-1989) drained the resources of the country. With Khomeini's death Iran has continued to be under the rule of the Islamic state headed by President Rafsanjani. The treatment of religious pluralism and religious freedom will need to be observed. The Baha'i did not fare well during the time of the revolution. Missionaries from western churches left Iran. Much data is needed on the current happenings in Iran.

Religions in action in Iran offer an intriguing exploration into the concepts of theocracy, religious pluralism, religious freedom, and the day-to-day relationships among religious communities. From 1941 to 1979 a primary conflict resided between the shah and the ayatollahs. They both claimed to be spokesmen for Allah, to know Allah's will, and to have the directions to develop the nation along sound religious lines. Both fought for the loyalties and allegiances of the people using the symbols and institutions of Shi'ite Islam. The shah ultimately relied on the rights of his theocratic claim, on the backing of his armed services, his secret police, and on the western support of his regime through the supply of weapons, technology, industrialization, and tens of thousands of international advisers, managers, and workers, to implement his modernization dream.

On the other hand, the ayatollahs relied upon the traditional religious establishments of the Muslim clerics, the mosques, the teachings of the Qur'an, the disenchantment of the intellectuals and the student generation, the dissatisfactions among the middle class merchants and bazaar merchants, and especially a deep latent hostility of a huge segment of the population against the shah, his family and his regime. Both the shah and the ayatollahs, in different ways and degrees, claimed to be speaking in the name of God, with a religious program sanctioned by God. Hence, they competed within a theocratic pattern. The shah restricted the religious freedoms of the ayatollahs and persecuted many of them, thus denying them some of the guarantees established in the constitution. The shah, then, had his difficulty with Shi'ite Muslims on constitutional, political-religious, and religious lifestyle grounds.

On the other hand, as long as ethnic-religious minorities acknowledged the shah and his rule with affirmation and patronage, they were encouraged in their religious communities and expressions. The basic test of the shah's policy of religious freedom came in his relations with the majority religion of the country, the constitutional religion of Shi'ite Islam.

In conclusion, Iran and the Middle East offer contrasting styles of religious expressions from those of the American tradition. Islam is both a religion and a politic, and where the constitution of a country like Iran or Saudi Arabia recognizes an official religion to be legally valid, it has to contend with possible prophet-statesmen who have religious-political based ideologies and programs. Consequently, there is not separation of church and state, and religious freedom is under the constraints of the legal majority religion. Freedom of religious choice and mobility across religious-ethnic lines are often prohibited and are usually carefully regulated. Given the tribal and ethnic groupings in Iran with religious and political flavors like the Sunni Muslim Kurds, Assyrian and Armenian Christians, all with historical and some with contemporary aspirations to have certain national identities, the added dimension of complexity faces the Iranian situation, as it does other countries in the Middle East.

Beneath shahs, ayatollahs, constitutions, and a host of complexities across the Middle East, there is the element of personal relations between individuals and communities of varying religious persuasions. Some of these relations have already been indicated. They could be multiplied by countless narrations of Jews and Muslims in Palestine, of Christians and Muslims in Lebanon and Iran, and among a host of other individuals in other Middle Eastern lands.

10

CHRISTIAN PERSPECTIVES
AND WORLD RELIGIONS

A classroom scene of the recent past at the Muslim seminary of the University of Teheran offers a poignant portrait of the levels of interaction of peoples of diverse religions. I was lecturing in comparative religions to a class of Muslim clerics, emphasizing the servant ministry style of Jesus. That particular day was a fasting day for Muslims, and during my lecture the call to prayer from the nearby mosque signaled the end of the fast day. The students asked permission to leave class to get food. One blind cleric remained behind. After explaining to me the deep meanings of the month of fasting for Muslims, indicating that fasting was a season of great devotion, sacrifice, and obedience, he posed a question to me: "Do Christians have greater obedience in their religion than Muslims?"

In our contemporary religious communities people are encountering one another eyeball to eyeball with searching questions and confrontive religious beliefs and life-styles. Scholars, missionaries, ministers, and laypersons of Christian churches and communities are experiencing a fresh challenge of the major religions. Throughout the history of Christianity there have been various interpretations of the beliefs and practices of other religions, and these interpretations have affected the relationships between Christians and peoples of other religions.

One Christian perspective on other religions has been that they are devoid of truth. Other religions are considered false, and they are composed of pagans and idol worshipers. In this view Christianity is the superior religion, and others have little worth in their beliefs, values, institutions, and lifestyle. Since other religions are false, there is little that can be learned from them.

This perspective fails to take seriously the cultures of other peoples, and it forgets the biblical views found, for example, in the New Testament Gospel of John, that states that Jesus is the light that enlightens every person. It also overlooks the testimonies of many Christians throughout history of the knowledge of God's mercy, righteousness, and justice which they have evidenced in their relationships with neighbors of other religions.

Another perspective views Christianity as the religion which fulfills all others. Religions have primitive or more advanced concepts of God and religious values and institutions, but it is in Christianity that these features are completed. Other religions are fragmented and partial. The Christian religion brings balance and wholeness to all the parts. This view tends to be evolutionary and progressive. For example, the spiritual values found in the Buddhist understanding of suffering are completed in the Christian's understanding of the suffering of Jesus in the crucifixion. However, this view demands a mathematics that adds up the parts of varying religious traditions to arrive at a summation in Christianity. It ignores the Christian understanding that all traditions, including Christian traditions, stand under the revelation of Jesus. The bits and pieces of the various religions do not add up to the gospel whose standards judge all religions. This perspective also ignores the complexity of each religious system and the integrity of each system that does not necessarily relate to others.

A variety of other perspectives exists among Christians and within Christian communities. Among Roman Catholic scholars there are several views. One is that the Roman Catholic Church is the conserver of God's truths in their completeness. The greater distance a religious community is from the Roman Catholic Church, that is, other Christians, Jews, Muslims, or atheists for example, then the less truth that community has. Another view among certain Roman Catholic scholars is that God's revelation and salvation knowledge is available in religions other than Christianity. Thus, within Roman Catholicism there are diverse views toward religions.

A generalized view voiced by some Christians is that there is little difference in any of the religions in matters of ultimate significance. Each one does the same things for its peoples by pointing them to God, setting standards for living, and providing them with rituals and practices to live a secure life. This view says that Christianity is good for Christians, and Hinduism is good for Hindus. The unity within religions is greater than its differences. Therefore, let each religion go its own way.

Another perspective is that all religions, including Christianity, stand under the judgment of God and the norms of the gospel as reflected in the life and teachings of Jesus Christ. Religious concepts, cultures, values, institutions, and lifestyles face the critique of the gospel. In this view, those who are closest to the truth may be the most hostile to the gospel, and those considered distant from the truth may be closer than one grants. This perspective places great emphasis on the confirmation, confession, and pilgrimage of the Christian in Christian community. At the same time the Christian is open to the possibilities and struggles of peoples of other religions. The tensions between revelation and reason, law and love, and within belief, faith, and sin are recognized. Ultimate matters like judgment and salvation are left in the prerogatives of God and the gospel for the Christian as well as for others.

Within Christianity, then, there are diverse views of the significance and meaning of other religions. These views have been shaped by various means. The Bible has been a source book for shaping the attitudes and relationships toward religions. Theological interpretations of Biblical content have become schools of thought about religions. Christian missionaries have lived among peoples of other religions and have provided insights into the meaning of culture and religion. Religions have experienced revitalization and revival and have influenced Christian scholars, missionaries, pastors, and laypersons to attempt to understand them. Not only are views shaped by the Bible, theology, missions, and the presence of religions in close proximity, but also relationships are affected. According to the view held, relationships may be based on hostility, suspicion, distrust, curiosity, openness, and friendliness. Relationships may take the form of aggressive proselytism, persuasive evangelism, intense dialogue, open friendliness, forceful isolation, and indifference.

In the following pages a Christian perspective will be developed that takes seriously the gospel and God's creation of diverse human populations with their religious meanings. The attempt will be made to penetrate beneath religions to religious persons. Religions may be viewed as theological and philosophical systems, as institutions, and as value systems. These characteristics are important; however, they may lead to a static view of religion. People are religious. People pray, worship, raise families, cry, laugh, suffer, wage war, and seek peace in the context of religion. People have dreams, imaginations, aspirations, and stories of life, death, and afterlife that are dynamic and open to interpretation and change. Thus, persons are the stuff of religion, and persons are created in the image of God.

A Christian pilgrimage will be explored in a brief and selective encounter with the history of Christianity. The theme will rest upon the conflict of God and the gospel with the various gods and goddesses, and with patterns for the resolution of the conflict. Then interpretations and applications of the gospel toward persons of other religions will ensue, including select major religions discussed in the preceding pages.

Theologies and Religious Pluralism

Throughout the history of Christianity there have been various diverse orientations toward people of other religions and their relationships to truth, salvation, and human destiny. Some theological views have been exclusivistic, seeing little if any revelation, knowledge of God, or redeeming values of people of other religions. Other views have been more inclusive.

These various orientations have focused on discussions of religious authority, revelation, knowledge of God, Jesus Christ, faith and unbelief, church, kingdom of God, history, culture, and religious experience. The focus of most of these discussions has been on the nature and function of Jesus Christ and the relationship of Jesus Christ to God and to humankind in the meanings of life and human destiny.

A brief, limited overview of various expressions of these orientations follows. Spokespersons from the Roman Catholic Church, various Protestant communities, and Eastern Orthodoxy are presented. There is no attempt to be comprehensive or entirely representative.

Early Christianity grew up as a minority religion in the Greek and Roman world. Early church theologians used the language and cultural forms around them to express biblical concepts. Tertullian employed Greek terms such as *homoousios* (of like substance) and *homoiousios* (of similar substance) to discuss the divine and human natures of Jesus Christ in his relationship to God. Justin Martyr, Origin, Clement of Alexandria, and Cyprian showed deep appreciation for Greek philosophy and indicated that the Logos (Word incarnate in Jesus Christ) was grasped as truth by the philosophers.

There were other church theologians who dissented from any association of Christianity with Greek philosophy or of Jerusalem with Athens. The Roman Catholic Church from the time of the early church to the twentieth century fluxuated between two beliefs about faith and salvation of peoples: God's universal love and desire to save, and the necessity of the church for salvation.

As Christianity became the established religion in the Roman Empire, it became synonymous with western culture. Salvation was closely related to the church and its sacraments, and the doctrine emerged that outside the church there was no salvation. Medieval Christianity launched attacks, persecutions, inquisitions, and heresy trials against Muslims, Jews, and dissenters within the church. The crusades of the eleventh and twelfth centuries attempted to dislodge Islam from the heartland of Christianity.

The Protestant Reformation of the sixteenth century fragmented the church, resulting in the pluralism of Protestant communities. Islam, which had begun in the seventh century A.D. in the Arabian peninsula and had spread as a missionary religion to most continents, remained relatively unstudied and unapproached by the churches. In the eighteenth and nineteenth centuries, Christianity, through its missionaries, began to take seriously the languages, ideas, and values of peoples of other religions.

World missionary conferences were held in the twentieth century in Edinburgh (1910), Jerusalem (1928), and Madras (1938). The agendas of the conferences included the evangelization of the world, the rising tide of secularism, the relationship of the churches to non-Christian religions, and the unity of the church.

Various Theological Perspectives

The dialectical theology of Karl Barth, the Swiss theologian, served as a giant hinge upon which many theologians and missiologists hung their presuppositions and strategies towards religious traditions. Barth placed revelation over against reason and religion, viewing religion as unbelief. However, he saw Christianity, though standing under the judgment of God's revelation, as the true religion in which the church is the locus of the miracle of grace, where the sinner is justified before God.

Hendrik Kraemer, the Dutch theologian and missiologist, standing upon the theology of Barth, in 1938 offered his ideas of biblical realism and radical discontinuity. He saw a distinction between God's revelation through the biblical tradition and that of general religious experience. For him revelation in Jesus Christ was unique. Non-Christian religions may be studied, but Kraemer emphasized the discontinuity between the religions and the revelation which comes through Jesus Christ. He asserted that the Christian missionary is the point of contact between the gospel and the non-Christian.

Another stream of theological inquiry focused on the theology of Paul Tillich. Tillich viewed religion as a state of being in which humankind was grasped by an ultimate concern which qualified all other concerns as preliminary. He saw revelatory experiences as universally human. Thus, peoples of all faiths deal with some ultimate concern that points them to the being of God. Tillich asserted that the appearance and reception of Jesus of Nazareth as the Christ is a symbol that stands for the decisive self-manifestation in human history of the source and aim of all being. Conversations with peoples of other faiths bring about the quest for spiritual freedom and spiritual presence.

Post World War II brought other writings about peoples of other faiths. In particular, theologians of the church and philosophers of Christian backgrounds considered the nature of salvation and the role of Jesus Christ in relationship to all humankind.

The Roman Catholic Church made major changes in its views and relationships with people of other religions. The Church softened its doctrine of no salvation outside the Church. The councils of Vatican I and Vatican II, along with Catholic theologians Karl Rahner and Hans Kung, raised new discussions on the nature and extent of truth, revelation, and salvation outside the Church. The Church established secretariats to relate to non-Christian religions, to Jews, and to non-Catholic Christians. Rahner's "anonymous Christians" and Kung's sympathetic view of possibilities of grace in other religions served as stimuli in theological reflections over the roles of Jesus Christ and salvation in relation to other religions.

Missionaries of various churches living among people of other religions offered their theologies. Christian thinkers of indigenous churches, some of whom had converted from their native religions, expressed their views.

Kenneth Cragg, a missionary and a missiologist who lived among Muslims, wrote about the Muslim faith as a human surrender to God. He viewed the role of Jesus Christ as the fulfiller of the Muslim's surrender and redemption. The role of the missionary to the Muslim is to unveil Jesus Christ, who is already present among people of religions. Raymond Panikkar, born of Roman Catholic and Hindu parents, wrote *The Unknown Christ of Hinduism*. Panikkar stated that the meaning of Jesus Christ is to be revealed and unveiled in the context of Hindu symbols and values.

Lesslie Newbigin, church administrator and missionary to India, wrote *The Finality of Christ*. His theology is that in Jesus Christ there is communication with non-Christians; but the communication calls for radical repentance and conversion from all pre-Christian religious experience. The clue to history is not the finality of Christianity but the finality of Jesus Christ.

Two native theologians of India, Paul Devanandan and M. M. Thomas, place the revelation of God in the "cosmic Christ." They view salvation history as not confined to the church but available in all histories.

Theologians in the developing nations offered liberation theology, emphasizing the salvific expressions of the gospel in relationship to the human conditions of dignity, justice, and peace. Gustavo Gutierrez, a Latin American theologian, wrote of the awakening of the poor and the dispirited masses of people and linked a revolutionary gospel of change with peace and justice.

Other contemporary theologians have offered views on other religions. John Hick has called for a Copernican revolution in shifting emphasis in theology from Christ to God, from a Christo-centric approach to a theocentric one. Wilfred Cantwell Smith has introduced the ideas of a cumulative tradition alongside a personal faith in understanding religion and religious experience. Smith sees faith as both revelation and personal discovery, which is available among all people.

Wolfhart Pannenberg emphasizes that the revelation of God comes through human experience that is historical and is always in process. In Jesus Christ God's future appears. Only in Jesus Christ is the final goal of salvation seen and understood, although the histories of other religions may demonstrate revelatory aspects of God.

The "Frankfort Declaration," formulated by Peter Beyerhaus and affirmed by a convention of theological evangelicals in 1970, makes a statement about Jesus Christ, salvation, mission, and other religions. The Bible is the primary document for understanding and evaluating other religions. Salvation is based on the crucifixion of Jesus Christ and is received only in participation in faith. All Christians are called upon to be missionaries to all non-Christians. The statement by evangelicals was made out of a perceived crisis of certain church bodies and theologians adopting positive views to other religions and seeing salvific possibilities in them. Harold Lindsell, an evangelical theologian, asserted that non-Christians perish if they die without knowledge of Jesus Christ.

Another congress of evangelicals was held in Lausanne in 1974. Theological statements were issued emphasizing the authority of the Bible, the uniqueness of Jesus Christ, and the need for evangelism. The congress rejected any efforts by the churches or Christians implying that Jesus Christ spoke equally through religions or that there was any possibility of salvation in other religions. Yet it recognized the need for a dialogue with people of other religions in order to understand them better and to meet their needs both physically as well as spiritually.

Eastern orthodox Christianity also has its spokespersons on the matter of Christianity and other religions. Georges Khodr, metropolitan of Lebanon, stresses that the work of salvation is carried on in Jesus Christ through the Holy Spirit throughout religious traditions and in diverse cultures.

From this brief and limited glimpse one may see various and diverse views of Christians have been shaped by the Bible, by the history and traditions of the churches, by Christian theology, by culture, and by living with and among people of other religions. Orientations of exclusivity, inclusivity, and moderation between the two have been seen.

In the following pages there will be presented Christian ideas and practices which relate to and are challenged by people of other religions. Primarily, there will be presentations on Hindus, Buddhists, and Muslims. Again, these orientations of Christians toward people of other religions are not comprehensive. They are intended to be brief and general in order to point the reader to issues and challenges that may be pursued in depth by further reading and study.

God and the Gods

The spiritual heritage of Judeo-Christian history knows about the battle of God and the gods. The ancient Sumerians insisted that the gods built the cities and brought the arts of civilization. As the cities grew and prospered, the gods departed, leaving the king to rule in the absence of the gods. The king ruled in power, and the people lived not in the fear of the gods but in the fear of the king and his power. The gods became secondary. Thus, the Sumerian view was as follows: The gods rule. They depart and the king rules in behalf of the distant gods. Then, the king rules. The themes of theocracy and secularism are echoed here.

About this time Abraham, a patriarch of the Old Testament, left the sophisticated urbanism of the Sumerian city of Ur to go "unto a land that I will show thee" (Gen. 12:1). Abraham moved across the desert at the bidding of God.

Perspective of the Old Testament

In its development the people of the Old Testament, by the time of the great prophets, became quite exclusive and anti-syncretistic toward the concepts of gods. How do the gods of other nations like Ashur and Baal originate? The Old Testament does not treat gods as symbols. They are idols made with human hands. People fell into vain imaginings, and images were made. The Hebrew idea of the utter transcendence of God conflicted with all images and stones. The God of Abraham, Isaac, Jacob, the prophets and the Hebrews was One, Righteous, Just, and Covenant-making. Gob gave the Law and sent the prophets. The Ten Commandments became the religious framework for the Hebrews. The Old Testament also painted a portrait of the coming of a Messiah, the Anointed One of God.

Perspective of the New Testament

It is the New Testament that points to the Christian's particular history. It paints religious life on a canvas with its roots in the Old Testament and its shape for the present and the future in the gospel of the teachings and life of Jesus Christ. There are three foci of the gospel and religious life.

The first focus is on God, humanity and family, relationship possibilities, and rebellion and sin. The themes of creation, the Garden of Eden, the responsibilities of humankind to God, and rebellion are evident. Humankind was to be responsible to God, to each other, and to nature. Rebellion against God brought severance of relationships and disharmony between God, humankind, and nature. The serpent-Satan played the role of a god, and humankind focused on the sin of denial and disobedience in its relationship to God. There is much more in this focus, but the central theme has been set.

The second focus is on God and the gospel. It is on the life-death-life of Jesus Christ. It is on the one named Immanuel, Son of God, Rabbi, Master, Teacher, King of the Jews, Lord, and the Lamb who takes away the sins of the world. The focus is definite, sharp, and historically and culturally penetrating. Jesus walked the dusty roads of the countryside of Palestine and the stones of the city streets of Jerusalem. He taught the commandments of love and the Sermon on the Mount. His teachings and his presence along the dusty roads and city streets sharpen the focus of integration of both Old and New Testament covenants between God and humankind. They have implications for Adam and Eve (every man and woman), for King Cyrus of Persia as a servant of God, for Peter and Paul being nursed along into spiritual maturity, and for the acceptance of a thief on a cross in the deepest moment of his rejection. The crucifixion on a cross and the resurrection which left open a heavy rock tomb door focus on the overcoming by God through Jesus Christ of hate by love and of sin and death by salvation and life.

The third focus is upon the Christian individual or anyone of humankind. It is the paradoxical experience of being created from the womb and yet still being created; of loving and dying; of using and misusing; of being proud and ashamed; of needing and being needed; of claiming and disclaiming; of lording over and being lorded over; of being lost and being found. It depicts a universal condition. And this focus projects a universal solution, the gospel.

All three foci present God, the gospel, and the individual, in a significant pattern of relationships. The data of the gospel are persons and their specific needs and possibilities. There is no strategy to relate to another religion. The focus is on persons who may be religious and whose religious aspirations, loyalties, and commitments may be misplaced. Thus, the spiritual heritage of the Judeo-Christian pilgrimage has been one filled with the initiatives which God has taken through the gospel to benefit humankind.

Perspective of Church History

The history of Christianity, as well as the history of humankind, has been conditioned by the battle between God and the gods. John Calvin wrote that the human mind is a permanent factory of idols. It is also a permanent factory of fears, as well as brilliant ideas. Idols are not merely statues of stone, but they are also divided loyalties and misplaced faith in the context of the three foci discussed above.

During the *first three centuries* of Christianity three crucial issues developed. One was the confrontation between the emerging Christian community and the Roman government, sometimes popularly called the issue between Christ and Caesar. The imperial Roman cult, centering around the Caesar Emperors, required religious worship, commitment, and loyalty from Christians. This was a classic struggle between God and the gods. Another issue was the introduction of the philosophy of Gnosticism into Christian theology and into the practice of the church. This philosophy taught that the creation was evil, that God was an evil creator, and that Jesus Christ was not human. Another battle between God and conflicting ideologies ensued. A third issue was the introduction of elements of the mystery religions from the eastern world into the life of the church. Vegetation gods and goddesses and fertility cults impinged upon the church. The Easter bunny and the Virgin Mary became symbols and practices bordering on fertility rites and goddesses. Thus, in the early centuries peoples of various religious and cultural backgrounds entered the church, and the church grew. It also held church councils to weed out heresies and the problems of idolatry.

During the crusades in the *medieval ages* the militarization of Christianity was greatly pronounced. The popes and Christian kings led the warriors of the church to liberate the lands of Palestine held by Muslims. They preached that the church's enemy is God's enemy. They preached that the church must convert those who worship other gods, out of love for the salvation of their souls, or the church must kill them out of its love for the salvation of others who might be contaminated by these religious enemies. The church of the crusades allowed no other religion the right to exist. Later, the church established the Inquisition and used its own torture chambers to extract confessions from the heretics and turn them over to the state to be burned. At the time of the Reformation the church had experienced great periods of corruption under certain popes. Pope Leo X said, "God has given us the Papacy. It is ours, so let us enjoy it." The cult of the Caesars and the cult of certain popes had become quite similar.

With the *modern era* there came the enlightenment, the age of reason, and the great technological discoveries. The American, Thomas Paine, uttered that enlightened spirit as a sign of the times when he said, "If the devil had carried Jesus on the mountain and showed him the kingdoms of the world, why didn't he discover America?" Not too far behind Paine was the great German philosopher, Nietzsche, who in his book *Thus Spake Zarathustra* had Zarathustra speak to the old man who was performing his worship to God: "Has he not heard that God is dead?" The age of unbelief and secularism had sprung up in the heart of Christian populations.

The history of Christianity also has demonstrated the faithful response of countless followers to live according to the light and love of God given through the gospel. Polycarp, bishop in the early church, refused to divide his loyalty to God and obey the cult of the Caesars, and went to his martyrdom saying, "Eighty and six years have I served my Master. How can I deny him who has done me no wrong?" Francis of Assisi in the medieval ages had love for Muslims when the church at large knew them only as distant idolaters. Martin Luther initiated the Reformation when his head and his heart became troubled over the church's teachings and practices, and he preached that the just should live by faith. The church has grown over the centuries and ministered to the needs of diverse populations and assisted humankind to overcome divided loyalties and misplaced faith. The church has found its place among peoples of the globe, even among peoples of other religions, because of its attachment and faithfulness to the gospel.

The challenges to Christians who live by the gospel are great. Confused minds, hurting hearts, and hungry bellies cry out and reach out for words of understanding and healing and for nutrition for their bodies. Often, they will follow any god or any person who promises liberation from misery and death. The challenges to Christians in the contemporary era are opportunities which help to intersect the gospel in the midst of various religious traditions and of gods.

Four Confessional Statements

In concluding this section on God and the gods four confessional or faith statements are made.

1. *The God and Father of Jesus Christ is active in the world through both obvious and mysterious ways.* The obvious ways have been described. Yet, in all the obvious, concrete, material and tangible ways, there is a mystery of the gospel. It is something like the light of God in the eastern sky which the Wise Men followed across a barren and vast desert wasteland to come to a birthplace and lay gifts at the presence of the child named Jesus. It is something like seeing through a mirror dimly and knowing there is more to see. It is like leaving all the ultimate decisions about salvation to the God of salvation and being a disciple in the light and love of the gospel.

2. *On the Christian path there is a rhythm of exile, dispersion, and gathering.* The Christian is a pilgrim. Moses left Egypt and went into the desert, not to stay there forever, but to find the transforming space under God to return and create a new people in the Exodus. Jesus journeyed into the wilderness to confirm his Father's directions for him and to battle the gods, chief of whom was Satan. He rejected the ruse of the gods to become a magician, a king, or a giver of false promises. His ministry as Messiah was to be a servant. Jesus returned among the people to proclaim release to the captives and the healing of the hurting and the for-

giveness of sin. He gathered the disciples to be a community of likemindedness.

3. *Like John the Baptist, the Christian is to prepare the way of the Lord.* The way is more than reason, knowledge, propositional truth, or the disclosure of divine facts. The way is a way of confessional revelation.

4. *Confessional revelation is based on the incarnation, the crucifixion, and the resurrection of Jesus Christ.* The climax of all religious mystery (whether of creation, revelation, prophethood, or law) is Immanuel, God with us. God returned to the garden in order to save. In Jesus Christ the Word became flesh and dwelt among the peoples. The crucifixion is an essay in universality, a suffering and giving quality of God's love that surpasses all other gods. Through it comes the healing of the whole human family. It is a mysterious destiny of death. At the time of Jesus' death, no one wanted to hand him over. Only Jesus knew what was really going on and what he was doing. His death identifies with the sin, alienation, and split state of all peoples. It is also the redemption.

What is the resurrection? There is no end to anything until God finishes it and begins it again. On the evening of the resurrection day, the resurrected Jesus met some men walking to Emmaus and said something like this to them, "Here is what I kept trying to tell would happen. Now I have come to claim the nations. Wasn't it in the psalms, prophets, my teachings and conversations about life, death, resurrection, repentance, forgiveness, and reconciliation?" Thus, in the incarnation, the crucifixion, and the resurrection confession is made to all peoples that here is the Lamb that takes away the sin of the world. Here is the Lion of Judah, the Suffering Servant, the Light, the Bread, the Water, the Prince of Peace. In the following sections these outlines of a Christian perspective will inform a brief discussion on the specific contexts of peoples of other religions.

A Note on Hindu Peoples

Hindus hold to various religious beliefs and practices. A simple person may worship one of a million gods. A family may offer sacrifices of food at an elaborate temple ceremony. An intellectual may discuss deep philosophical principles. An older man may spend the remainder of his days in meditation practices. A person like Gandhi may devote much of his other energies to improving the daily life of the people. Hinduism offers a variety of ways for people to experience religious meaning in life. Hinduism is very tolerant of other religions, including Christianity.

Gandhi once said that Jesus Christ belongs to the whole world, no matter how people worship him. Within Hindu tolerance Christianity is another path that leads to salvation, and Jesus Christ is another god who expresses the ultimate meanings of the universe. Hinduism, then, as a religion, is adept at absorbing diverse concepts and values and incorporating them into itself. It, however, has limits to its tolerance. Christianity would need to conform to the various systems of Hindu thought and practice.

A Christian perspective toward Hindus is aware of their rich diversity of religious experience. It also knows that Hindus differ in the ways that they claim knowledge and inspiration from their traveled paths toward God, truth, and a religious life. It can appreciate, for example, the intense religious fervor and commitment of Hindus to the best teachings of the Bhagavad Gita, or of the Hindu's quality of respect for nature. A Christian perspective, then, would acknowledge that Hinduism is a reservoir of religious truths with Hindus in various conditions of religious thought, practice, and commitment. A proper way to learn about the religious status of a Hindu is to meet the Hindu in the practice of Hinduism, careful not to heap all the components of Hinduism upon him.

A Christian perspective also recognizes that there are sharp differences with Hinduism in its grander views of God and truths, as well as in the minutiae of religious devotion. Since there is no founder, no creed, and no unique expression of revelation as are found in the mainstream of Christianity, Hinduism often is difficult to describe and understand.

However, there are several understandings within Hinduism which a Christian perspective particularly notes. A basic view of Hinduism is a unitary universe. There is a little distinction between a creator-god and creation. *God*, divine principle, humankind, animals, and nature are all basically one. A primary goal of Hinduism is union or absorption of all the parts into the whole. This view becomes explicit in the Hindu concept that in the karma-transmigration cycle, one may take the form of animal or human. Nothing actually disappears. It just takes a different form with the underlying goal that at some point in time and space all forms may become one. Some Hindus may speak of this unity or form as God, as an impersonal principle, or as the reality for which the Krishna god stands.

God in the Christian view is the personal creator of the universe. God's creation includes humankind, a special creation, along with animal and natural orders. The relationship between God and humankind is intended to be based on personal, responsible, and fellowship principles. Unlike Hinduism's basic view of reality, a *person is* distinct from the natural orders, is created to be responsible to God and is gifted with a will and intellect and emotions to communicate with God. There is no karma-reincarnation cycle.

There is a Christian sense of *history*. History has a beginning. It moves purposefully toward the intentions of God, its originator. History has a conclusion. History, then, has meaning. More particularly, it has ultimate meaning for the individual who relates to God in his life. History is demonstrative of the individual's unique existence.

The Hindu view of history is conditioned by endless time. Time is like a circle or a spiral. An individual may come in and out of time and history in various forms. Through the transmigration of souls in reincarnation, an individual may have life in many historical periods.

One may observe at this point that there is divergence between a Christian view and a Hindu view of God, person, nature, history, and life. The divergence becomes more pronounced in the views of *human destiny* and its challenges and fulfillment. A classical Hindu view sees the primary difficulty of human life as a problem of knowledge and ignorance. One may reach God and attain union or absorption through the right understanding of the nature of reality. To overcome ignorance with enlightenment is a solution. One may also attain union through good works and sacrifices and devotion to particular gods. Time is on one's side to achieve this kind of salvation through various cycles of reincarnation. For a Christian view the essential problem for humankind is not degrees of knowledge or ignorance. Sin, moral rebellion, and evil are the problem. Individual disobedience to God through willful choice is the difficulty. The seriousness of humankind's dilemma is its rejection of the will of and love of God, and the context of the dilemma occurs in each individual's personal history.

Christian and Hindu views differ on the nature of *the human problems*, and they differ on its solution. Hindus have many paths for attaining salvation, including a work ethic, mystical knowledge, meditative exercises, and devotion to deities. All the paths are valid. Some may aid one's arrival at salvation quicker than others. Some are based on individual, save-oneself methods. Others rely on the advice and example of a Guru religious master. Some depend on the benevolence of a godlike Krishna. In fact, Hinduism allows for nine incarnations (avatars) of the god, Vishnu, including a deer, a turtle, and Krishna. In the background of all of these paths there is the view of union of all things.

In a Christian view the solution of the human dilemma focuses on the relationship between God and the individual in the context of the gospel. The gospel is the ultimate significance and meaning in Jesus Christ and his teachings. The individual cannot solve his dilemma alone. Human sin is dealt with by God in the incarnation, life and teachings, crucifixion, and resurrection of Jesus Christ. Sin is forgiven through the individual's acceptance in faith of the will and love of God demonstrated in Jesus Christ. Jesus Christ is unique. Salvation is a gift of God through Jesus Christ to the individual. It is experienced in the historical existence of the individual and in an eternal fellowship with God. The incarnation demonstrates God as He is in relationship to humankind. The crucifixion shows the seriousness of humankind's sin and the availability of God's forgiveness. The resurrection portrays the eternal possibilities of life in the overcoming of death and the establishment of a fellowship and a kingdom of God which begins in history.

Thus, Christians and Hindus have distinct beliefs and practices that challenge each other with their differences and provide opportunities to learn from one another. Hindu respect for nature, for tending to the needs of the interior life through reflection and meditation, and for attempting to find unity and wholeness in life and in the universe are challenging patterns. The concept and practice of nonviolence (ahimsa) as a religious duty, expressed in the life of Mahatma Gandhi and learned by Martin Luther King from Hindu teachings, is worthy of consideration. The Hindu writings like the Vedas, the Upanishads, and the Bhagavad Gita contain many noble ideals which have contributed to humankind's development. A Christian perspective toward Hindus acknowledges the vast reservoir of religious meanings which they present to the world.

Mahatma Gandhi said that Jesus Christ belongs to the whole world. In a Christian sense that is the inclusiveness of the gospel. The gospel has unique and ultimate meanings for Hinduism. However, in a Christian view the gospel is also exclusive in that Jesus Christ is not just another incarnation (avatar) in the Hindu sense. Jesus Christ is the incarnation of God, unique in historical expression and salvific in meaning for all religious traditions.

A Note on Buddhist Peoples

When the teachings of classical Buddhism are examined, one notes that the emphasis is on humankind and not on God. The concerns of the Buddha were not so much metaphysical and speculative about the existence of God as they were about the psychological and ethical nature of humankind. However, beside classical Buddhism there developed a movement which emphasized concerns about metaphysics, gods, and salvation. It is important in a Christian perspective toward Buddhists to know that Hinayana Buddhists adhere more closely to classical teachings, while the Mahayana Buddhists have interpreted or changed these teachings to include faith and practice in gods of salvation.

Hinayana Buddhists

A Christian perspective toward Hinayana Buddhists is primarily focused on the Four Noble Truths and the Eightfold Path as taught by the Buddha. In these truths and path there is no concept of God. Emphasis is placed on the individual who through appropriate understanding, ethical actions, and mental discipline may overcome the difficulties of life and enter Nirvana, an indescribable state. The major problem of life is suffering, which is initiated through misplaced desires. There is no soul concept, and there is no describable state of existence after life. Buddhists continue to believe, as Hindus do, in the karma-reincarnation cycle, but without a belief in the soul concept. This denial of soul (anatta) raises questions of what transmigrates from one historical era to another. Thus, a Christian has little basis of similarity within Hinayana Buddhist thought-forms to communicate about God, soul, and a transcendent reality like eternal life.

Hinayana Buddhists place great importance upon the concept and the experience of *suffering*, and they design methods by which suffering may be overcome or eliminated. A Christian perspective views suffering in the context of God's creation, humankind's sin, evil, and the crucifixion of Jesus Christ. Meaning can be found in and through suffering. The crucifixion of Jesus Christ demonstrates a way in which suffering is met, not by escaping it, but experiencing it and consequently overcoming it. The deeper meanings attached to suffering, like evil and death, are also overcome in the crucifixion and the resurrection of Jesus.

For the Buddhist all the responsibility for suffering rests upon the individual. There is no help from God. There is no hope based on a future life. Yet, the Buddhist believes that ethical actions of good will (*metta*), benevolence, and compassion (*karuna*) will help eliminate suffering. Buddhist monks serve as mediators in assisting Buddhists with the problem of suffering. Since monks have more time for the practice of the higher ethical ideals and mental disciplines, Buddhists reward them with gifts, so that the merits of the monks might be transferred to the Buddhists themselves. Thus, there is a mediatorial system in Hinayana Buddhism.

A Christian view of Hinayana Buddhists acknowledges their anxiety and frustration with the complex problems of living in the world. Suffering is real. One may appreciate the high ethical doctrines of Buddhism which stress honesty, integrity, peacefulness, and ecological balances within nature. The responsibility which the individual must assume for one's actions and the freedom of individual choice are admirable beliefs and practices. However, the Christian world view is not atheistic or agnostic. It acknowledges God and a good creation. It affirms the potentialities of humans as well as a sinful humanity. Ethics is centered in the relationship between a God of justice and love and humankind, and Jesus Christ is the mediator-reconciler of humankind to God. The world is not a place from which to escape, but a place in which to live affirmatively.

Mahayana Buddhists

Mahayana Buddhists build upon the foundations of the teachings of the Buddha, but they have different interpretations and practices. These

Buddhists elevate one central teaching. It is the idea of a savior-god, the bodhisattva, who aids individuals to attain salvation. The bodhisattva is a holy person who has attained enlightenment but who delays entrance into Nirvana in order to help others attain it. The individual, through faith, relies on the grace and compassion of the bodhisattva to affect salvation. The Buddhists of the Pure Land movement worship Amida, who promises them an afterlife of paradise.

A Christian view notes that there are key differences between Hinayana and Mahayana Buddhists. Mahayana Buddhists view the individual not so much as autonomous but as dependent. A religious experience founded upon belief, faith, grace, and salvation is prominent. A world view which includes a savior-type and an afterlife is important.

There are several concerns which a Christian view has of Mahayana Buddhists. In the classical teachings of the Buddha the existence of God was of no importance. In fact, the place of religion with its beliefs and rituals was basically irrelevant. However, Buddhists move in the direction of believing in a reality beyond themselves, while the Christian view holds that God is the reality.

The Buddhist idea moves from emphasis upon the individual to the importance of the relationship of the individual to one another and to a bodhisattva. A Christian view confirms the religious need of the individual for community and for the proper relation to God. Among Mahayana Buddhists one may ask what has happened to the self concept. If the self is not real, as classical teachings imply, why is such importance attached to preserving it? Why not let it flicker out, expire, become extinct. If the self is an illusion, why is it worth preserving by the bodhisattva in another existence? There is the value among Buddhists of disinterested good will, of doing good for others without consideration for one's own welfare. Yet, there is the primary teaching to cease desiring and craving and to exit the world unattached to thoughts, emotions, or human relationships.

Like Hinduism, Buddhism offers choices to its followers. In religions where knowledge of the gods may be esoteric and ways to attain salvation may be complex, religions become adaptable. A Christian perspective notes that changes occurred in Buddhism from a system built on philosophy and psychology to one with religious beliefs and practices. Throughout Buddhism, however, the idea of karma-reincarnation remained. For the Hinayana Buddhists the monks became the saints to help the masses escape the rebirth cycles more rapidly through a merit system. For the Mahayana Buddhists the bodhisattva became the gods offering salvation during a lifetime which could break the rebirth cycle and provide an eternal afterlife.

A Christian view toward Buddhists denotes tensions and possible contradictions within their teachings and lifestyles, but this may be true in all religions. Buddhist psychology is complex and is often difficult to translate into other cultural forms and terminologies. One can appreciate the serious empirical and pragmatic quest of Buddhists as they delineate the problems inherent in the human situation and as they attempt to validate their answers from personal experience. They continue to have concerns about God and transcendent reality, human nature, evil, salvation and liberation, and a savior. A Christian perspective would invite Buddhists to consider the full meaning of the gospel as it is presented in Jesus Christ and his teachings.

A Note on Muslim Peoples

Of the major religions, Islam is experiencing a peculiar history in the contemporary world. Hundreds of thousands of Muslims travel the globe to study in colleges, universities, and research centers; to work in industries; to transact business opportunities from their oil wealth; to be tourists and to visit families and friends. They have a story to tell of their families, their nation, their religion, and their aspirations for the future. Some Muslims are excited about their religious faith and practice, about the growing importance of Islam in the world, and about the publicity which current events bring to their religion and native countries. Other Muslims are anxious about rapid change in their home countries as they become more modern. What will change do to their religion, family, and nation? Some Muslims are seriously seeking meaning for their fragmented and confused lives.

Christian and Muslim peoples have been interacting with one another for some thirteen hundred years. Islam grew up in an environment with tinges of Christian churches. The prophet Muhammad was in contact with Christian peoples, and he parlayed many aspects of the narratives of the New Testament into the Qur'an.

During the Christian dark ages in medieval Europe, Islamic art, architecture, literature, science, mathematics, and medicine flourished in the Middle East. Islam preserved both philosophical works of Christian scholars during this period, which became a renewed heritage of the church in the late medieval ages. The crusades marked a low ebb in relations between Christians and Muslims, and the crusade era still remains ingrained as a negative force in contemporary Christian-Muslim relations.

Christians and Muslims have a variety of similar theological ideas and religious values and practices which they can explore for meanings. Theological concepts such as monotheism, revelation, prophets, salvation, judgment, eschatology, law, and ethics afford opportunities for exploration. The very fact that Islam builds its religious foundations upon Hebraic-Christian backgrounds offers similarities of ideas and ideals. The Muslim emphasis upon prayer, community worship, stewardship, preaching, and scripture gives the Christian points of contact for communication.

A Christian view toward Muslims can appreciate several Islamic doctrinal statements. Their statements of the nature of God including oneness, mercy, compassion, righteousness, and justice can be reflected upon with meaning by Christians. Muslims emphasize a prophetic religion in which God communicates through individuals called prophets. Their world view includes creation by God, a decisive historical experience in which individuals live life and make decisions with ultimate consequences for an afterlife, and a final judgment. Belief and unbelief, religious commitment, and ethical decisions are important to Muslims.

These Muslim foci of belief and practice provide the Christian with ample means of communicating on a belief and faith level. A Christian view may also appreciate the discipline and commitment observed in many Muslim lives. Muslims give much time and human resources to prayer, both formal and informal. Seasons of fasting are observed. The indigent are a responsibility of the stewardship of the Muslim faithful. The Muslim community has the responsibility to gather for worship and prayer at stated times. In the Muslim view these disciplines are not optional. They are Muslim expressions of devotion to and praise of God.

Perhaps more than any other religious group, Muslims have specific views toward Christians. These views have developed out of the close proximity of Christian-Muslim backgrounds and similar ideas and practices. There are several understandings Muslims have of Christian faith and practice that have caused misunderstandings between the two peoples. Muslims emphasize the unity of God (Allah) in nature and attributes. They view the Christian concept of God as fragmented and disunited, as they think that Christians believe in three gods. They have misunderstood the Christian statement of the Trinity and the reality of the Christian experience of which the statement speaks. Christians are monotheists. They believe in the oneness and unity of God, and oneness and unity are confirmed in the revelation of God and in Christian experience.

Muslims consider Christians, as well as Jews, *people of the book*. They understand that the revelation of God has come to both Jews and Christians through prophets of God such as Moses and Jesus. However, Muslims believe that these peoples misunderstood and distorted the revelation. Consequently, the Torah (Old Testament) and the Injil (New Testament), or the Bible for both Christians and Jews contain corruptions, not the faults of the prophets but of the peoples. Muslims believe that God gave the final and pure revelation through the final prophet, Muhammad. This revelation is contained in the Qur'an. The Qur'an contains the corrected content of the revelation from the Torah and the Injil. Therefore, Christians and Jews live under the distortions and falsehoods of their Scriptures. This view of Christians as people of the book has meant that Muslims have granted Christians certain special standings in Muslim communities, such as religious freedom to worship.

A Christian view of revelation, prophets, and Scripture varies from that of the Muslim. The revelation of God is seen in nature, in human history, and in the content of the Bible. The Bible itself becomes the reservoir for the patterns of the revelation of God. More specifically, the Bible and the gospel, meaning Jesus Christ and His teaching, become the anchor points for revelation. Prophets are the messengers of the revelation of God. However, a Christian view holds that the revelation of God is uniquely and ultimately expressed in Jesus Christ. A Christian view may appreciate any truth that is evident among Muslims, including the thoughts and teachings of Muhammad and the sayings in the Qur'an. However, a Christian view does not refer to Muhammad as the seal of the prophets or to the Qur'an as the most recent, supreme, and corrective revelation of God.

Perhaps the most discussed view between Christian and Muslims is the nature and meaning of *Jesus*, and it may be the most volatile and tension-filled point of contact between the two. Muslims demonstrate a deep appreciation for Jesus, as recorded in the Qur'an and in their various written traditions and verbal expressions. The Qur'an refers to the virgin birth of Jesus, and it associates miracles with Him. Descriptive words about Jesus in the Qur'an are servant, spirit, Messiah, prophet, messenger, sign, parable, witness, righteous, and blessed. There are more titles of respect given to Jesus than to any other prophet in the Qur'an. The Qur'an differs with the Bible in its narrative concerning the crucifixion of Jesus. According to the Qur'an, Jesus was not crucified on the cross, for someone took His place; and there was no resurrection. Thus, Muslims view Jesus out of the context of what is written about Him in their scripture and literature.

As already indicated, Christians have their anchor points in the God who revealed Himself in Jesus Christ. The biblical narratives of the incarnation, the crucifixion, and the resurrection of Jesus are the touchstones not only of Christian teachings but of Christian experience. The tough issues between Christians and Muslims focus on the nature of revelation, authority, and the nature and role of Jesus. These issues are also problematic within and between other religions. Christians and Muslims use words whose historicity and semantics refer to the Palestine of Abraham, to the Nazareth and Jerusalem of Jesus, and to the Mecca and Medina of

Muhammad. Sometimes they use the same words that convey the same meanings. At other times they speak the same words which have altogether different meanings. There is a language of words and there is also a language of relationships. A balanced Christian view acknowledges the difficulties attached to the use and meanings of words between Christians and Muslims, while at the same time opting for a language of relationships built on trust, patience, and service.

11

REFLECTIVE EXERCISES AND SUGGESTED READINGS

Chapter 1 Overview of Peoples and Their Religions

Reflective Exercises

1. List and discuss four reasons why a study of world religions is meaningful.

2. What are the differences between monism, animism, polytheism, and monotheism?

3. Why are sacred writings important to religious people? Why is your scripture important to you? How would you explain your scripture to another person?

4. Are there similar principles and practices among the major religions? What makes them similar or dissimilar?

5. What are the basic challenges to the survival and growth patterns of religions? Which do you think are the most important? Why?

6. Write a brief essay on the topic: "My perspective toward other religions is. . . ."

7. Choose one or several of the following for a research project:

   a. Ask a person of another religion to explain his/her view of God.

   b. Interview a person of another religion about that person's view of scripture and religious life derived from scripture.

c. Take a world map. Trace the origins and expansions of the major world religions. Which religions are more missionary than others?

Suggested Readings

Bouquet, A. C. *Sacred Books of the World* (Baltimore: Penguin Books, Inc., 1959).
A good overview of scriptures of major religions.

Eerdman's Handbook of the World Religions
Published by Wm. B. Eerdman's Publishing Co. in 1982 in Grand Rapids, it is a good overview of world religions with good photography and graphics.

Elwood, Robert S. Jr. *Words of the World's Religions* (Englewood cliffs: Prentice-Hall, Inc., 1977).

Great Religions of the World
This is a publication of the National Geographic Society, 3rd ed., 1978. It is excellent for its photography of the peoples, rituals, and institutions of the major religions of the world.

Lewis, James F. and William G. Travis. *Religious Traditions of the World* (Grand Rapids, Zondervan Publishing House, 1991).

Major Religions of the World
This is a filmstrip of fifty-eight frames including cassette, manual, and response sheets written by George W. Braswell, Jr. and published by Broadman Press, 1981. It is excellent for older youth and adult study and discussion.

Swanson, Guy E. *The Birth of the Gods* (Ann Arbor: The University of Michigan Press, 1968).
This book presents a background study of monotheism, polytheism, ancestral spirits, reincarnation, and the concept of the soul. It is written from an anthropological viewpoint.

Chapter 2 Hinduism

Reflective Exercises

1. How can one account for the diversity of beliefs in Hinduism?

2. Explain the Hindu devotion to the cow. How does this devotion make sense to the Hindu?

3. What is the caste system to Hinduism? How does devotion to Krishna affect the caste system?

4. Hindus pray in the name of Lord Krishna. Christians pray in the name of Jesus Christ. What does the Hindu mean? What does the Christian mean?

5. What are the meanings of terms like:

a. Avatar

b. Brahma

c. Brahman

d. Atman

e. Karma

f. Moksha

g. Transmigration

h. Four ways (margas)

i. Veda

j. Bhagavad Gita

6. Choose one of the following:

a. Interview a Hindu and determine his/her view and loyalty to a Hindu deity, his/her pattern of worship at home and in a temple, and his/her view of an afterlife. What does it take for the Hindu to attain an afterlife?

b. Visit a Hindu temple, observe the ceremonies, talk with the Hindus, and write up the experience as if you were a journalist preparing an article for the next day's newspaper.

c. How would you explain your religious faith to a Hindu? What features of Hinduism would you find easier to approach in discussing your faith? What features of Hinduism would you find more difficult?

Suggested Readings

Koller, John M. *The Indian Way* (New York: Macmillan Publishing Co., 1982).
There is good material on the major religious traditions of India. The chapters on Hinduism are good, including the Vedas, Upanishads, Bhagavad Gita, Yoga, and Devotional Hinduism.

Renou, Louis. *Hinduism* (New York: George Braziller, 1962).
An anthology of significant Hindu scriptures.

Ross, Nancy Wilson. *Three Ways of Asian Religion* (New York: Simon and Schuster, 1966).
It focuses on Hinduism, Buddhism, and Zen. Its graphics on Hindu art forms are good.

Sen, K. M. *Hinduism* (London: Penguin Books, 1965).
Sen, a native son of India, describes Hinduism from a native son's perspective.

Weber, Max. *The Religion of India* (Glencoe: The Free Press, 1962). A classic presentation of the sociology of Hinduism.

Chapter 3 Buddhism

Reflective Exercises

1. Define or identify the following:

   a. Buddha

   b. Three Vows

   c. Four Noble Truths

   d. Eightfold Path

   e. Hinayana

   f. Mahayana

   g. Bodhisattva

   h. Zen

   i. Nichiren Shoshu of America

   j. Tripitaka and Sutra

2. Was the Buddha a reformer of Hinduism? How?

3. What does the word Buddha mean? What, if any, are the differences of the view of Gautama Buddha and the word Buddha among the Hinayana and the Mahayana?

4. How would you describe the Bodhisattva and how would you compare the term Bodhisattva with the term avatar in Hinduism?

5. What does Nirvana mean? Is there a difference in its meaning among the Hinayana and the Mahayana. What, if any, is the difference?

6. Is Buddhism a missionary movement? Explain.

7. What are the major forms of Buddhism in America?

8. Choose one or several of the following:

   a. Trace the movement of Buddhism from its native soil to America on a map. Note the major forms of Buddhism in the different countries.

   b. Visit with a Buddhist. If possible, attend a Buddhist ceremony at a temple. Learn from the Buddhist what he/she considers to be the primary beliefs and practices by which he/she lives out Buddhism.

   c. Who had you rather explain your religious faith to: A Hinayana Buddhist or a Mahayana Buddhist? Why? How would you do it?

   d. Examine the concept of Bodhisattva. Write a brief essay on its meaning and the meaning of Jesus Christ.

Suggested Readings

Burtt, E. A. *The Teachings of the Compassionate Buddha* (New York: The New American Library, 1955).

Gard, Richard A. *Buddhism* (New York: George Braziller, 1961).

Humphreys, Christmas. *Buddhism* (London: Penguin Books, 1964). Humphreys served as the President of the Buddhist Society of London for forty years. He gives a candid study of the world of Buddhism.

Swearer, Donald. *Buddhism in Transition* (Philadelphia: The Westminster Press, 1970). It focuses on Buddhism as a religion, as a politic, and as a challenge to Christianity.

Chapter 4 Chinese and Japanese Religious Traditions

Reflective Exercises

1. Define or identify the following:

   a. Confucius

   b. Lao Tzu

   c. Five Confucian Relationships

   d. Tao

   e. Yang and Yin

   f. Shinto

   g. Kami

   h. Analects

   i. Rice Gods

   j. Li

2. Who was Confucius? A teacher, philosopher, and/or religious leader?

3. What is Taoism? How does it differ from Confucianism?

4. How does Shintoism affect the individual, the family, and the nation of Japan?

5. What is the relationship between Buddhism and Shintoism in Japan?

6. Choose one or several of the following:

   a. Write a brief essay on the impact of Confucianism on present day China.

   b. Compare the ceremonies held in Confucian, Taoist, and Shinto temples and shrines. How are they similar and dissimilar? Make a chart of the characteristics.

   c. Write a brief essay on the place of ancestors in Chinese and Japanese religions.

Suggested Readings

Earhart, H. Byron. *Religions of Japan* (San Francisco: Harper & Row Publishers, 1984).
Consideration is given to nativistic influences on Japanese religion, as well as Chinese influences. Buddhism and Shintoism are also covered.

Overmyer, Daniel L. *Religions of China* (San Francisco: Harper & Row Publishers, 1986).
A brief and comprehensive overview of Chinese religions.

Thompson, Laurence G. *Chinese Religion* (Belmont: Wadsworth, Inc., 1979).
Chinese animism, ancestor veneration, Confucianism, and Taoism are treated in their historical contexts.

Chapter 5 Judaism

Reflective Exercises

1. List the religions that had their beginnings or very important happenings about the sixth century B.C. Why do you think this was a productive time in the development of religions?

2. Define or identify:

   a. Torah
   b. Talmud
   c. A Prophetic religion
   d. Messiah
   e. Reformed Judaism

   f. Conservative Judaism
   g. Orthodox Judaism
   h. Maimonides
   i. Israel
   j. synagogue

3. What is Judaism? Who is a Jew? What major tenets of belief and practice are a part of Judaism?

4. What are the implications of the formation of the nation of Israel in 1948 in terms of the history of the people of Israel, the people of Palestine, Jews of the world, and other nations?

5. What is the meaning of the city of Jerusalem in the history of Israel, in Christian history, and in Islamic history?

6. Choose one or several of the following:

   a. Outline the history of the Jews from Old Testament times to the present.

   b. Visit a synagogue during Jewish worship and write an essay on your observance.

c. Interview a rabbi on his/her life experiences, including decisions to enter the rabbinate, training as a rabbi, and the work of a rabbi.

d. Write an essay on the meaning of monotheism in the context of Judaism, Christianity, and Islam.

e. Interview several Jews on the meaning of Messiah in Jewish thought.

Suggested Readings

Hertzberg, Arthur. *Judaism* (New York: George Braziller, 1962).
An anthology of significant Jewish writings.

Neusner, Jacob. *The Way of Torah* (North Scituate: Duxbury Press, 1979).
An excellent overview of the history, theology, and practices of Judaism.

The Bible (Various translations are available).

Chapter 6 Christianity

Reflective Exercises

1. Define or identify:

   a. New Testament   f. Roman Catholicism

   b. Trinity   g. Eastern Orthodoxy

   c. Four Aspects of Church   h. Paul the Apostle

   d. Martin Luther   i. Book of Acts

   e. Messiah   j. Jerusalem

2. Outline the major historical periods of the Christian church.

3. Write a brief essay on the roots of the Christian tradition as it arose out of Judaism.

4. What is the meaning of the following terms given to Jesus of Nazareth: Savior, Lord, Christ, Son of God, Son of Man?

5. Is Christianity a missionary religion? How? Compare it to Hinduism, Buddhism, and Judaism with regard to their status as missionary religions.

6. Choose one or several of the following:

   a. Compare the major beliefs and practices of Roman Catholicism, Eastern Orthodoxy, and Protestantism. What are their greatest similarities and differences?

b. How does church architecture differ? What does church architecture communicate in terms of its physical arrangements and symbolism?

c. How do the roles and functions differ of a Roman Catholic priest and a Protestant minister?

d. Salvation is a term used in Christianity. How is the term salvation used in Hinduism, Buddhism, and Judaism, or what are its equivalents?

Suggested Readings

Brantl, George. *Catholicism* (New York: George Braziller, Inc., 1961).
An anthology of the major teachings of the Roman Catholic Church.

Dunstan, J. Leslie. *Protestantism* (New York: George Braziller, Inc., 1962).
An anthology of the major teachings and expressions of Protestantism.

Latourette, Kenneth Scott. *A History of the Expansion of Christianity* in seven volumes copyrighted in 1944 and published by Zondervan Publishing House.
An excellent and thorough treatment of the growth of Christian missions and outreach from the first century of the church to the present century.

Chapter 7 Islam

Reflective Exercises

1. The religion, Islam, began in the seventh century A.D. What influenced its beginning?

2. Define or identify:

a. Muhammad	g. Mecca
b. Ali	h. Medina
c. Six Pillars of Islam	i. Jerusalem
d. Sunni	j. Qur'an
e. Shi'ite	k. Imam
f. Sufi	l. People of the Book

3. Compare the Jewish, Christian, and Muslim views of Yahweh, God, and Allah, respectively. What criteria do you use to evaluate someone's view of divine being?

4. Compare the major beliefs and practices of Jews, Christians, and Muslims. Make notes of the similarities and differences.

5. What role does Jesus have in Islam? Why do Muslims repeat the phrase, "Please be upon Him" after they say the names of Jesus and Muhammad?

6. Choose one or several of the following:

   a. Trace on a world map the missionary expansion of Islam from the seventh century A.D. until the present. What countries have significant populations of Muslims?

   b. Why do Muslims call Jews and Christians "People of the Book"?

   c. Why is Jerusalem important to Jews, Christians, and Muslims?

   d. Visit a mosque. Observe the worship patterns. Write a brief essay detailing the architecture and ceremony.

   e. Interview a Muslim. Determine his/her view of God, prophet, prayer, law, love, and Jesus.

Suggested Readings

Arberry, Arthur J. *The Koran Interpreted, Vol. 1, 2* (New York: The Macmillan Company, 1971).
A very significant work of Qur'anic translation.

Donohue, John J. and John L. Esposito, eds. *Islam in Transition Muslim Perspectives* (New York: Oxford University Press, 1982).
A collection of articles written by Muslim scholars of various nations on diverse subjects like Islam and nationalism, Islam and social change, and Islam and its re-emergence.

Fry, George C. and James R. King. *Islam: A Survey of the Muslim Faith* (Grand Rapids: Baker Book House, 1980).
A brief overview of major historical, doctrinal, and practical expressions of Islam.

Pickthall, Mohammed Marmaduke. *The Meaning of the Glorious Koran* (New York: Mentor Books, 1953).
A popular reading of the Qur'an by a convert to Islam.

Williams, John Alden. *Islam* (New York: George Braziller, Inc., 1962).
An anthology of significant Islamic writings.

Chapter 8 Other Select Religious Traditions

Reflective Exercises

1. Define or identify:

   a. animism

   b. Mahavira

   c. Nanak

   d. Khalsa

   e. ahimsa

   f. Zeus

   g. ziggarat

   h. Zoroaster

   i. Oladumare

   j. Baha'ullah

   k. Avesta

   l. House of Justice

   m. mystery religions

   n. ancestors

   o. fire temple

   p. Among-Re

2. What influences did the Mediterranean religions have on the development of Christianity?

3. Jainism and Sikhism arose in India. What were the influences of Hinduism on Jainism, and what were the influences of Hinduism and Islam on Sikhism? How did each differ respectively from Hinduism and Islam?

4. Was Zoroastrianism a monotheistic and ethical religion? How and/or how not? Compare your findings in relationship to Judaism and Christianity.

5. African Traditional Religion has been described as monotheistic. What is your understanding?

6. The Baha'i faith has been described as the latest world religion. What do you think? What is its relationship in its origins to Judaism, Christianity, and Islam?

7. Choose one or several of the following:

   a. Write a brief essay on the impact of one of the following religions upon the world population: Jainism, Sikhism, Zoroastrianism, Baha'i, or African Traditional Religion.

   b. What were the similarities and dissimilarities of the role of the prophet, Zoroaster, for his time and place with those of the Hebrew prophet, Amos; with the enlighted one, Buddha; and with the Muslim prophet, Muhammad?

   c. Visit a Sikh or Baha'i temple or meeting place and observe its surroundings. Interview a Sikh or a Baha'i about his/her beliefs and practices. Write a brief essay on your findings.

Suggested Readings

Duchesne-Guillemin, Jacques. *Symbols and Values in Zoroastrianism* (New York: Harper & Row, 1966).
A scholarly overview of the thought and practice of Zoroastrians.

Esslemont, H. E. *Baha'ullah and the New Era* 4th ed. (Wilmette: Baha'i Publishing Trust, 1980).
A good documentation of the history of the Baha'i faith.

Idowu, Bolaji. *African Traditional Religion* (Maryknoll: Orbis Books, 1973).
A good overview of African religions written by a native son.

Jackson, A. V. W. *The Hymns of Zarathustra* (London: John Murray, 1952).
A good collection of the sacred writings of the Zoroastrians.

Kramer, Samuel Noah. *Mythologies of the Ancient World* (New York: Doubleday, 1961).
Please see chapters on ancient Egypt, Mesopotamia, Greece, and Rome.

Perkins, Mary and Philip Hainsworth. *The Baha'i Faith* (London: Green Printers, 1980).

Smart, Ninian. *The Religious Experience of Mankind* (New York: Charles Scribner's Sons, 1984).
Please see chapters on The African Experience and Religion in the Ancient Mediterranean World and on The Indian Experience.

Chapter 9 Religions in Action:
A Case Study of the Middle East

Reflective Exercises

1. Name the major religions of the Middle East. Describe their places of greatest strength.

2. What major movements or influences are affecting religions in the Middle East? What are their significance?

3. Write a brief essay on several of the following:

   a. religion and politics in Lebanon

   b. Judaism and the state of Israel

   c. religious freedom in the Middle East

   d. Kemal Ataturk and Reza Shah

   e. American religious traditions and Middle East religious traditions

4. Write a brief report on several of the following:

  a. Shi'ite Islam in Iran

  b. Christianity in Iran

  c. Minority religions and religious freedom in Iran

  d. Religion in Iran: power and politics

  e. Muhammad Reza Shah Pahlavi and Ayatollah Khomeini

5. Projects for further research:

  a. Choose a country in the Middle East and study its religious communities noting the patterns and styles of religious pluralism and religious freedom.

  b. Consider conflict and tension as they are expressed in religion and between religious communities in the Middle East. What are the sources of conflict? Project ways in which conflict may be resolved.

  c. Religion characterizes nations, communities, families, and individuals. Consider religion's meaning of each entity above in the context of the Middle East and of the United States.

Suggested Readings

Arjomand, Said Amir. *From Nationalism to Revolutionary Islam* (Albany: State University of New York Press, 1984).
It focuses on social, religious, and politic movements in the Middle East.

Braswell, George W., Jr. *To Ride a Magic Carpet* (Nashville: Broadman Press, 1977).
Iranian life is depicted in city and village while the author lived in Iran from 1968-1974. Shi'ite Islam is described in both its theology and in the daily lives of Iranians. The clash between the Shah and the Ayatollahs is explained. The interaction of a Christian missionary-professor and Shi'ite Islam is presented.

Burke, Edmund, III and Ira M. Lapidus. *Islam, Politics, and Social Movements* (Berkeley: University of California Press, 1988).
It includes chapters on Egypt, Iran, and the Palestinians.

Coon, Carleton S. *Caravan: The Story of the Middle East* (New York: Holt, Rinehart, and Winston, 1958).
A well written account of the history and culture of Middle Eastern peoples to the 1950s.

Gulick, John. *The Middle East: An Anthropological Perspective* (Pacific Palisades: Goodyear Publishing Company, Inc., 1976).
An excellent overview of Middle Eastern institutions and cultural values is given including family, religion, and national identity groupings.

Keddie, Nikkir. *Religion and Politics in Iran* (New Haven: Yale University Press, 1983).
Considerations are given to the history of Shi'ism and politics, to recent religio-political leaders, and to the revolution.

Waterfield, Robin. *Christians in Persia* (London: George Allen and Unwin, 1973).
Written by an Anglican missionary, it presents in a continuous narrative the history of Christians in Persia from the second century A.D.

Chapter 10 Christian Perspectives and World Religions

Reflective Exercises

1. Formulate a list of statements which characterize your major beliefs. Discuss them with another individual or with a group.

2. List and reflect upon various Christian perspectives toward other religions.

3. Write a brief essay on the topic: "My perspective toward other religions is . . ."

4. Which religion do you consider to be the greatest challenge to Christianity? Why?

5. In this exercise you may role play with members of a group or you may imagine the situation and think what you would do. Imagine a faithful, outgoing person of another religion like Hinduism, Buddhism, Islam, or Baha'i becoming your neighbor. That Hindu, Buddhist, Muslim, or Baha'i is eager to talk with you about his/her religion and may invite you to a religious meeting. This person may be a missionary to you.

   a. What are your initial feelings about this encounter?

   b. What do you imagine that person's assumptions to be?

   c. Describe your thoughts about that person's beliefs, religious practices, and invitation to you.

   d. What would be your response to that person based on your own religious faith, belief, practice, and values?

6. The year A.D. 2000 is nearing. With your study of world religions make some educated guesses about the following as the end of the century approaches:

a. Which of the religions will grow? Why? Where?

b. Describe the status of Christianity among world religions.

c. What part will religious freedom play among the religions and the nations?

Suggested Readings

Anderson, Gerald H. and Thomas F. Stransky. *Mission Trends No. 5 Faith Meets Faith* (New York: Paulist Press, 1981).
This is an invaluable source of brief statements written by Christians from four continents on Christian witness to peoples of various religions. These statements represent various theological views and methodological principles. Hindu, Jewish, and Muslim peoples are included in the discussions.

Braswell, George W., Jr. *Understanding Sectarian Groups in America*; Revised Edition (Nashville: Broadman Press, 1994).
It includes chapters on Hinduism in America, Buddhism in America, and Islam in America and Christian perspectives in relating to these peoples.

Cragg, Kenneth. *Christianity in World Perspective* (London: Luttersworth Press, 1968).
Cragg addresses the topic of religious pluralism and theological reflections upon it. He specifically writes about issues within Judaism and Islam and applies Christian perspectives to them. Cragg has written two outstanding books on Islam and Christian encounter with it, namely, *The Call of the Minaret* and *Sandals at the Mosque.*

Dyrness, William A. *How Does America Hear the Gospel?* (Grand Rapids: Eerdmans, 1989). It focuses on hearing the gospel in the midst of religious pluralism.

Knitter, Paul F. *No Other Name? A Critical Survey of Christian Attitudes Toward the World Religions* (Maryknoll: Orbis Books, 1985).
Knitter presents select proponents within the evangelical, mainline, and Roman Catholic communities and presents their views toward other religions. He concludes with his own view.

Newbigin, Lesslie. *The Finality of Christ* (Richmond: John Knox Press, 1969).
Newbigin first went to India as a missionary. Later, he became Bishop of the Church of South India. He states in this book that the gospel is an announcement of an event which demands that all persons make a decision for or against it. The gospel, he argues, is the clue to history.

Niles, D. T. *The Preacher's Task and the Stone of Stumbling* (New York: Harper & Brothers, 1958).
Niles, a Ceylonese minister and scholar, presented this material as the Lyman Beecher Lectures at Yale. The chapters include preaching in the context of a Hindu refusal, a Buddhist refusal, and a Muslim refusal.

Walker, Arthur L. *Educating for Christian Missions* (Nashville: Broadman Press, 1981).
Articles by various authors including George W. Braswell, Jr., on "The Shape of Things to Come," Glenn A. Inglehart on "Impact of World Religions on American Culture and Education," and Gerald H. Anderson on "Christian Faith and Religious Pluralism."

NOTES

1. From Nicol MacNicol, *Hindu Scriptures* (London: J. M. Dent and Sons, 1938), 1. First published by E. J. Lazarus & Co., Benares. Notes omitted.

2. Ibid., 36-37.

3. R. E. Hume, *The Thirteen Principal Upanishads* (Daryaganj, New Delhi: Oxford University Press, 2nd ed., 1931). Reprinted with permission of Oxford University Press.

4. From New American Library, Mentor Edition of *How to Know God: The Yoga Aphorisms of Patanjali*, trans. Swami Prabhavananda and Christopher Isherwood.

5. G. Buhler, trans., *The Laws of Manu* (Oxford,: The Clarendon Press, 1886), 24-28. Notes omitted.

6. W. W. Hunter, *Orissa* (London: Smith, Elder and Co., 1872), 132-34.

7. F. Edgerton, trans. *The Bhagavad-Gita* (London: George Allen & Unwin, 1944), 65-67, 108-119; cited in *Hinduism*, Louis Renou, ed. (New York: George Braziller, Inc., 1961), 135-38.

8. Henry Clarke Warren, *Buddhism in Translations* (Cambridge, MA: Harvard University Press), 159-60, 162-63, 165-66. Reprinted by permission.

9. F. L. Woodward, *Some Sayings of the Buddha* (Walton Street, Oxford: Oxford University Press, 1973), 143-44. Used by permission.

10. The Ven. Balangoda Ananda Maitreya, "Buddhism in Theravada Countries," in Kenneth W. Morgan, ed., *The Path of the Buddha*. (New York: Ronald Press Company, 1956), 144-52. Reprinted by permission of the Ronald Press Co., for John Wiley and Sons, Inc.

11. A. C. Bouquet, *Sacred Books of the World* (London: Pelican Books, 1954), 153-54. Reprinted by permission of Penguin Books Ltd.

12. Personal notes from a Zen Buddhist Master, Bhikku Bodhi, who lectured in Tehran, Iran, on November 1, 1970.

13. Archie Bahm, *The Heart of Confucius* (New York: Harper & Row, 1971), 69-71, 78-79, 92-95. Notes omitted. Reprinted by permission of John Westerhill, Inc.

14. Wing-Tsit Chan, ed. and trans., *The Way of Lao Tzu*, Library of Liberal Arts (Indianapolis: Bobbs-Merrill Co., Inc., 1963), 144.

15. Reprinted with permission of Macmillan Publishing Co., Inc. from Arthur J. Arberry, trans., *The Koran Interpreted* (New York, 1955), 29.

16. Ibid., pp. 50-52.

17. Ibid., p. 73.

18. Ibid., p. 83.

19. Ibid., p. 135.